THE ULTIMATE GUITAR BOOK

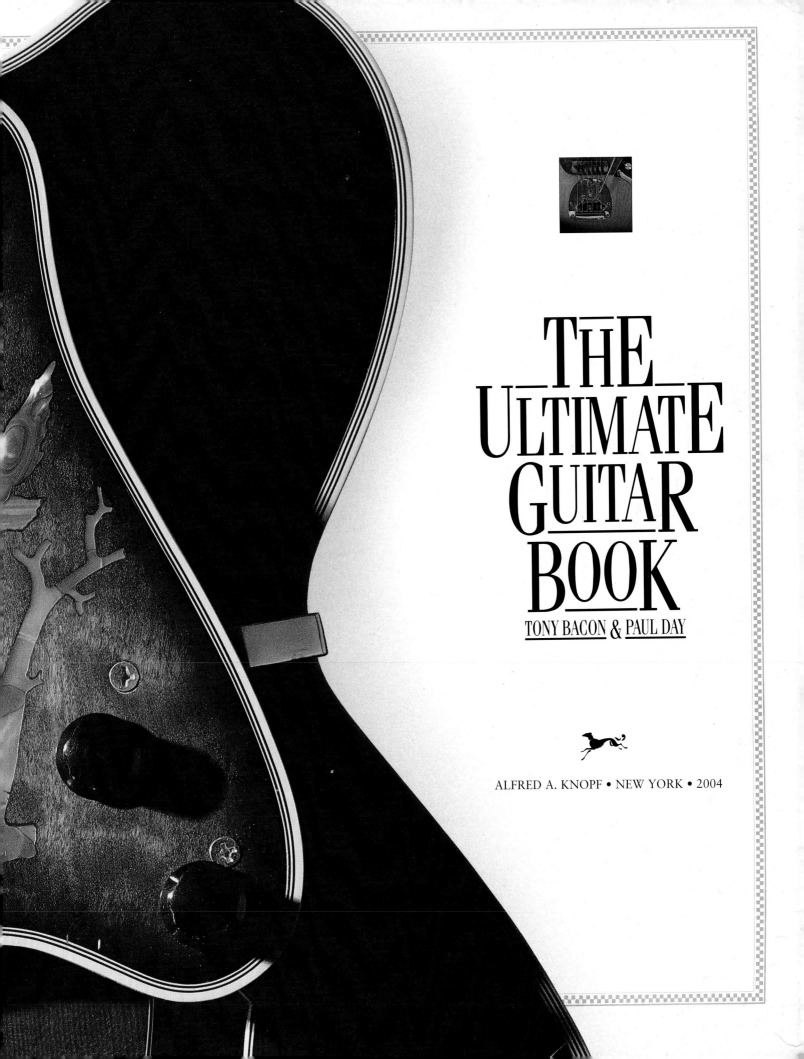

THE ULTIMATE GUITAR BOOK

TONY BACON & PAUL DAY

ALFRED A. KNOPF • NEW YORK • 2004

This is a Borzoi Book
Published by Alfred A. Knopf, Inc.

Published September 27, 1991
Reprinted Twice
Fourth Printing, February 1994

ISBN 0-375-70090-0
Library of Congress Number 91 052714
First American Edition Published
September 27, 1991
Reprinted Once
Third Printing, January 2004

Conceived and produced by Dorling Kindersley Limited

Senior Editor Josephine Buchanan
Managing Editor Carolyn King
Managing Art Editor Nick Harris

ART DIRECTOR
NIGEL OSBORNE

PROJECT EDITOR
JUDY MARTIN

DESIGNER
SALLY STOCKWELL

Typesetting by Midford Typesetting Ltd., London W1
Reproduced by Colourscan, Singapore
Printed and bound in China by L.Rex Printing Co., Ltd.
D.L.TO: 916-1997

SPECIAL THANKS
Tony Bacon would particularly like to thank the following, who helped greatly in shaping this book: Julie Bowie; Doug Chandler; Richard Chapman; Paul Day; Bill Marsh; Charles Measures; Will Meister; Barry Moorhouse; Bill Puplett; and Raymond Ursell. This book would not have been possible without music.

*This book is dedicated to the
memory of Leo Fender (1909-1991)*

INTRODUCTION

This book tells the history of the guitar, using photographs of over 450 choice instruments. The guitars we have chosen to show range from mass-produced beginners' boxes to unique custom models for the professional player. What links them all is their ability in talented hands to make music, whether humble, or radical, or just plain pleasurable. Remember, as you delve into these pages, that without musicians there would be no musical instruments. So before we start, here are six guitarists to help set the scene for the fascinating story of the world's most versatile musical instrument, the guitar.

66*Guitar players have long needed a champion, someone to explain to the world that a guitarist is something more than a robot pluckin' on a gadget to keep the rhythm going.*99

CHARLIE CHRISTIAN writing in **DOWN BEAT**, December 1939

66*I pride myself only in having been a daring, tireless prober of the subtle beauty of the guitar, in conquering for it the love of millions in the world ahead.*99

ANDRES SEGOVIA writing in his autobiography, 1976

66*Let's be realistic about this, the guitar can be the single most blasphemous device on the face of the earth. That's why I like it. . . . The disgusting stink of a too-loud electric guitar, now that's my idea of a good time.*99

FRANK ZAPPA quoted in **SOUND INTERNATIONAL**, April 1979

66*Certain songs just seem like they were written for guitar and nothing else. Take something like 'You Really Got Me' or 'Substitute'. I'm sure you could arrange them for keyboards, but they just wouldn't compare.*99

JERRY HARRISON, Talking Heads, quoted in **ONE TWO TESTING**, March 1985

66*All the kids made their own git-tars. Made mine out of a box and bit of stick for a neck. Couldn't do much with it, but you know, that's how you learn.*99

MUDDY WATERS quoted in **CONVERSATION WITH THE BLUES** by Paul Oliver, 1965

66*Sometimes I jump on the guitar. Sometimes I grind the strings up against the frets. The more it grinds, the more it whines. Sometimes I rub up against the amplifier. Sometimes I play the guitar with my teeth, or with my elbow. I can't remember all the things I do. . . . And when we play, people just see what their eyes see, and forget about their ears.*99

JIMI HENDRIX quoted in **HENDRIX** by Chris Welch, 1972

Herringbone inlay on a Martin D-28.

Stromberg Ultra-Deluxe.

Gibson Firebird VII.

Chet Atkins: "We all have a different touch when we play . . ."

To illustrate the story of the guitar, we have brought together the best collection of guitars ever seen in one book. You will see guitars from the late sixteenth century to the late twentieth century, from cheap acoustic guitars to vastly expensive instruments designed to link guitars with synthesizers; and all from as many guitar-producing countries as could be identified.

The book shows hollow-body, semi-solid and solid guitars and basses; acoustics, electrics, and marriages of the two. Laid out before you are great guitars, silly guitars, guitars to make you catch your breath, and guitars to make you smile. Here are famous guitars, everyday guitars, valuable guitars, battered guitars, guitars from museums and guitars from the stage, guitars that make the pop charts scream, and guitars that soothe the ear.

The human touch

The guitar's essential simplicity offers a challenge to anyone who chooses to make one guitar, 1,000 guitars or 100,000 guitars: how do you improve on such a straightforward, practical object?

People from many different backgrounds have risen to the challenge, building instruments that they hope will bring guitarists nearer to their ultimate guitar. Some of these designers have been musicians, like the inventive and influential Les Paul, bringing a player's mind to bear directly on the nuts and bolts of the guitar. Other makers have been engineers, keen to apply their natural skills with raw materials or with electronics to an object that links craftsmanship, science and art – just as radio-repairman Leo Fender did in the 1950s when he showed how to take the guitar into the age of mass-production.

This book shows how hundreds of makers, from the one-man workshop to the vast corporate factory, have put their own improvements into practice. It demonstrates precisely how each of them has taken the basic designs that have inspired all who build guitars. Some ideas have succeeded, many more have failed. This book is intended to show the

The beauty of simple design: a Martin D-42.

Italian factories adopted their own fresh style in the 1960s.

successes and the failures, as well as plentiful examples of the countless guitars which fall somewhere between the two.

Crossing barriers

The guitar is an attractive musical instrument, and most of those who pick it up for the first time find it a simple matter to achieve a relatively successful sound from some rudimentary chords. In this respect it is an easy instrument for the beginner. But as with all musical instruments, there are very few players who can be said to have mastered the guitar. This opposition of simplicity and difficulty is at the root of the guitar's popularity. Another reason for the guitar's

Handicraft lives on as assembly methods change.

huge popularity is its almost universal musical adaptability. It is arguable that no other instrument has been used regularly in such a wide variety of music, with the possible catch-all exception of "percussion." Try to imagine an absence of guitars in rock, flamenco, blues, heavy metal, rhythm 'n' blues, country, punk, bluegrass, jazz, folk, rock 'n' roll, pop, reggae, or even (if you can remember) rockabilly. And in its "classical" form the guitar, a largely non-orchestral instrument, has its own solo repertoire. It has also occasionally been placed in ensemble and orchestral settings, as in the well-known works of twentieth-century Spanish composer Joaquin Rodrigo. Even the piano, the only other serious contender for the title of "world's most popular musical instrument," does not feature in quite so diverse a range of styles and forms.

Given this universality, one might imagine that the guitar would help establish common ground between the various musical styles. But the interchange between players involved in the broadly defined "classical" and "popular" areas is limited. Eric Clapton, certainly among the best-known of modern blues/rock guitarists, drew large audiences to his performances of a concerto for electric guitar and orchestra, written for him in 1989 by Michael Kamen. And in the late 1970s the renowned classical guitarist John Williams formed Sky, using a rock group line-up to perform updates of classical pieces. Both examples are exceptions; not everyone is prepared to recognize that music is music, and a fine player is a fine player, whatever the style.

In the United States in particular, young musicians learning the guitar are encouraged to amass knowledge on the technical aspects of playing, to fill their heads with scales, arpeggios and impressive licks. Many are urged to study widely, too: as a New York classical guitar teacher told *Guitar International* in 1984: "Many of [my students] are involved in pop music. Today I have two or three that play incredibly well who play in groups as a sideline. Then they come and play Bach. In America that's very common."

The negative aspects of this admirable diversity come when fledgling players begin to wonder about taking their playing beyond the merely technical. Technique is of course essential, but not if it is at the expense of the most valuable quality a guitarist can possess – what some call feel, or soul, or spirit.

Whatever it is, Richard Thompson, a superb British guitarist and songwriter, successful in the USA, expressed a popular view in a 1986 interview with this author for *Making Music:* "Here [Britain] there's more innovation in music, more invention and ideas. In America it's more of a linear tradition . . . There's more accent on musicianship there, and that's a good thing *if* you have an open mind and don't become a slave to it. Some American guitar players do. They can be staggering in their technique but what they're actually saying is fairly insignificant." All this should not, of course, be construed as criticism only of American players. These tendencies are prevalent elsewhere; they just happen to be easier to spot in a country where thousands of young hopefuls take up the guitar every year.

A big body and f-holes for dance-band volume.

The most versatile instrument

The guitar is a unique musical instrument; no other combines in such a portable package such inherent harmonic, melodic and rhythmic potential. Even played on its own, the guitar offers a remarkable range of harmony to the player, who has continuous access to over three octaves (four on many modern electrics), with polyphony limited only by the guitarist's dexterity and the musical context. The guitar's ability to sustain is also of great importance. Julian Bream put it like this in an interview in *Making Music* in 1989: "Plucked strings have a slightly exotic quality, because the note always decays from the moment it's struck. It has an extraordinary death in a way.

Unlike every instrument that's in the orchestra, except perhaps for drums."

The overall musical potential of the guitar is kept in a continual state of development by pioneering players. Just one example from many will suffice: during the 1980s, a two-handed "tapping" style was extended and updated by a number of jazz-fusion and heavy-metal guitarists. It gave

Publicity material for two Swedish-made brands.

them the ability to play with rapid, violin-like leaps, impossible with normal playing techniques. As Joe Satriani told this author in a 1990 *Making Music* interview: "With guitar, you have four fingers on a bunch of strings, and if you have to jump up and down from, say, the second to the twenty-fourth fret, the movement is going to taint what you're able to do. Suddenly, with tapping, you could get lines going that sound effortless, yet have the width and breadth of a larger range."

The rise of "tapping" is also interesting because it highlights the constant interplay between guitarists and those who design and make guitars. Tapping benefits from a long fingerboard; suddenly, guitars were regularly

Collectors call this black-and-white humbucker a "zebra".

seen with 24 frets (and more in some cases). But which came first: the player's need, or a totally new kind of guitar? Often it is hard to work out the source of such developments. Is it the new type of instrument that inspires a style of playing, or do guitarists' new methods provoke new kinds of guitars and hardware? Did Floyd Rose and Dave Storey's locking vibrato systems encourage the new breed of "tapping" guitarist to start using extreme vibrato techniques? Or were these designers trying to provide a device that could do things players were trying unsuccessfully to achieve with existing systems? Did dance-band musicians lead the way to electric guitars in the 1930s and 1940s, or was it the guitar companies looking to expand their market?

At the end of the eighteenth century, was it players or guitar-makers who decided that a six-string instrument should supersede the contemporary guitars with five or six doubled courses? It has always been a mixture of both, and as long as this dialogue between guitarists and guitar-makers continues – and each side listens to what the other is saying – then the future of the instrument should be healthy.

The people's instrument

The guitar has been fashionable on and off since the 1600s, but during the twentieth century it became one of the most popular of all musical instruments.

Rickenbacker's new guitars keep alive their idiosyncratic 1960s style.

Until recently in the USA, more guitars were sold than any other instrument (although since 1985 the new mini "portable" keyboards have taken over the lead). The number of guitars sold in the United States is still greater than that of virtually all other popular instruments.

The National Association of Music Merchants (NAMM) collects sales statistics from various sources in the USA. For 1989 they recorded over 1,400,000 guitar sales, compared to

Charlie Christian and his guitar, Gibson's 1930s electric ES150.

about 350,000 woodwind, some 320,000 synthesizers, and around 138,000 pianos (the last two figures include exports). Portable keyboard sales were over three million units.

NAMM's guitar sales figures, which come from the US Tariff Commission and industry estimates, also reveal the huge boom in guitar playing that occurred in the early 1970s. This boom seems to have peaked in 1972 when over 2,500,000 guitars were sold in the wake of the folk and rock music revolution that was absorbing the nation's youth. American guitar sales fell gradually after that, hit a low in 1983 (mirroring economic decline and the emergence of popular keyboard instruments), and climbed

again until 1988, the last year for which we have figures at the time of writing.

Combined domestic and export sales statistics from the Ministry of International Trade and Industry in Japan show that in April 1990 some 54,500 guitars were sold, ahead of synthesizers (26,500), pianos (25,000), and woodwind (19,500), but well behind portable keyboards (102,000) and electronic keyboards (166,000).

This string-switching gadget did not last.

During the 1980s the guitar began to lose its dominance of popular music to keyboard-based instruments, primarily the synthesizer and, later, the sampler (a device which enables real sounds to be recorded digitally and replayed at any pitch by a keyboard). The use of the computer as a compositional tool to control synthesizers and samplers became commonplace by the 1990s, and this change of musical emphasis in the production of popular music has meant a shift in fortunes for some guitar-makers.

This 1920s design used internal resonators to increase volume.

Some makers try to link guitars and synthesizers, to reclaim a place for the guitar among the computers and hardware of the modern studio, while others mix classic guitar designs to try to find a safe "new" combination. When Allan Holdsworth told Matt Resnicoff for *Guitar Player* in 1990: "Now, unfortunately, the music *business* is ahead of the music the little guys have to fight it, and that's what we're doing," he was talking about the musician's side of the operation. But he could just as easily have been talking about the problems of modern guitar-making.

Relative values

Many guitars have become collectable: as musical instruments, certainly – but also as historic objects, maybe even as pieces of industrial art, or cultural icons. Of course, we have tried to ensure that the guitars shown in this book are genuine

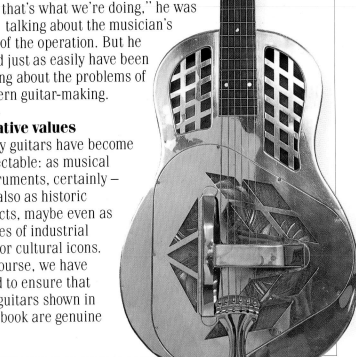

and — a great worry to collectors -- that wherever possible they are in original condition, without major modifications or restoration. To the musician this obsession with originality is absurd, as the very modification that might make a guitar more playable instantly devalues it in the eyes of the collector. To the collector any alteration is, at the extreme, an irreversible molestation of the past. It really all depends on

what the guitar has been bought for. Is it to play, or is it to hang on the wall? Ideally, both should be possible.

Value changes as soon as a guitar leaves the workbench.

Collectors and musicians were among the many observers who drew a deep breath in 1990 when a Fender Stratocaster once owned by Jimi Hendrix was sold at auction for very nearly £200,000 ($375,000), to a Hendrix fan who neither played nor normally collected guitars. The figure realized was by far the highest amount ever paid for a guitar, and many collectors were worried by the implications of the sale. It was some 200 times the normal market value of a Stratocaster of the period, and clearly was based on the association with Hendrix, generally considered by many to be the greatest and most influential of all rock guitarists. The assumption is straightforward: the auctioned Stratocaster was played regularly by Jimi Hendrix; this previous ownership is what makes it valuable. As if to underline this trend, a little later in the same year a personalized acoustic guitar once belonging to Buddy Holly was sold for $275,000 at another auction.

Collectors largely reject these value-by-association sales, and argue that a guitar is made valuable by its inherent quality as an instrument, its condition, its desirability among other collectors, its age, its rarity, and, probably last, who owned it. Musicians are sometimes left in the cold when guitars become

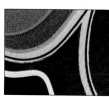

fashionable among collectors, who can push up prices to a level where players cannot hope to afford them. The choicest examples of the original Gibson Les Paul Standard (pages 82-83) can easily command five-figure sums in the United States and elsewhere,

Workmanship can add to a guitar's desirability.

so an example is unlikely to turn up on-stage at the average concert. Some of these guitars have, inevitably,

attracted the professional investor who considers them merely as commodities with a certain market value. So, far from reaching the stage, some rare instruments are more likely to be found locked in a bank-vault, an environment not usually noted for its musical stimulation.

There is also a degree of snobbery attached to the use of old guitars. "They don't make them like they used to" is a commonly heard defense, and while it goes some way in explaining the attraction of an aging or even obsolete model, there is no evidence that old is necessarily best. As Hank Marvin told John Tobler and Stuart Grundy for the BBC Radio One series "Guitar Greats" in 1983: ". . . age isn't necessarily a good thing in a guitar — it depends on how it's been treated and if it was a good one in the first place."

Makers will tell you that two guitars built in exactly the same way from exactly the same piece of timber can sound very different from one another. Move up a step or two to mass-production and, despite the consistencies of such a process, there are still the vagaries of timber and "the Friday-afternoon guitar" to deal with. Each batch of guitars has potentially good and bad instruments. Some say that an old worn guitar is the best bet, the theory being that it has been played because it is a good one. But it could be a bad one that has been abused by careless owners. So condition is not necessarily an indication of inherent quality.

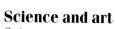

Science and art

Science can tell us a little about the way a guitar behaves as a physical object, but begins to flounder when it tries to advise guitar-makers about their craft. Of course, some makers do analyze in a scientific manner the nature of the instrument they are building, and react to that information in their production methods.

A special Anniversary edition from Fender.

There is a relatively recent example of a major guitar-maker taking science on board — and failing to capture musicians with the new guitars. In 1977 Gibson launched the Mark Series acoustic guitars. In the promotional literature for the four new models, the 35, 53, 72 and 81, the company explained how, in the past, improvements to instrument design had come about by trial and error, and luck. "That's why Gibson chose a new method in its search for a better acoustic guitar – the scientific method."

Gibson's two-year research plan involved

three scientists: a professor of acoustical physics, who recorded and analysed "voice graphs" of popular guitar designs; a chemical physicist (also director of an institute of molecular biophysics) to oversee structural design; and a professor of acoustics who devised new scientific measuring techniques and an environmental test chamber. But despite all this, the guitars did not prove

popular and were soon dropped from the Gibson catalogue. The company returned to their old, proven method of trial and error (and luck), and most players would argue that they returned to making good guitars as a result.

These oriental bass guitars absorb existing designs into their own.

Gibson's high-profile failure deterred many makers from the scientific route. Some have adopted such technologically inspired facilities as computer-controlled routing on their production lines, and while you are unlikely to see a craftsman tuning and carving an individual guitar top in a modern mass-production guitar factory, science has at least brought a greater degree of consistency to the still essentially human process of mass-production.

Science does have some benefits to offer the guitar-maker. Ned Steinberger (see page 174) certainly shook up the electric guitar industry with his successful use of synthetic materials for tiny, headstock-less guitars. Greg Smallman (see page 25) has yet to have such an influence on the much more conservative "classical" guitar world, but his use of carbon-fibre in the internal strutting of concert guitars is also beginning to turn a few heads.

The uneasy mix of science and art in musical instruments was accurately assessed by Professor Charles Taylor, who hosted a series of Royal Institution Christmas Lectures, televised by the BBC in 1989.

In the lecture on stringed instruments, the amiable professor concluded by considering how science might help makers achieve the "perfection" of the Stradivari often seen as the pinnacle of violin design.

"We're still on the absolute fringe of development [of stringed instruments]," he said. "Scientifically speaking,

A selection of catalogue cover art from Germany.

I think we're beginning to help makers to achieve more uniform instruments. We're not necessarily helping them all to achieve the quality of a Strad, for example, because we frankly don't know what the real quality of a Strad is." While he chose to use the Stradivari as an example, he might just as easily have said Torres, or Martin, or Fender.

Great guitar designs are not quantifiable, and that in itself is part of their greatness. The ultimate guitar has yet to be produced, but this book will acquaint you with most of the others.

A collector would object to this 1952 ES295's replaced tuners; a player would prefer their efficiency.

Gibson's Chet Atkins was in effect an electric "classical" guitar.

THE 16TH AND 17TH CENTURIES

To appreciate more fully the modern guitars dealt with in the main body of this book, it is useful first to consider the early history of the guitar. To begin, a simple definition: the guitar is a plucked, stringed instrument that has a "waisted" body with incurved sides. There is, according to experts on its history, little evidence of such an instrument existing before the fifteenth century. That is not to say that broadly similar stringed instruments did not exist long before that time. But a barrage of confusing instrument names and hazy historical data cloud the issue, and even the experts disagree.

In this book we are concerned with surviving guitars, and the late sixteenth-century instrument shown on this page (right) is among the earliest that are still in existence.

Four-course guitar
The earliest guitars had four "courses" (a single, double or even triple string), as on this guitar shown in a book from 1552 (right). The four-course "treble" instrument, despite being surpassed by the five-course guitar, lasted until at least the seventeenth century.

Frets *Early guitars generally had tied-on gut frets: eight to ten for plucked playing, fewer for strumming.*

1614 Matteo Sellas five-course guitar
The five-course guitar had appeared by the mid-sixteenth century, and lasted until the late eighteenth century. Tunings suggested by the surviving music varied widely, as did the use of unison or octave doubled courses.

Tunings *Until the mid-eighteenth century "re-entrant" tunings were common. Strings are not tuned successively higher but in a pattern of rising and falling pitches.*

Size *String length (nut to bridge) of this guitar is 71cm (28in).*

Body *Matteo Sellas, working in Venice, used a vaulted construction of laminated strips for this guitar's back.*

QVATRIESME LIVRE
CONTENANT PLVSIEVRS FANTASIES,
Chanfons, Gaillardes, Paduanes, Branfles, reduictes en Tabulature de Guyterne,
& au ieu de la Ciftre, par Maiftre Guillaume Morlaye,
& autres bons autheurs.

A PARIS,
De l'imprimerie de Michel Fezandar, au mont fainct Hylaire, a l'hoftel d'Albret,
1552.
Auec priuilege du Roy, pour dix ans.

Rose *This is the original rose, made from laminated parchment. It shows the beginnings of the later popular "stepped" design.*

Body *The top is a modern renewal; the (original) back is flat.*

Bridge *This unit with tied strings is typical of the period.*

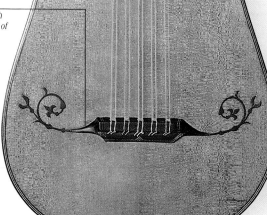

c1590 five-course guitar
This is probably the oldest surviving "full size" guitar, according to its owner Robert Spencer. Construction and decoration are very similar to a small guitar dated 1581 by Portuguese maker Belchior Dias that is in the Royal College of Music collection, London.

Frets *The guitar has ten tied-on gut frets.*

Neck *Cut down at one time, this has been restored to what is considered to have been its original length. String length is 68cm (26³⁄₄in).*

1627 Giorgio Sellas chitarra batente

The chitarra batente was a form of guitar popular in Italy at this time. The name means "guitar played with a plectrum," and the instrument was distinguished by its metal strings. Many also had fixed frets. Giorgio Sellas was from the same Venetian guitar-making family as Matteo (opposite page).

Tuning pegs *All guitars of this period have "friction" pegs, kept in position by the friction of peg and hole.*

Fingerboard *Guitars of the period have body tops projecting on to the fingerboard for strength.*

Neck *It is covered with inlaid designs in mother-of-pearl. The frets are missing.*

Back *This is highly decorated with ivory on ebony. Note the depth and the steeply curved shape.*

Decoration *The top is beautifully embellished, as is the typically recessed rose hole.*

Strings *Metal strings pass over the bridge, and are fixed on the bottom edge of the body. String length is 68cm (26³/₄in).*

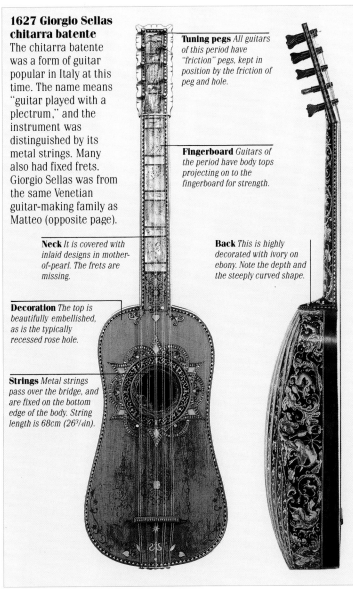

Craftsmanship

Some early guitars feature superb decoration, as on this seventeenth-century Italian example (close-up, left). These guitars, probably owned by the wealthy, may have survived more for their charm as objects than as instruments. The guitar was a great popular success at this time, yet peasants' guitars rarely survive.

1680s Stradivari five-course guitar

This is one of a handful of guitars made by the renowned Italian maker of violins, Antonio Stradivari. It shares the plainness and elegance of Stradivari's violins, in marked contrast to some contemporary guitars. The date on the back of the headstock (right) is either 1680 or 1688.

Fingerboard *This is ebony, as are the frets. String length is long at 74cm (29in).*

Frets *These continue on to the body. The position of the twelfth fret near the neck/body join is not usually seen until later.*

Stradivari guitar

The back recalls the maker's violins, using attractive "curly" maple. The joins are inlaid with ebony.

Body *Unlike many guitars of the period, decoration is limited to the rose hole and the tiny inlay below the bridge.*

Headstock *Six tuning pegs are surmounted by a decorated brass plate.*

Arms *These are purely decorative, and do nothing to enhance or diminish the sound.*

Strings *Lyre guitars generally came with six single strings, though others had up to nine, or six doubled courses.*

*c*1805 Thibout lyre guitar

This was made by Amedée Thibout in Caen, northern France. There was a vogue in Europe for these instruments from the 1780s to the 1810s. Popular at the same time was the similar harp-guitar, but the wealthy ladies at whom both instruments were aimed soon turned to the newly mass-produced piano.

*c*1760 Preston "English guitar"

This was not a guitar at all, but a type of cittern. John Preston worked in London around the 1750s and made many "English guitars," which were more popular in Britain at this time than the conventionally shaped guitar.

Tuning *Turning a watch-key in holes above the strings moved the string hooks laterally, thus adjusting tuning.*

Capo tasto *This shortens the string length to play in higher keys. The neck is drilled to give four positions.*

Early oddities

The two instruments shown on this page are not mainstream guitars, but each highlights an interesting European tributary.

Principally in France and as a result of the so-called "classical revival," the lyre guitar (left) rather fancifully adopted the shape of the ancient Greek lyre – an outline often used in the West as a symbol of music. It has been suggested that its great popularity around the early nineteenth century, mainly with amateur players, influenced the move at this time by many makers of conventional guitars to six single strings.

The "English guitar" (right), with six metal-strung courses and a small, rounded body shape, was very popular in Britain from the middle of the eighteenth century to the early 1800s, when it was ousted by the conventional Spanish-style guitar.

Body *The two soundholes in the top were common on such instruments. Decoration here is tastefully minimal.*

Size *The string length (nut to bridge) of this typical lyre guitar is quite short: 59cm (23¼ in).*

Strings *"English guitars" usually had six courses of metal strings, and very short string lengths – here 42cm (16½in).*

Bridge *A unit securing the strings with pins was becoming popular at this time.*

c1760 Salomon modified five-course guitar

This guitar was made in Paris by Jean-Baptiste Dehaye Salomon. It has been modified with two added tuners and an extra bridge channel, designed to accommodate a sixth course. There is no room on the neck for more strings, so the sixth course probably ran free of the neck on the bass side, over an extended nut.

Tuners *These two pegs were added later to the center of the headstock.*

Frets *The instrument has tied-on gut frets.*

Size *String length is 67cm (26¹/₂in).*

Vieyra guitar

This guitar is undated, but despite the general move from five to six courses around the end of the eighteenth century, some six-course guitars were made earlier.

Size *String length is 68cm (26³/₄in).*

c1804 Pagés six-course guitar

This instrument was made in Cadiz, south-western Spain, by Josef Pagés. He was among the first in Spain to use a fan-strutting system, later developed by Antonio de Torres (see pages 20-21).

Body *This highly decorated guitar was the work of Antonio dos Santos Vieyra, of Lisbon, Portugal.*

Frets *Twelve full-size metal frets lead to shorter "treble" frets on the body.*

Size *String length is 64.5cm (25¹/₂in).*

Soundhole *Around the early nineteenth century makers were moving from the rose hole to the open soundhole.*

Further developments

As we have seen, guitar makers had begun by the mid-sixteenth century to adopt five courses and a generally larger instrument than the early "treble" four-course guitar. Tunings of the "baroque" five-course guitar varied widely, but by the middle of the eighteenth century had started to become standardized toward A/D/G/B/E – in other words, as the top five strings of the modern guitar.

At about the same time as a vogue (primarily in France and Britain) for some unusual instruments related to the guitar, conventional makers started around the late eighteenth century to move from five to six courses on their guitars, with the extra course tuned to a low E. From there a simple refinement was made, at first in Italy and France, to six single strings: the result, adopted widely elsewhere, was an instrument looking and sounding a little closer to the modern guitar.

To continue the evolution which followed in the Spanish-style guitar, refer to the European "classical" section beginning on page 20. For the development of the acoustic guitar in the United States, see pages 26-31 (Martin flat-tops) and pages 36-37 (Gibson archtops).

❝At its simplest an acoustic guitar is a box with a neck, but the best examples have an unadorned elegance that is both practical and beautiful.**❞**

ACOUSTIC GUITAR

1931 MARTIN OM-28, courtesy Guitar Gallery (UK).

ANATOMY OF THE ACOUSTIC

There are principally two kinds of acoustic guitar, the flat-top and the archtop. The general description of a flat-top with a round soundhole covers classical nylon-strung instruments as well as steel-strung "folk" guitars, while the archtop acoustic was a later development. As explained later in this section, the archtop style of acoustic was designed to increase the volume of the basic instrument.

Here we examine the construction of a flat-top acoustic, this one from the workshop of English maker Andrew Manson. The workmen pictured are at the Martin factory in the USA. Of course, each guitar-maker has his or her own particular tastes in use of materials and application of design, but this overall view applies to the majority of guitars of the type.

Bending the sides
To make guitar rims, wood is soaked and then shaped over a heated pipe (shown here at Martin).

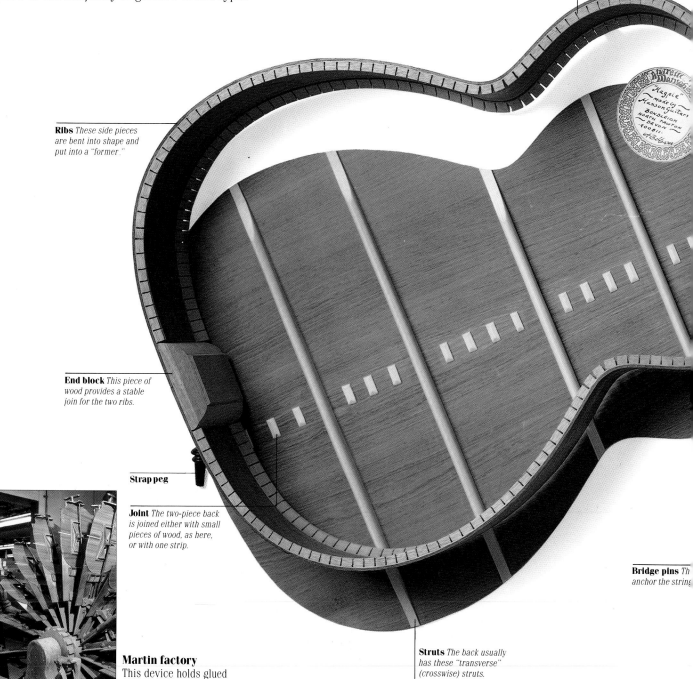

Lining These strips ease the joining of the sides to top and back.

Ribs These side pieces are bent into shape and put into a "former."

End block This piece of wood provides a stable join for the two ribs.

Strap peg

Joint The two-piece back is joined either with small pieces of wood, as here, or with one strip.

Bridge pins Th anchor the string

Martin factory
This device holds glued guitar backs.

Struts The back usually has these "transverse" (crosswise) struts.

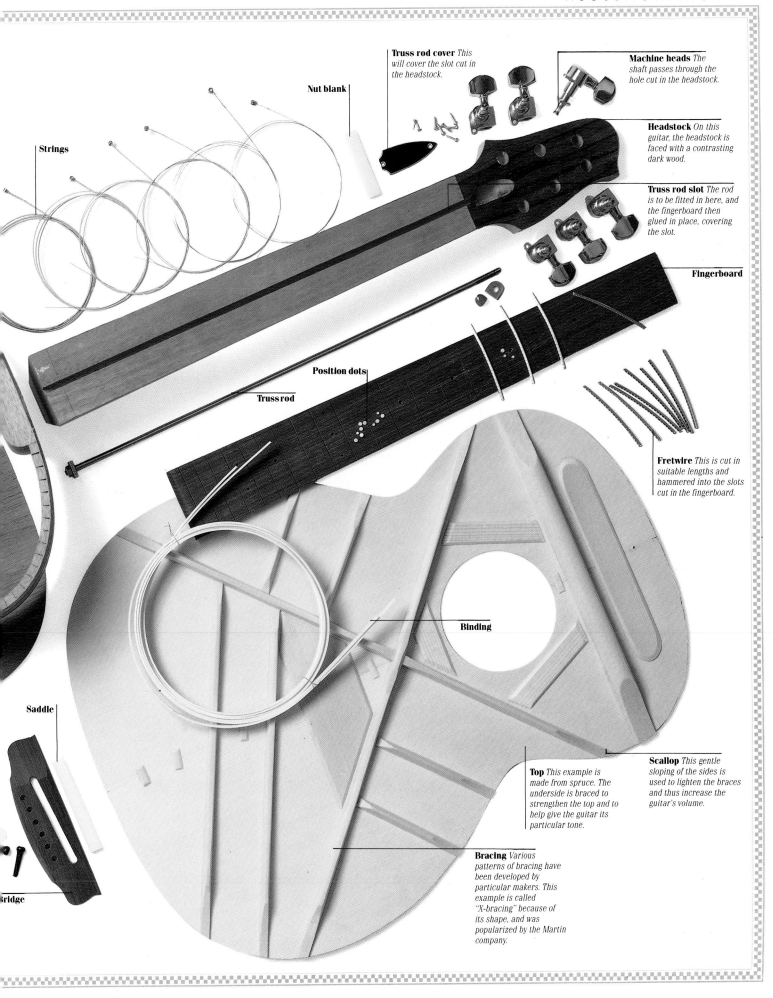

Truss rod cover *This will cover the slot cut in the headstock.*

Nut blank

Machine heads *The shaft passes through the hole cut in the headstock.*

Strings

Headstock *On this guitar, the headstock is faced with a contrasting dark wood.*

Truss rod slot *The rod is to be fitted in here, and the fingerboard then glued in place, covering the slot.*

Fingerboard

Position dots

Truss rod

Fretwire *This is cut in suitable lengths and hammered into the slots cut in the fingerboard.*

Binding

Saddle

Scallop *This gentle sloping of the sides is used to lighten the braces and thus increase the guitar's volume.*

Top *This example is made from spruce. The underside is braced to strengthen the top and to help give the guitar its particular tone.*

Bridge

Bracing *Various patterns of bracing have been developed by particular makers. This example is called "X-bracing" because of its shape, and was popularized by the Martin company.*

ANTONIO DE TORRES

During the nineteenth century the guitar began to develop into the instrument generally referred to now as the "classical" guitar. The maker most responsible for this development was Antonio de Torres. Around 1800, the European guitar had moved away from five courses (see pages 12–15) to six single strings. Many of the early six-string instruments had relatively small bodies with transverse strutting inside the top, such as the 1830s guitar (shown right) made by the Frenchman René Lacôte. Torres, however, introduced a bigger but not heavier body with wider bouts, and established the fan-strutting pattern inside the top of the body as the most effective for the Spanish guitar. Torres's methods produced a tonally more wide-ranging instrument, particularly in the bass, and his ideas for an integrated guitar were widely adopted in Spain and far beyond.

1835 Lacôte
René Lacôte was making guitars in Paris during the first half of the nineteenth century. He is sometimes credited with the invention of the scalloped fingerboard. The machine heads of this guitar are completely enclosed in the headstock. The short fingerboard is more often seen on earlier instruments.

1836 Louis Panormo
The son of an Italian violin-maker, Louis Panormo ran a prolific workshop in London in the early nineteenth century, advertising himself there as the "only maker of guitars in the Spanish style." He was one of the few outside Spain using fan-strutting, a better type of which was later popularized by Torres.

Decoration Note the attractive inlay work on the body.

Bridge This is of the early "pin" type without a saddle.

Body This top is made from two pieces of spruce.

Rosette A middle-range example of Torres's decorative work.

Bridge Torres ratified the use of the separate saddle.

Antonio de Torres (1817-1892)

Torres was born near Almeria in Spain, and worked in Seville (1852-69) and Almeria (1875-92). His designs developed his theory that the guitar's top was the key to its sound.

Torres' fan-strutting pattern for the top's underside, his characteristic "doming" of the lower bout, his shifting of the bridge proportionately further up the body, and his uses of relatively thin woods all combined to produce strong but not heavy guitars with a responsive, rounded sound and an elegant plainness.

The most famous contemporary guitarist to use Torres instruments was Francisco Tarrega (1852-1909) who was among the first to establish the guitar as a "serious" musical instrument. José Romanillos, in his thorough, intelligent study *Antonio de Torres – Guitar Maker*, estimated that Torres made some 320 guitars during his two active periods, of which 66 have been traced.

Headstock *Wood has been added here, presumably to accommodate the new machine heads.*

BACK AND SIDE
Torres generally used rosewood, maple, or cypress for the backs and sides of his guitars. For this instrument he used a dark Brazilian rosewood. The back has an attractive three-piece construction with the outer pieces "bookmatched" – the wood is split and opened out to give a symmetrical "reflected" grain.

Body *The three-piece top is of spruce: back and sides of cypress.*

1876 Torres
Originally an 11-string, this is one of three that Torres is known to have made, with five extra bass strings. It was converted to a six-string in 1945.

Six strings *It was converted to six by Marcelo Barbero in Madrid.*

1860 Torres
Guitars like this underline the view that Torres originated the modern style of flamenco guitar (see page 23). Note the body shape, tuners, and materials.

Body *The top is spruce; the back is four-piece cypress, and the sides are also of cypress.*

Machine heads *These appear to have been added; the guitar possibly had peg-type tuners originally.*

Neck *This is made from cedar, and has a rosewood fingerboard.*

Label
One of two types used by Torres during his second "epoch" of guitar-making (1875-92), this shows the address 23 calle Real, Almeria; the guitar is numbered 28, and dated 1882.

1882 Torres
This Torres guitar was discovered in South America in 1989. Like most Torres instruments it conforms to one of the several body shapes (*plantilla* is the Spanish term) that Torres used, all of which were related in overall proportions.

Andrés Segovia (1893-1987)

Born near Granada in southern Spain. Segovia did more than any other player to popularize the "classical" guitar on the concert stage. In 1912 Segovia replaced his first guitar (by Benito Ferrer) with a Manuel Ramírez (probably made in the Ramírez workshop by Santos Hernández). He changed in the late 1930s to the Hermann Hauser (main picture), which he used until about 1970, when he moved to new guitars by Fleta and José Ramírez.

1937 Hermann Hauser 1

The guitar shown was played for many years by Andrés Segovia. Based in Munich, Hermann Hauser (1882-1952) made a variety of stringed instruments. Some earlier guitars were in an older, non-Spanish style, but he soon adopted the Torres style. His son and grandson, both also named Hermann Hauser, have continued to make guitars. The guitar shown is now in the Metropolitan Museum of Art in New York.

Body *The top is spruce, neck mahogany with ebony fingerboard, and back and sides are Brazilian rosewood. There is a penciled dedication to Segovia from Hermann Hauser under the guitar's top.*

CLASSICAL AND FLAMENCO

The influence of Torres (see pages 20-21) spread throughout Spain and into the rest of Europe. Madrid became the center of guitar-making expertise, and instruments from some of the most famous of these *guitarreros* (the Spanish word for guitar-makers) are shown on the opposite page. For some time into the early twentieth century the flamenco guitar was the most popular kind of Spanish guitar. It was not until the great Andrés Segovia began to perform widely during the 1920s and 1930s that the idea of the serious "classical" guitar took root, since when this instrument has become the dominant type of Spanish guitar. There have also been important makers outside Spain: for example in Germany and France.

Bridge *The strings on this typical "classical" type are looped and tied at the rear.*

Body *Bouchet used very thin tops that add to his guitars' superb sound.*

1954 Barbero flamenco
Marcelo Barbero (1904-55) was another of the great flamenco makers.

1913 Manuel Ramírez flamenco
Manuel Ramírez (1864-1916) is highly regarded, for both "classical" and flamenco guitars. His workshop spawned many later great makers. Early guitars were in the style of his brother José Ramírez I, but Manuel soon defined his own style.

1923 Santos Hernández flamenco
Hernández (1873-1942) was a brilliant pupil of Manuel Ramírez.

Body *This is made from traditional flamenco guitar materials: spruce top, cypress back and sides.*

Headstock *Wooden "friction" pegs help lighten the guitar.*

1934 Esteso flamenco
Domingo Esteso (1882-1937) trained at Manuel Ramírez's workshop in Madrid, later setting up in that town in his own right, to wide praise. This Esteso, owned by guitarist Juan Martin, is quite deep for a flamenco.

Label
Ramírez's title "Luthier," as shown on the label, was awarded by the National Conservatory of Madrid.

Label
Engraved by Bouchet, this indicates guitar 31, made in 1954.

Flamenco guitar
"Flamenco" is the word generally applied to the folk music of the gypsies of Andalusia, southern Spain. The form combines song (*cante*), dance (*baile*), and guitar playing (*toque*). The percussive guitar style includes rhythmic tapping of the guitar's top (often protected by a plastic *golpeador*, or tap plate) and requires an attacking sound with little sustain. Differences from the "classical" guitar include the extreme lightness of the flamenco guitar, and the low action of the strings to aid percussion and speed. Recent performers tend to use instruments combining flamenco and "classical" guitar.

Golpeador *This is a "tap plate" that protects the top.*

Fingerboard *This is made from ebony.*

Headstock *Bouchet engraved his machine heads and hand-carved their ivory buttons.*

Back *Fleta used varnish inside, intended to brighten the sound.*

1976 Fleta (below)
Ignacio Fleta (1897-1977) set up a workshop in Barcelona in 1927, later developing his typically wide-waisted guitars.

1954 Bouchet (above)
Painter Robert Bouchet (1898-1986) was a keen guitarist. He began making guitars in Paris in 1946, impressive instruments produced in small numbers.

Body *Fleta always added a diagonal strut under the treble side of the top to increase volume.*

TWENTIETH-CENTURY CLASSICALS

Visually, most modern "classical" guitars bear the shape and general characteristics of Torres's nineteenth-century designs, though some makers now use bigger bodies. Efforts for change have also taken place inside the guitar, principally in the layout of strutting under the guitar's top, crucial to its overall tone and volume. It is the production of the latter quality, while retaining or even improving upon the former, that has exercised many maker's minds, as Segovia pointed out in Christopher Nupen's 1969 film about the great guitarist: "When I arrived in the musical world I began to play in very big halls, and from that moment all the makers tried to do a guitar that sounds better and stronger. To have this instrument with the strong sounds, and mellow, it is really a great achievement of the guitar makers."

1968 Rubio (right)
Englishman David Rubio lived and worked in Madrid, apprenticed at the workshop of Domingo Esteso (maintained by his nephews). He built guitars in New York from 1961, then set up a workshop in England from 1967 (at first on Julian Bream's farm). Makers from Rubio's workshop such as Paul Fischer are now respected in their own right. This Rubio is owned by British guitarist John Mills.

Body *Rubio often used a "nodal bar" inside, designed to produce distinct treble and bass.*

Fingerboard *This is made of ebony, on a mahogany neck.*

Rosette *Romanillos's guitars have beautiful decorations here and at the headstock.*

Catalogues
José Ramírez is one of the few large "classical" manufacturers to publish catalogues.

Body *This is spruce. Some modern Ramírez guitars use western red cedar, a replacement used by a few makers.*

Label *This was signed by the current head of the family, José III.*

1985 Romanillos "La Buho" (left)
José Romanillos was born in Madrid in 1932, and has lived in Britain since 1959. He set up a workshop near Julian Bream's home in England in 1970; by 1987, Romanillos estimated that he made about 17 guitars a year. Bream played Romanillos guitars among others from 1973, and used the guitar shown until he sold it at a London auction in 1990.

1990 José Ramírez 1A
The Ramírez dynasty began with brothers José I (1858-1923) and Manuel. The business passed to José II (1885-1957) and José III (born 1922), the latter heading the workshop that produced the guitar shown. In 1982 there were 17 workers producing around 1000 guitars a year.

Body *The top is made of two-piece spruce, while the back and sides are of Indian rosewood.*

1987 Smallman
Greg Smallman lives and works in isolation in the rain forest of New South Wales, Australia. Interest in his guitars was boosted when John Williams began to use Smallmans in the 1980s. The most unusual constructional aspect of Greg's guitars is the lattice-like strutting made from wood and carbon fiber, under a very thin, usually cedar top – all designed to increase volume. A few makers have in recent years moved from the traditional spruce top to one of cedar.

Body *This has a cedar top and rosewood sides and back, which is gently curved and without braces.*

1987 Gilbert
John Gilbert is based in California, south of San Francisco. Originally a tool-maker, he turned to guitar-making in 1966 and has developed a loud, responsive instrument. The distinctive feature of Gilbert guitars is the bridge (now adopted by some British makers), designed to give strength where it is needed, and John's original pin saddles. Also noticeable visually is the rosette style, with "squared-off" sections.

Scale-length *Smallman uses the standard 65cm (25^1/$_2$in).*

Saddle *A steel pin gives definition to each string. Gilbert uses a different design now.*

1973 Kohno
Masaru Kohno is, at the time of writing, the leading Japanese "classical" guitar-maker. At first, he studied guitar-making in the Madrid workshop of luthier Arcángel Fernández. Kohno then went on to set up his own operation in Tokyo during the late 1960s. Note that the two small screws visible near the bridge of this guitar are from a pickup added by owner Steve Howe.

Body *The top is of sitka spruce; back and sides are Indian rosewood.*

Bridge *Smallman's bridges are slightly smaller than usual, to minimize weight.*

Hernández Y Aguado
These record sleeves present us with evidence of two interesting duos, one from guitar-making, the other from guitar-playing. Manuel Hernández and Victoriano Aguado teamed up to make guitars in Madrid in the 1960s. The superb

British guitarists John Williams (above left) and Julian Bream (right) are seen playing the same Hernández y Aguado instrument, which they each owned at various times. Williams and Bream themselves teamed up during the 1970s, to perform as a very successful duo.

MARTIN GUITAR FEATURES

For more than 150 years the Martin company has been producing some of the finest acoustic flat-top guitars in the world. Martin's designs for the shape of the guitar's body, its internal bracing, and its decorative inlay work have influenced virtually every maker of acoustic guitars, both directly and indirectly.

The company has been in the hands of the Martin family since the very beginning, when Christian Frederick Martin emigrated from Germany to set up a music store in New York in 1833. He soon moved to Nazareth, Pennsylvania, where Martin's headquarters and factory are based today.

Arguably, Martin's real success started in the 1930s and was consolidated following World War II, but many of their classic designs were formulated well before that time. A number of fine guitars were made by the company before the start of the twentieth century.

Christian Frederick Martin (1793-1873) Founder of the Martin company.

The Martin family
Christian Frederick Martin was born in 1796 in Germany, the son of a guitar-maker. He worked for his father and other makers, including Stauffer in Austria, but emigrated to the United States in 1833. The business was moved from New York to Pennsylvania, a factory established, and Christian Frederick Martin's grandson, Frank Henry Martin, took over the running of the company in 1888. Since then, successive generations of Martins have headed the company. The most recent is C. F. Martin IV, who became Chairman of the Board in 1986.

Binding *The decorative inlay features a repeating black-and-white pattern.*

Bridge *Martin's design here is already beginning to show traces of their classic "pyramid" type.*

Body *It measures 43.8cm (17¹/₄in) long and just over 28cm (11in) at its widest. The top was most likely made from spruce, as have been the vast majority of Martin guitars.*

Labels *Stuck to the back of the guitar are the labels of Martin and of their sales agent, Ludecus & Wolter.*

X-bracing

In the period up to the end of the nineteenth century Martin's guitars started to shed obvious European influences such as the Stauffer-style headstock (main picture). The company began to formulate their own designs and schemes, including the famous "X-bracing."

This refers to the pattern of wooden strips inside the top of the body, which contributes to the particular quality of tone produced by an acoustic guitar. Martin developed their X-shaped pattern in the 1850s and have used it ever since – as have most other acoustic-makers.

The Nazareth stamp

Another significant change a little later in the nineteenth century was when Frank Henry Martin, who had taken charge in 1888, decided no longer to use Martin's New York distributor, Zoebisch. Frank began to sell guitars direct to dealers in 1898, giving Martin more control over their own business. So it was at this time that the brand stamp changed from "C F Martin & Co, New York" to "C F Martin & Co., Nazareth PA." Zoebisch had insisted on retaining the "New York," despite Martin's move to Nazareth some 40 years before.

1880s Martin
This Size 1 Martin has a "C F Martin & Co. New York" stamp, used from 1867 to 1898. The company's famous "herringbone" inlay in the rosette around the soundhole and on the back was a feature of Style 21 guitars made by the company.

1860s Martin
The "C F Martin New York" stamp inside the soundhole was used only until 1867. The body is Size 2½ (meant for beginners). Note Martin's ebony "pyramid" bridge, named after the raised decorations either side of the saddle and pins.

SIDE AND BACK

Martin probably used rosewood for the back and sides of this guitar. Just visible on the back of the body, near the neck, is the C F Martin stamp, an identifying trademark still used in modified form today.

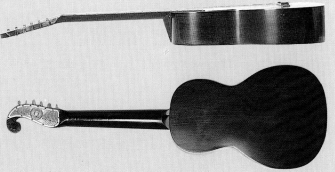

Early Martin guitar (below)
This instrument, like several built by Christian Frederick Martin soon after his immigration to the USA, bears a striking curved headstock of European influence. The guitar dates from the late 1830s and is typical of the small-bodied "parlor" guitars that Martin was making at this time.

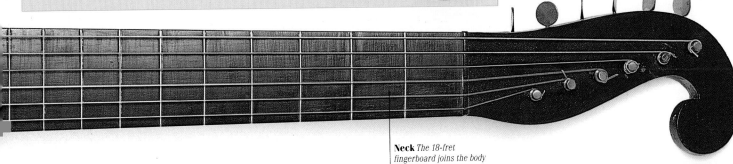

Neck *The 18-fret fingerboard joins the body at the twelfth fret.*

Labels

These are visible through the soundhole of this early guitar. The large label is for C F Martin, giving the company's address as 212 Fulton Street, New York, and this probably dates the guitar to 1838 or 1839. The smaller label is from a company called Ludecus & Wolter, which at the time acted as Martin's sales agent.

Headstock
This was directly influenced by maker Johann Stauffer, who employed C. F. Martin Snr in Vienna in the 1820s. The curved shape, and the rear metal cover, are typical of Stauffer.

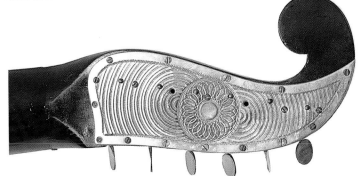

MARTIN'S STYLES AND SIZES

Two very significant changes came to Martin guitars in the 1920s and 1930s. First, the guitars were adapted to use steel strings rather than the previous gut types. To take the greater strain, during the 1920s Martin's guitars were braced more strongly, the tougher "belly" bridge was added around 1930, and necks were strengthened in the mid-1930s.

Second, the neck was moved further out of the body to make the playing of higher frets easier. The more playable design with fourteenth-fret body join first appeared on the OM models (1929) and was quickly adopted for other Martins. It became a standard for acoustic guitar design.

Model codes

Martin's simple model-number system has a number or letter code before the hyphen that gives the size of the body (see opposite page). The number following the hyphen refers to Martin's body "Style"; generally, a higher number means fancier finishing.

SIDE AND BACK
This model, the 0-45, has Martin's normal rosewood back and sides, and a mahogany neck.

Style 45 inlay
This model was first offered by Martin in the early 1900s. Its pearl inlay extends around the back and side of the guitar, creating a luxurious feel. The Style 42 looks similar from the front, but does not share this all-round inlay.

Soundhole *There is delightful pearl inlay work here, and all over the body.*

Pearl inlay *This continues around the edge of the fingerboard.*

1980 00-18
The Style 18 is among the plainest of Martin's guitars, with very little decoration. This instrument has had an internal bridge pickup added to make it more suitable for stage use: note the volume control visible on the upper side of the body.

1926 000-45
The Size 000 is favored by players who want a guitar without the bass-heavy sound of the Dreadnought size, but with a larger body than the 0 and 00 sizes. The ebony bridge was added to Style 45 in 1919, and this guitar's bracing for steel strings was an option, not becoming standard until 1928.

1930 2-17
This guitar illustrates how the depression of the 1930s in the USA hit some Martin models. This plain and spartan instrument was made from mahogany, with simple bridge and minimal inlay. It sold for $25, compared to $80 for a 000-28. Eight years earlier, Style 17 had been the first Martin made for steel strings.

1931 OM-28 (above)
The OM, new in 1929 and standing for Orchestra Model, was Martin's first guitar with a neck joining the body at the fourteenth fret. Such guitars, referred to as "14-fret" models, give better access to higher frets than "12-fret" types. The OM had a body like that of Size 000, but a longer scale length, and was made until 1933.

1929 0-45 (below)
Style 45 is Martin's top of the line, and has the most decorative inlay work. Immediately obvious is Style 45's so-called "torch" inlay on the headstock, though from the 1930s this was changed to a long C F Martin logo in pearl. Also distinctive is the amount of inlay work on the fingerboard.

Fingerboard *The pearl markers on the ebony board of some 45s are nicknamed "snowflakes".*

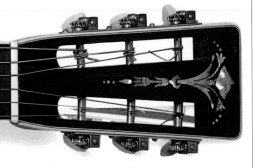

Martin body sizes
The measurements given are only approximate. The first figure is for the body height; the second is across the widest part of the body. There are some differences in size between 12- and 14-fret versions.

Size 2 *(12-fret)*
46.4×30cm
(18¹/₄×12in)

Size 1 *(12-fret)*
48×34.4cm
(18⁷/₈×13³/₄in)

Size 0 *(12-fret)*
48.5×34.3cm
(19¹/₈×13¹/₂in)

Size 00 *(14-fret)*
48×36cm
(18⁷/₈×14⁵/₁₆in)

Size 000 *(14-fret)*
49×38cm
(19³/₈×15in)

Size D *(14-fret)*
51×39.5cm
(20×15⁵/₈in)

MARTIN DREADNOUGHTS

The Dreadnought acoustic guitar is among the most famous of Martin's models, and like many innovations from the company has been of great influence on other makers. It has a distinctive square-shouldered, wide-waisted look. The bass-heavy tone designed for vocal accompaniment has been widely adopted by country and bluegrass players.

The Dreadnought, named after the British battleship of the time, was designed in 1916 by Frank Henry Martin and Harry Hunt, who was at the time manager of the Ditson music store in New York. Originally, Ditson sold the early Dreadnoughts exclusively. When the store went out of business in the late 1920s, the Martin company went on to experiment with the basic design. The archetypal Martin Dreadnoughts, the D18 and D28 models, came into general production in 1935, while the classic D45 was made in limited numbers at this time.

BACK AND SIDE
These views again show the thrashing that the guitar got in Presley's hands – and also it seems, given the back's centralized damage, from an intrusive Elvis belt buckle.

Damage *There is evidence here of Presley's hard strumming style.*

Body *Martin's plain Style 18 first appeared in Size D in 1935.*

Stick-on letters
Presley's personal touch of kitsch. The "S" has long been missing.

1988 D-45

The first D-45 was made in 1933 for singing cowboy star Gene Autry. An early D-45 is among the rarest of Martin's guitars: only 91 were built until the model was stopped in 1942. Demand led to its reintroduction in 1968, and the guitar remains in production today. It combines Martin's biggest body size with its best, most ornate style. The retail price of a D-45 in 1938 was $200; in 1990, $5,330.

1988 D-28S

A few early Martins and the Ditson Dreadnoughts have a twelfth-fret body join, but a fourteenth-fret join soon became standard. Reissues of the "12-fret" type, judged by some to have a sweeter tone, began in the 1960s with the D-18S, D-28S, and D-35S.

Neck *The twelfth-fret join pushes more fingerboard on to the body.*

Logo *The type with "C F Martin & Co." curved over "Est. 1933" is attributed to models from 1933.*

1989 Brazil D-41LE

Style 41 appeared in 1969, like a 45 but with marginally less inlay on the top. Only 31 were made that year using Brazilian rosewood sides and back before Martin switched to Indian rosewood. This 20th anniversary export limited edition uses Brazilian rosewood.

DATING GUITARS
Labels

The earliest Martins have paper labels, often mentioning associates such as Schatz, Coupa, and Bruno.

Stamps

The C F Martin stamps are found in one or more places: on the center strip inside the back, visible through the soundhole; on the neck block further inside the body (sometimes upside down); and on the back of the headstock (or on the outside back near the neck/body join). The center-strip stamp gives the approximate date of manufacture as follows:

C F Martin New York 1833-1867
C F Martin & Co, New York 1867-1898
C F Martin & Co, Nazareth PA 1898-date. "Made in USA" was added from the 1960s.

Serial numbers

Usually found on the neck block inside body.
1898-1909: up to 11018
1910-1919: up to 14512
1920-1929: up to 40843
1930-1939: up to 74061
1940-1949: up to 112961
1950-1959: up to 171047
1960-1969: up to 256003
1970-1979: up to 419900
1980-1989: up to 493279

Brand stamp
The "C F Martin New York" type was used from 1833 to 1867. The stamp, on the back-strip, is seen here through the soundhole.

"& Co" 1867 to 1898.

Nazareth since 1898.

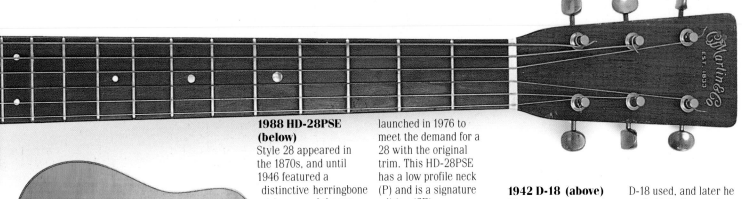

1988 HD-28PSE (below)

Style 28 appeared in the 1870s, and until 1946 featured a distinctive herringbone trim around the top edge. The HD-28 was launched in 1976 to meet the demand for a 28 with the original trim. This HD-28PSE has a low profile neck (P) and is a signature edition (SE).

Herringbone
After a drop in the marquetry quality, Martin stopped using the trim in the mid-1940s.

1942 D-18 (above)

This Martin was used by Elvis Presley during the early part of his career, probably around 1954 and 1955 when he was recording for Sun Records of Memphis, Tennessee. From the date of the instrument's manufacture, it is clear that Elvis bought the D-18 used, and later he traded it in for another guitar (at O.K. Houck's music store in Memphis). The guitar, used by Elvis at a time when his music still had strong country influences, was in 1974 donated to the Country Music Hall of Fame, Nashville.

D'ANGELICO AND D'AQUISTO

D'Angelico guitars are among the most highly rated of all archtop jazz guitars. John D'Angelico (1905-64) began working in New York during the 1930s. Come the 1950s, many top American jazz players, such as Johnny Smith and Chet Atkins, had discovered the beautiful tone of D'Angelico's guitars. By that time John was offering two cutaway-equipped models, the Excel and the New Yorker, but he also made variations as directed by individual players. After D'Angelico died his flair and style lived on in the instruments of Jimmy D'Aquisto, who had worked for D'Angelico since 1952.

1950 D'Angelico Excel (above) This has a smaller body than usual, perhaps a special order. In the 1960s it was refurbished by Jimmy D'Aquisto.

1961 D'Angelico Excel (above) Note how the machine heads, truss-rod cover, pickguard and tailpiece conform to the "stepped" design theme.

Bridge *These inlays are more often seen on New Yorker bridges.*

Stain *Sometimes seen on jazz guitars, this comes from a small cork circle on the underside of a (since removed) pickup.*

Pickguard *Original 1950s units tend to crystalize and emit a gas that damages the guitar. So most are replaced.*

Tailpiece *This "two-bar" type is the one most often seen on Excels.*

1948 D'Angelico Excel (above) This natural "blonde" D'Angelico Excel was John's equivalent of the Gibson L5. Generally, the Excel had less decorative work than the New Yorker (see right).

Jimmy D'Aquisto

After John D'Angelico became ill in the early 1960s, Jimmy D'Aquisto began to take on the more important parts of the guitar-building process. When John died in 1964, Jimmy lost the right to use the D'Angelico name, but began making guitars in New York under his own name. As the two archtop instruments (boxed right) show, Jimmy gradually modified his D'Angelico-influenced designs to incorporate his own ideas.

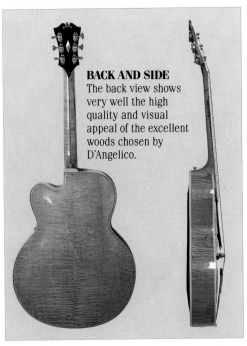

BACK AND SIDE
The back view shows very well the high quality and visual appeal of the excellent woods chosen by D'Angelico.

D'Aquisto "New Yorkers"
These two examples show how Jimmy D'Aquisto added his own touches to the D'Angelico style. The 1968 example (left) has a small pickguard and smooth-sided "f-holes." By 1986 (right) D'Aquisto's "New Yorker" has a spruce top and the original metal tailpiece is now wooden.

1978 D'Aquisto Flat Top Delux (right)
As well as his archtop acoustics, Jimmy D'Aquisto has also made solid electrics and flat-top acoustics. He built eleven examples of this Delux model between 1976 and 1981.

Pickguard *D'Aquisto's distinctive small type.*

Hardware *The tailpiece and large bridge are made from ebony.*

Fingerboard *D'Angelico occasionally used this pointed flourish where it meets the body.*

Inlays *Most Excels feature block markers, while most New Yorkers have "split blocks."*

Machine heads *The Grover Imperials suit the "stepped" theme.*

1954 D'Angelico New Yorker (below)
The "New Yorker" was bigger than the Excel; compare also the fingerboard inlays and tailpieces.

Headstock *Some have this ornate shape, others are smooth-topped (like the "New Yorker's" below).*

Back view (below)
The back of the 1954 "New Yorker" reveals D'Angelico's superb sunburst work.

Receipt
This is John D'Angelico's original receipt for a 1952 Excel model.

EPIPHONE AND STROMBERG

The Epiphone brand began in 1928, named after guitar-maker Epaminondas Stathopoulo – Epi for short. His Greek immigrant father, Anastasios, built flutes and violins and had founded the House of Stathopoulo in New York.

Epaminondas was president of the company when in 1928 they changed their name from the House of Stathopoulo to the Epiphone Banjo Corporation. The principal products were guitars, mandolins, and banjos (in that order), and the best of their archtop acoustic models established during the 1930s were quickly taken up by many leading jazz guitarists. These fine guitars have since become widely sought after.

As well as the superb Emperor and Deluxe instruments shown here, Epiphone made a number of other significant archtop acoustics, some of more humble manufacture. These included the Broadway, Triumph, Royal, Spartan, Blackstone, Devon and Zenith models.

The magic did not last. Epi Stathopoulo died in the early 1940s, and Epiphone never really took off again after World War II. Business complications in the early 1950s led to a series of changes, including a move out of New York to Philadelphia. Although still in production, during this period Epiphone were reportedly making guitars from existing parts. In 1957 Epi's brother Orphie, who had taken over as president, sold Epiphone to Gibson.

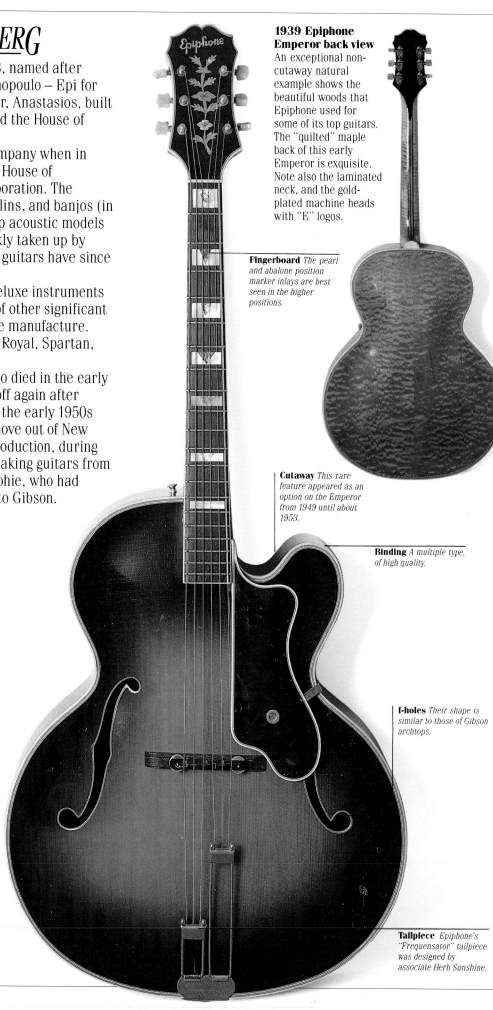

1939 Epiphone Emperor back view
An exceptional non-cutaway natural example shows the beautiful woods that Epiphone used for some of its top guitars. The "quilted" maple back of this early Emperor is exquisite. Note also the laminated neck, and the gold-plated machine heads with "E" logos.

Fingerboard *The pearl and abalone position marker inlays are best seen in the higher positions.*

Cutaway *This rare feature appeared as an option on the Emperor from 1949 until about 1953.*

Binding *A multiple type, of high quality.*

f-holes *Their shape is similar to those of Gibson archtops.*

Tailpiece *Epiphone's "Frequensator" tailpiece was designed by associate Herb Sunshine.*

Epiphone Broadway
This is the headstock of a 1930s Broadway model from Epiphone's early so-called "Masterbilt" series. Note the asymmetrical shape, and the attractive scrolls and vine inlay. This guitar has been recently overhauled, which is the reason for the new tuners (originally cheap small-button types) and block fingerboard inlays.

1942 Epiphone Emperor (right)
Epiphone launched this top-of-the-line archtop acoustic around 1936, as a response to the huge new Super 400 produced by Gibson, Epiphone's chief competitor. The Emperor, too, was enormous and was apparently so named as Epiphone wanted a "royal" word to tie in with the news in 1936 of Edward VIII's abdication from the British throne. The example shown is a rare cutaway model, introduced in 1949 and in production for only a few years.

Epiphone logo *This is an early type; note the pointed-end p and opened e.*

1941 Epiphone Deluxe

The Deluxe was originally part of the early 1930s Masterbilt series. But this version with a bigger body first appeared at the end of that decade, again in response to Gibson, who had recently increased the size of their L5. In competitive terms, the Deluxe vied with the L5, and the Emperor with the Super 400.

Markers *Called "cloud" inlays, these early divided types look more like fans.*

Body *This example has a natural "blonde" finish.*

f-holes *Some Epis, mainly mid-period examples, have "squared-corner" f-holes.*

Bridge *Individual bridges were carved to match the arch of each guitar's top.*

1951 Epiphone Deluxe Emperor

This hybrid model was made from around 1949. The guitar's label says Deluxe, but the body is of Emperor proportions. Other features are Deluxe-like, such as the headstock shape and the "cloud" inlays.

Ultra-Deluxe headstock

A close-up of the main guitar's headstock shows to good effect Elmer Stromberg's notable attention even to minor detail.

Stromberg Ultra-Deluxe

This guitar was made in Stromberg's Boston workshop, probably in the late 1940s, and ranked third in the maker's range. Note the beautiful checkered binding on the body, and the decorated fingerboard inlays (including a personalized block at the seventeenth fret).

Stromberg G1 Headstock

The G1, while a lesser model than the Ultra-Deluxe, still displays charming evidence of handcrafted inlay, especially the fine work around the Stromberg logo.

STROMBERG

The Stromberg business was based in Boston: Charles Stromberg, a Swedish immigrant, made banjos and drums, while his son Elmer made guitars. All Strombergs were built to order, but from the early 1930s to the mid-1950s, when Elmer's guitars became popular with jazz players, he offered about seven basic models. In descending order, they were the enormous Master 400 (wider even than the Gibson Super 400), Master 300, Ultra-Deluxe, Deluxe, G3, G2 and G1.

GIBSON ARCHTOPS

When Orville Gibson began to build his first musical instruments at the end of the nineteenth century, they had arched tops. Gibson's beautiful carved-top creations were to have a long-lasting effect on the later Gibson company's output, and for decades Gibson led the way with archtop guitars. Their classic archtop acoustics, the L5 and the Super 400, were designed for big volume. But demand for acoustic jazz guitars waned as the electric guitar took over, and the non-cutaway Super 400 and L5 were dropped during the 1950s; cutaway versions were made in small numbers until the early 1980s.

Orville H. Gibson
Gibson's founder was born in 1856, the son of a British immigrant. A skilled instrument-maker, he formed the Gibson company in Kalamazoo, Michigan in 1902.

BACK AND SIDE
The very first L5s had backs and sides made from birch, but this example, like most L5s, is of maple. Note the gold-plated tuners and the rich sunburst.

Bridge *The stepped saddle part is recent.*

Tailpiece *This is a simple "trapeze" unit.*

Body *The original L5 (dating from about 1923 to 1936) has a relatively small body. At its widest, this type measures a little over 40cm (16ins).*

Top *This is made from spruce, and the rich, dark color was called cremona brown by Gibson.*

1916 Style O
Introduced in 1903, this was Gibson's leading archtop until replaced by the L5 around 1923. By about 1907 the unusual scroll decoration and flat cutaway had appeared. "The Gibson" was added to the headstock after 1916.

1924 L4
This early L4 looks similar to the first "pre-scroll" Style Os. It was introduced in the early 1910s; the oval soundhole is an Orville Gibson trademark. Mid-1920s L4s have this "snake-head" headstock.

1939 Super 400
In about 1937 Gibson increased the size of the upper body of the already large Super 400. This example also features the alterations made in 1939 to the design of the tailpiece. This natural "blonde" finish was introduced as an option in 1939, although most Super 400s were still made in the traditional brown sunburst coloring.

1936 Super 400
Gibson's largest archtop when launched in 1934, this extravagant model had new flourishes like the headstock's "split blocks." The upper body of this early type measures 32cm (12½in), later enlarged.

Upper body *By 1939 this measured about 33.5cm (13½in) across.*

Tailpieces *The early type (above) has a hinged base and a "sharp" Y. The post-1939 version (left) is one-piece with a "curved" Y.*

Gibson factory
A 1937 view of the Kalamazoo workshops.

Dating Gibson guitars before 1947
Between 1902 and 1947, most Gibsons have a serial number on a white paper label inside the soundhole or f-hole. As a rough guide: 1902-09 up to 6975; 1910-19 up to 53800; 1920-29 up to 89750; 1930-39 up to 96050; 1940-47 up to 99999. Some guitars made around 1939–40 have a special number with an "EA" prefix. Some models also carry a factory order number.
For information on dating from 1947, see page 133.

Headstock *The "snake-head" type is narrower at the top than the base.*

Fingerboard *The original dot inlays gave way to blocks in about 1929.*

1940s L5 (below)
This model has the big post-1934 body. Dating this blonde is tricky: the logo puts it pre-war, but serial number indicates 1947.

1928 L5 (above left)
Launched around 1923, the radical L5 defined early archtop acoustic style. This guitar was designed mainly by Gibson's Lloyd Loar, and some early examples bear his signature on the internal label. Loar's innovative guitar was among the first to feature f-holes rather than circular soundholes, and a pickguard raised from the guitar's top.

1947 L5P (right)
The P stands for Premier, a term Gibson used to indicate a cutaway guitar. The option first appeared on L5s and Super 400s in about 1939. The suffix changed to C for cutaway around 1949.

GIBSON FLAT-TOPS

Gibson's traditions lie in the making of archtop guitars, and it wasn't until the late 1920s and into the 1930s that the company appeared to consider flat-top acoustics seriously. No doubt this decision was influenced by the growing success of Martin guitars, whose "Dreadnought"-shaped instruments appeared in the mid-1930s (see page 30). The debut in 1928 of the Gibson Nick Lucas flat-top produced one of the first guitars named after a musician. While the SJ200 (or J200) was a flashy flat-top aimed squarely at the country musician, plainer acoustics were made by Gibson under their own logo and also in their cheap Kalamazoo line.

BACK AND SIDE
Gibson used rosewood for the back and sides of the prototype and the following production models. After World War II, the company switched to maple for the back and sides.

Bridge *Shaped like a cow's horns, this type was nicknamed the "moustache."*

Body *A spruce top with sunburst finish.*

Pickguard *This prototype is without the decorated plate later applied.*

Gibson J45 (left)
This 1940s example was a relatively cheaper model from Gibson's developing flat-top "Jumbo" range (hence the J). Gibson tried with these models to compete with the popular Martin "Dreadnought" acoustics.

Pickup *The single-coil unit sits at the end of the fingerboard.*

Mounting holes *At later stages, further pickups here been added and removed.*

Body *Like other J series flat-tops, this has a spruce top with mahogany back and sides.*

1962 J160E
This guitar, owned by George Harrison, was used on many classic Beatles recordings throughout the 1960s. Although Harrison and John Lennon each owned a J160E, the guitars were swapped around in the studio, and the instrument shown would have been used by both Beatles guitarists.
Gibson's J160E was launched in 1954 to give an approximate version of amplified acoustic guitar from its on-board single-coil pickup and associated controls. It could, of course, still be used unamplified and was often miked-up to combine the acoustic and pickup sounds. The J160E ceased production in 1977.

Control knob *This alters tone; above is the J160E's volume control.*

1963 Everly Brothers (right)
The pop vocal duo were rarely seen on stage without their special Gibson acoustics, in general production from 1962 to 1973. The guitars' curved pickguard, smaller on later models, make them easy to spot.

1970s Dove (left)
Gibson's Dove was launched in 1962 as number two in their acoustic line, below the J200. It has a spruce top with maple back and sides, and features a distinctive, beautifully decorated pickguard.

Fingerboard *Whitley's guitar has a narrower board than later 200s.*

Position markers *Inlaid western scenes feature on this prototype.*

1937 SJ200 (above)
This is the prototype of Gibson's top-of-the-line flat-top acoustic guitar. It was made specially for one of Hollywood's earliest singing cowboys, Ray Whitley. He suggested to Gibson several ideas to enhance the guitar's bass sound. The 200 went very quickly into general production.

1952 J200
Called variously the Super Jumbo 200, the SJ200, and the J200.

Gibson's "King of the Flat-top Guitars" is seen here in scarce "blonde" finish.

NORTH AMERICAN GALLERY

The steel-strung flat-top acoustic guitar is such an important part of American music, particularly in bluegrass, country, and blues, that it is no surprise to note the huge numbers of such instruments made by American companies.

We have already seen how much makers such as Martin and Gibson have contributed to the now accepted specifications of shape and size of the instrument, and most builders in the US and Canada adhere to these rules. Variations are subtle, limited to minute details such as the delicacy of inlay work on the body or fingerboard.

The archtop tradition, however, owes much to another musical form popularized in America – jazz. The innovations of the prime US makers, principally Gibson, have already been described, and here we chart the impressive instruments of some smaller names.

Machine heads *These are gold-plated Schallers.*

1979 Guild F212CR-NT (right)

Guild's 12-string flat-tops also have a strong following. Some models in the F series were offered with this sharp cutaway during the 1970s. This example is the better appointed version of the standard F212, with rosewood back and sides, and an ebony fingerboard and bridge.

Harmony Sovereign (left)
This model from the Chicago-based Harmony company, well known for budget guitars, was a mainstay of 1960s acoustic strummers. An earlier, plainer version led to this type with decorated soundhole and "cow-horn" bridge in the late 1960s.

Markers *The inlays are mother-of-pearl.*

Fingerboard *Made from ebony, this has inset binding.*

Body *The top is spruce. The F50R's back and sides are rosewood, the F50's maple.*

Bridge *This unit is made from ebony.*

1975 Guild F50R-NT (right)
The Guild company's early reputation was based on electric acoustic archtop jazz guitars. But following Guild's move to New Jersey in the 1950s, the company also became known for high quality flat-top acoustics, especially in the 1960s and 1970s. The big F50R was billed as the "finest six-string flat-top."

1990 Taylor 712-C
Bob Taylor began building guitars in Lemon Grove, California, in 1974, founding Taylor Guitars with partner Kurt Listug. Since then Taylor instruments have been used by players such as Bruce Springsteen. This cutaway ("C") model was launched around 1985.

1990 Larrivee C10
Canadian maker Jean Larrivee, based in North Vancouver, British Columbia, began building guitars in 1968. The company is still owned by Jean and family. The C10, with spruce top and sharp cutaway, was launched in 1971.

1990 Norman B50
The Canadian Norman company was started in the late 1960s by maker Jean-Claud Norman, and is now owned by Robert Godin (see also page 47). This B50 is the top of Norman's B series models, all of which are offered with optional L. R. Baggs pickups (also used on Godin guitars).

1990 Santa Cruz Tony Rice Model D
Santa Cruz guitars began in 1976, made by Richard Hoover in California. This 1980-launched model is based on a Martin D28 owned by jazz/bluegrass player Tony Rice which once belonged to Byrds guitarist Clarence White.

Vega (left)
This brand has appeared on a huge variety of guitars since it began in Boston in 1903, as well as on banjos, ukuleles, amplifiers and brass instruments. Some guitars were made by Vega themselves, but others were bought in. Little is known about the curious model shown, which inside bears a tiny typewritten slip that reads "patented 1930."

Vega brochure
This contains a range of Harmony-like electric and acoustic guitars.

Epiphone Frontier FT110
After Gibson's acquisition of Epiphone in 1957, all Epis were made by Gibson until the late 1960s. This is one of the 1960s Gibson-built steel-strung flat-tops: the Excellente and Bard models were higher priced; the Troubador, Eldorado, Serenader, Texan, Cortez and Cabellero were lower-cost models.

Pickguard *Note the lassoes and cacti, in keeping with the Frontier theme.*

Gretsch Synchromatic
Gretsch is best known for its electric acoustic guitars of the 1950s and 1960s. But guitars had been important to the company as early as the 1930s, and the acoustic archtop Synchromatic was among the first models. It appeared in many further versions.

Rick Nelson
The pop singer is seen here in the late 1950s with a Rickenbacker 390 archtop acoustic. Seated to his right is session guitarist James Burton.

EUROPEAN GALLERY

The flat-top acoustic guitars produced in Europe have tended to follow the patterns set by US makers. The direct simplicity of the designs established by Martin leave little room for innovation by other makers, so builders in Germany, Britain, Sweden, and elsewhere in Europe have created few surprises. In addition to the makers shown here, another popular European company which definitely merits a mention is Eko, from Italy. Eko has produced a large range of mainly budget-priced flat-tops, principally since the 1960s.

A very different acoustic instrument was the Selmer guitar designed for the Parisian company in the 1930s by an Italian called Mario Maccaferri. Although his association with Selmer was shortlived, Mario's unusual ideas for an internal sound chamber gave the guitar a distinctive, cutting tone. This, combined with the small numbers made, and its use by Django Reinhardt, has led to a rare and desirable guitar.

The archtop by Fleta illustrated here is a very rare instrument, and an uncommon example of a European "classical" maker dabbling in the jazz archtop field.

Machine heads *These are the original sealed types.*

Zero fret *This sets string length and height; the nut merely supplies spacing.*

Neck *This has built-in strengthening plates of an aluminum alloy.*

Body *The top is spruce; back and sides are laminated rosewood. Inside is a soundbox suspended from four fixing points.*

Fingerboard *The extended section gives 24 frets for the high E-string.*

Bridge *Selmer offered seven different bridge heights on this model.*

Tailpiece *This will take either ball-ended or looped strings.*

1963 Framus 5/98 King

This was a budget-priced flat-top. The King was a cutaway version, but a similar non-cutaway guitar, the 5/97 Jumbo, was also available. The King's top was made from pine, the back and sides from mahogany.

Hofner 491

This big bodied flat-top appeared in 1966 (it is also known by its Selmer London model number, 5154). It had a spruce top and mahogany back and sides. There was a 12-string version, and both models were available with a pickup built into the end of the fingerboard.

1932/3 Selmer Maccaferri (right)

Mario Maccaferri was an Italian "classical" guitarist turned guitar designer. The French Selmer company adopted his designs for a series of instruments in the 1930s. The type shown includes an unusual internal sound chamber to increase volume and give a smooth tone. However, a dispute meant that fewer than 300 such guitars were made. Maccaferri moved to the USA and in the early 1950s made an innovative if unsuccessful range of plastic guitars.

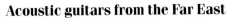

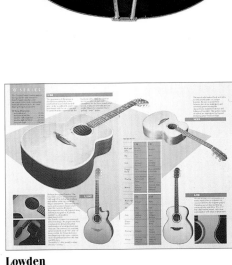

Levin Goliath (above)

Of the two well-known Swedish guitar makers, Hagstrom are recognized for their electrics. while Levin are best remembered for their fine flat-top acoustics. The affordable Goliath was extensively used during the 1960s.

1970s Levin (right)

The US Martin company bought Levin in the 1970s, and this guitar bears clear signs of Martin influence. Levin ceased trading at the end of the 1970s.

Acoustic B-bender

Pushing the handle bends up the B-string by a pre-determined interval.

1987 Manson

This guitar, made by Andrew Manson of Devon, England, has two extra fittings. At the nut is Manson's Slideslammer device, which raises the strings to a higher action for slide playing. At the bridge is a B-string bender, giving pedal steel effects and more usually associated with electric Telecasters.

1980 Tom Mates

British maker Tom Mates built this guitar for Dave Pegg (of Fairport Convention and Jethro Tull). The headstock, fingerboard and top are inlaid with mother-of-pearl, abalone, awabi, and synthetic ivory.

Fleta jazz guitar

This very unusual guitar was built in Barcelona by the renowned "classical" guitar-maker Ignacio Fleta. It is thought that Fleta experimented with the construction of a few archtop jazz guitars toward the end of World War II.

Lowden

A spread from the 1990 catalogue of this noted Northern Ireland maker.

Acoustic guitars from the Far East

Most of the large guitar-makers in Japan, Korea, Taiwan and elsewhere in the Far East have in their acoustic guitar ranges followed the usual pattern of copying western designs. In fact, because there is so little room for innovation or "improvement" in acoustic design, instruments from the Far East have, in general, stuck to the task of doing the job required at a reasonable price.

Logos that have appeared on acoustic guitars from oriental makers include most of the big names – such as Yamaha, Washburn, Takamine, Aria, Hohner, plus a host of importer-specified brands.

Many flat-top acoustics from these sources have laminated tops rather than the superior solid tops of the more expensive flat-tops, and consequently do not improve with age.

THE OVATION PRINCIPLE

For the touring band of the 1960s, accurate amplification of acoustic guitars on-stage was a constant problem. A microphone in front of the guitar was inefficient, and tied the performer to one spot. An electric guitar pickup stuck in an acoustic guitar gave little of the original sound quality of the adapted instrument.

In the late 1960s the Ovation company, based in Connecticut, came up with a new idea: the electro-acoustic guitar. Ovation built a special type of six-way pickup into the bridge which reacted to the mechanical movement both of the strings and of the top of the guitar. Amplified, this gave a sound claimed to be more like that of an acoustic guitar.

Ovation had been started in 1966 by Charles Kaman, a wealthy aeronautics engineer and keen guitarist. An electro-acoustic Balladeer model first appeared in 1970; Ovation made 100 and predicted failure. Today "Ovation" is almost synonymous with "electro-acoustic".

Body *Originally available in shaded blue, red, beige, or brown.*

1976 Ovation Custom Legend (above)
Ovation's standard guitars have a wooden top and Lyrachord fiberglass bowl-back.

Controls *This is volume; next to it is tone.*

Soundholes *These feature inlaid epaulets of exotic woods.*

1990 Ovation Collectors (below)

Beautiful maple was used for these limited-edition guitars. Note that "1990" is inlay displayed at the twelfth fret.

1990 Yamaha APX10

This has the usual transducer in the bridge, but adds another inside the body. It also offers a stereo output.

1990 Washburn EA40

This Japanese electro-acoustic has become popular with touring rock bands as a stage guitar. Note the slider controls.

SIDE AND BACK
The fiberglass bowl of the Adamas is slightly deeper than Ovation's normal "deep bowl." Some Ovations have a "shallow bowl," making a thinner guitar.

1990 Takamine Ltd-90

This limited-edition model was made by the Japanese Takamine company whose guitars are now distributed by Kaman.

Fingerboard *Triangular maple inlays are set into a walnut board.*

Headstock *A carved scroll design echoes detail on the bridge.*

Electro-acoustic pickups

"Transducer" is the name commonly given to the pickups popularized by Ovation and now used on many makers' electro-acoustic guitars. In fact, a transducer is any device which converts one form of energy to another, so the term applies to all guitar pickups, among other things.

The specific type of transducer used on electro-acoustics is a piezoelectric pickup, which incorporates special crystals that generate electricity under mechanical strain.

Ovation placed six individual piezo elements at the points where the strings cross the bridge saddle. Each element picks up the individual string's vibration from above, while all the elements combine to pick up from below the vibration of the guitar's top.

A small pre-amplifier inside the guitar boosts the signal from the pickups and sends it to the output socket. The guitar is then plugged into an amplifier or recording set-up.

The sound produced by a piezoelectric pickup is different from that generated by the normal electric guitar's magnetic pickup, which responds solely to metal strings moving in its magnetic field. The piezoelectric pickup responds to mechanical movement and is intended to give more "acoustic" character in its amplified sound.

1978 Ovation Adamas (above)

The Adamas model was added at the top of the Ovation range in 1975, furthering the company's use of synthetic materials. The top was made from a sandwich of carbon fibers and birch veneers, with 22 small soundholes replacing the usual central hole.

THINLINE ELECTRO-ACOUSTICS

Ovation's solution to the problem of amplifying the acoustic guitar has proved very successful, although many players argue that the amplified sound of electro-acoustic guitars still does not reproduce very accurately the pure sound of the acoustic guitar.

Ovation's "shallow bowl" guitars were aimed at attracting players used to solid electric guitars. But some guitarists wanted a combination of the sound of the electro-acoustic with a body based on solid electric styling.

During the 1980s various makers came up with instruments to meet such demands, offering the sound of the electro-acoustic in compact packages, and these guitars varied in quality and in the degree of compromise involved. Some produce a more natural acoustic sound, while a few are actually solid electrics with a bridge transducer; all are designed mostly for amplified use.

The success of these thinline electro-acoustic guitars relies on ease of use: they plug in just like an ordinary electric guitar, and they are styled so that players of solids will feel comfortable with them.

1990 Hohner TWP Western (left)
This has the soundhole of the traditional acoustic, but on a cutaway, thinline body with bridge transducer.

1989 Kramer Ferrington II KFS2 (right)
This was designed by maker Danny Ferrington, and launched by Kramer in 1986. There is also a Telecaster-shaped KFT model.

1988 Ibanez Artstar AE200 (below)
This combines a normal neck pickup with a bridge transducer. The body slots are a purely decorative feature.

Bridge *The six built-in piezo pickups are individually adjustable for volume.*

1983 Gibson catalog
This shows the Chet Atkins Classic Electric, described as "a nylon string solid body, all classic and all electric, all at the same time."

Body *The Chet Atkins models have two "tone chambers" inside to improve the sound.*

Fingerboard *Two types are offered. Model CE is of normal width (4.6cm/1¹³/₁₆in at the nut), while model CEC is of "classical" width (5cm/2in).*

1990 Gibson Chet Atkins CEC
Launched in 1982, this guitar was designed by Chet Atkins and Gibson as an electric version of a classical nylon-strung guitar.

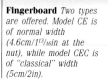

Chet Atkins
The well known country finger-picker is featured in a Gibson catalogue with the electric nylon-string guitar he helped to design.

1990 Shadow SHP1 (left)
While it appears to have no pickup, this German-made solid-body model has a transducer hidden in the bridge.

1990 Washburn SBT21 (right)
Like the Godin, this Washburn needs a second look before you can be sure it is an electric. But the six piezo elements are visible on the bridge.

1989 Godin L R Baggs (right)
This Canadian hollow-bodied guitar has a three-piece transducer under the bridge, and an active circuit.

Control panel *This has sliders for volume, bass, mid and treble.*

Bridge/tailpiece
Normal solid electric type, but with a transducer mounted in each saddle.

1990 Gibson Chet Atkins SST
This steel-strung version with body-mounted controls came out in 1987. Three years later, Gibson added a 12-string model.

Bridge *Dispensing with the usual bridge-pins, it secures the strings by threading them through from the back of the bridge.*

Body *This has a spruce top, with mahogany back and sides.*

Louder acoustics
Before Ovation came up with their piezo-electric bridge pickup, a number of guitar makers were offering flat-top acoustic models with ordinary magnetic pickups fitted into the soundhole. Some of these guitars even came with controls on the body (see, for example, the Gibson J160E on page 39).

Magnetic pickups retain virtually none of the acoustic character of the guitar in the resulting amplified sound. So musicians and sound engineers would combine the output from these pickups with that of a microphone placed in front of the guitar, aiming to return some of the lost acoustic quality.

Other experiments have been and still are practiced by players seeking the seemingly elusive sound of the accurately amplified acoustic guitar. Some use piezoelectric transducer "bugs" stuck to the guitar's body, inside or outside, usually in the form of circular dots or long plastic strips. These pickups will often have a lead trailing away from the point of contact, or may be more permanently wired into the guitar with a socket added to the body, perhaps replacing the end-pin strap button. A few players find the best bet is to use a combination of some of these methods. But while many are happy with Ovations and their thinline derivatives, some players feel that there is still nothing quite like an acoustic guitar.

RESONATOR GUITARS

In the 1920s and 1930s, most makers responded to musicians' calls for louder guitars by building bigger-bodied instruments, or by starting experiments with amplification. But a stylish, effective and portable solution was offered by the various "ampliphonic resonator" guitars made in California (later in Chicago) and commonly known as dobros. In fact these guitars, based on the principle that a resonating aluminum cone inside the body would greatly increase their volume, were popularized by two brands, Dobro and National.

The guitars have a distinctly brash sound thanks to the aluminum resonator and, very often, a metal body as well. In general, Dobro-branded models tend to have wooden bodies and Nationals have metal bodies, but there are exceptions. Cheap resonator guitars proved popular with some blues players, and a variation with a squared neck was used for playing Hawaiian or lap-steel styles. Today, oriental copies have appeared, while the early models are much sought after by collectors.

National Style O (right)
This example of the Style O, National's best-known resonator guitar, dates probably from the early 1930s. The Hawaiian scenes sandblasted on to the front and, particularly, the back suit some of the music made with these instruments.

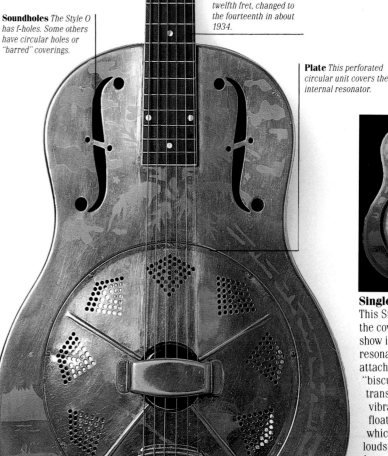

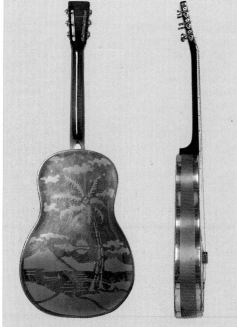

BACK AND SIDE
The back shows the attractive sandblasted decoration. This Style O has the conventional rounded-neck profile for use as a normal guitar. Compare its shape with that of the Tri-plate on the opposite page.

Headstock *This slotted type was replaced with a solid version in the later 1930s.*

Dobro
The Dobro brand began as an offshoot company from National, but the two merged again in the early 1930s. Later in that decade the Chicago-based Regal company was licensed to make Dobros. Many of the Dobro resonator guitars have wooden bodies, and some have two screen-covered soundholes.

Resonator *In the Dobro type the hidden unit is dished, with a raised center, and is fixed to the bridge by a six-legged "spider" (just visible through this cover).*

Neck *Early Style Os have a neck/body join at the twelfth fret, changed to the fourteenth in about 1934.*

Soundholes *The Style O has f-holes. Some others have circular holes or "barred" coverings.*

Plate *This perforated circular unit covers the internal resonator.*

Single resonator
This Style O has had the cover removed to show its single, spun resonator. The bridge is attached to a circular "biscuit." This transfers the strings' vibrations to the floating resonator, which moves like a loudspeaker to amplify the sound.

Tailpiece *This distinctively shaped unit is used on almost all National and Dobro resonator guitars.*

Mosrite D100 Californian

Semie Moselely bought the rights to make Dobro-based guitars in the 1960s. This was one result, a thinline electric with single resonator. (There was also a 12-string and a bass version.)

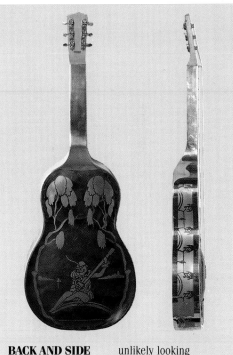

1965 Melphonic

The Chicago-based Valco company made some National guitars from the 1940s to the 1960s. These plastic-bodied types were made under various brands; this model also appeared with a National or Supro logo.

1950s National Resophonic (left)

This guitar was an earlier Valco-made National model. It had a wooden body covered in plastic, and was designed for playing by beginners who would be more at ease with its short-scale neck and single-cutaway body.

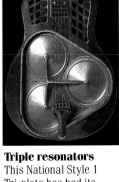

Late 1930s National Tri-Plate Model 35

The earliest National resonator guitars, launched in 1927, were made to this Tri-plate design, with three resonators suspended inside the body. The type is easily spotted by the large T-shaped support on the triangular cover.

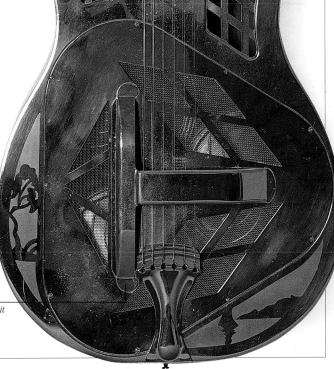

Soundholes *Tri-plates have this unusual "barred" effect.*

Company history

The name "dobro" comes from the inventors, five Czechoslovakian immigrants – the DOpyera BROthers. They started making Tri-plate resonator guitars with the National Guitar Co. in about 1927. John, Rudy and Ed then formed the Dobro company, making "spider" resonator guitars from 1929. Dobro and National merged in 1932, splitting again a few years later.

The Chicago-based Regal company was licensed to make Dobros in 1934; Mosrite in California bought the rights to use the Dobro name in 1965; and in 1967 Ed Dopyera's son Emil started making resonator guitars for his Original Musical Instrument (OMI) company. In 1985 this set-up was sold, and in 1990 resonator guitars were being made to the original designs by National ResoPhonic Guitars in California.

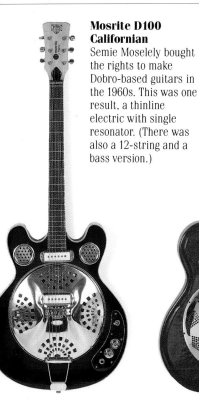

BACK AND SIDE The beautiful decoration on this model features a stylized Renaissance musician with an unlikely looking resonator guitar. This example, like many Tri-plates, has a squared neck designed for playing as a lap-steel.

Triple resonators

This National Style 1 Tri-plate has had its triangular cover removed, revealing the three pressed resonators. The bridge moves the T-section bar, which is connected to and vibrates the resonators, thus amplifying the sound.

Cover *The T-shape unit fits over the three resonators, visible through the grilles.*

LAP STEELS AND PEDAL STEELS

The steel guitar is played horizontally, on the seated player's lap or on a stand with attached tuning pedals. The strings are stopped over the neck of the guitar with a sliding steel bar (hence the name) held in the player's non-picking hand (sometimes a glass bottleneck, metal comb, or knife is used). Strings are raised off the neck, and "picks" are usually worn on the player's picking fingers and thumb to achieve a hard, attacking sound.

The steel guitar style was developed in Hawaii in the late nineteenth century. Local musicians hit upon a drifting sound obtained by sliding a metal object across the guitar strings, which they already customarily set to various open or "slack key" tunings.

Although no one person seems responsible for the style's invention, George S. Kanahele's *Hawaiian Music And Musicians: An Illustrated History* suggests that three early Hawaiian players, James Hoa, Gabriel Davion, and Joseph Kekuku, "may have discovered the technique independently." The style is also referred to as Hawaiian guitar, or slide guitar. Lap steel guitars enjoyed a vogue in the USA during the 1920s and 1930s, during which time they were much more popular than the "normal" guitar, usually referred to as the "Spanish" type.

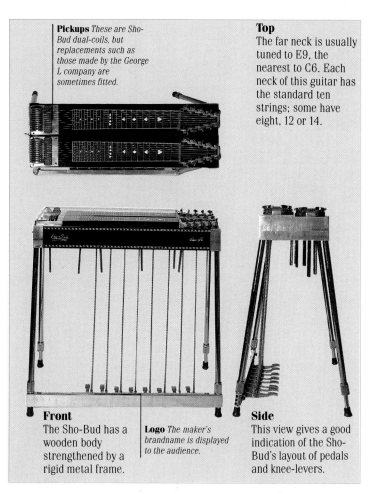

Pickups *These are Sho-Bud dual-coils, but replacements such as those made by the George L company are sometimes fitted.*

Top
The far neck is usually tuned to E9, the nearest to C6. Each neck of this guitar has the standard ten strings; some have eight, 12 or 14.

Front
The Sho-Bud has a wooden body strengthened by a rigid metal frame.

Logo *The maker's brandname is displayed to the audience.*

Side
This view gives a good indication of the Sho-Bud's layout of pedals and knee-levers.

Pedal steel

A distinction of the steel guitar style is the use of a variety of open tunings. In order to change instantly from one to another, players began to use multi-neck steel guitars. In the 1940s makers such as Bigsby added pedals to change tunings. Players would use the pedals to move to new tunings as if they had changed necks, but the idea of using the pedals to shift pitch during playing came later. Probably the first use of this "slurring" sound, now thought of as the pedal steel's trademark, was on Webb Pierce's *Slowly* (1954, played by Bud Isaacs). Pitch-changing knee-levers were later added to the instrument, giving even greater versatility to the steel player.

Late 1970s Sho-Bud Super Pro
Steel players Shot Jackson and Buddy Emmons started Sho-Bud in the USA in the 1950s. Sho-Bud still make pedal steels, improved versions of the 1950s design, in small numbers. In the early 1960s Buddy formed the Emmons company, which continues today.

Machine heads *The open tuning of the strings is usually adjusted here.*

Action *Note the height of the strings over the neck.*

Rods *These connect the pedals to the pitch-changing mechanisms.*

Pedals *The standard is eight pedals for a twin-neck instrument. Three serve the E9-tuned neck, and five the C6 neck, raising and/or lowering the strings' pitch.*

Rickenbacker Electro Model B
This guitar, made from Bakelite, first appeared in the mid-1930s. It was a very popular steel, lasting in various forms until the 1970s. This example, which probably dates from the 1950s, has volume and tone controls plus a "horseshoe" pickup.

Body *Most Silver Hawaiians were made from chrome-plated brass.*

Rickenbacher Electro Silver Hawaiian (below)
Rickenbacker's steel guitar made from sheet metal was launched in the late 1930s, and lasted about a decade.

Roller nut *This assists the strings' constant lateral movement.*

Changer *Each neck has a changer with ten "fingers" over which the strings pass. The fingers move as the pedals are operated, either pulling (to raise the pitch) or pushing (to lower) the string.*

Knee-levers *This Super Pro has six, although the standard is four. Like the pedals these are used to change the pitch of strings.*

Adjustable legs *The individual player adjusts these to suit.*

Lap steel
The earliest lap steels were simply "Spanish" guitars played on the lap, but soon musicians and guitar-makers were adapting that instrument; for example, by raising the strings off the neck with a high nut so that the object used to slide across the strings did not hit the frets. From the 1930s, players wanted louder lap steels: some used resonator guitars (see page 48) or even Los Angeles maker Weissenborn's loud, hollow-necked acoustic steel guitars. But soon electric lap steels were being made, including the very first electric guitar, the Rickenbacker "Frying Pan" (page 54). Above are two more Rickenbacker models, and below some electric lap steel guitars from other US makers.

Gretsch Electromatic
"Electromatic" was the name that Gretsch gave to some electric lap steel models. The one shown probably dates from around the late 1940s. It has the smaller, box-like body that became popular for lap steels.

Pickup *A "Charlie Christian" unit.*

Body *Note the beautiful curly maple top.*

1930s Gibson EH150 (above)
According to Andre Duchossoir in his "Gibson Electrics" book this model was, strictly speaking, Gibson's first electric guitar. The earliest examples of this lap steel appeared in 1935, just before the "Electric Spanish" ES150 (see page 56).

1930s Gibson Double Neck Electric Hawaiian (right)
This was in effect a twin-neck EH150. The 150 came with six or seven strings; the Double Neck was offered with six, seven or eight strings per neck.

❝In the United States during the 1930s and 1940s guitar makers, musicians and designers invented the 20th century's greatest musical instrument, the electric guitar.**❞**

ELECTRIC PIONEERS

1987 FENDER US VINTAGE 52 TELECASTER, courtesy Fender A&R Centre.

THE RISE OF THE ELECTRIC GUITAR

No one invented the electric guitar. Rather, the instrument evolved from a series of experiments and collaborations between musicians, makers and engineers, principally in the United States during the 1930s and 1940s. These people wanted a guitar which could project a louder but tonally accurate version of the acoustic instrument. At first, some designers came up with mechanical methods to achieve this, the best known of which are resonator guitars (see pages 48-49).

Gradually it became clear that the most practical answer was offered by the amplification of electro-magnetic pickups, an idea first put into practice by Rickenbacker. The method was applied very successfully to steel (or slide) guitars, which were used for the Hawaiian guitar style that had been enormously popular in the USA since the end of World War I.

Then came the application of electric amplification to the "Spanish" guitar, a term used at the time to identify the less popular "normal" guitar. Not long after that, a handful of visionary men – among them Les Paul, Paul Bigsby, Merle Travis, and Leo Fender – replaced the guitar's traditional hollow body with a solid construction. This reduced the body's interference with the guitar's tone, simplified production, and paved the way for the modern electric guitar as we know it today.

Adolph Rickenbacker
The founder of Rickenbacker was born in Switzerland, some time around the early 1890s. When still young he went to the USA, eventually settling in Los Angeles, most likely in the late 1910s. Early connections with guitar-making companies such as National led to an interest in musical instrument production. The modern Rickenbacker company came about when Adolph sold out to Californian business-man Francis Hall in 1953. Adolph Rickenbacker died in 1976.

Output *A two-core cord connects to these two screw-thread terminals.*

Body and neck *This prototype is maple; production models were cast aluminum.*

Pickup *It consists of two "horseshoe" magnets enclosing a magnetic coil under the strings.*

Frets *The solid maple neck has 25 metal frets. On a steel guitar they do not stop strings, but indicate positions.*

Rickenbacker and the Electric Guitar

The Rickenbacker name often arises among the claims and counter-claims of guitar historians keen to assign the invention of the electric guitar to one company or one inventor.

Three instruments related to Adolph Rickenbacker's companies of the 1930s are of great importance in the embryonic days of the electric guitar. The "Frying Pan" was among the first electric steel guitars; the Electro Spanish contends for the title of earliest electric-acoustic guitar; and the Rickenbacker Electro Model B could well be called the first solid-bodied electric guitar.

By 1925 Adolph Rickenbacker, a tool-and-die-maker in his early thirties and of Swiss extraction, had formed in California the Rickenbacker Manufacturing Company. One of the jobs he picked up, after meeting George Beauchamp, was to make metal parts for the National resonator guitars (see page 48).

Beauchamp, a guitarist and evidently an inventor too, had collaborated with National's founders, the Dopyera Brothers, to apply the resonator idea to the guitar. (The extent of this collaboration is the subject of one of the many disputes that cloud the story of National, Dobro, Rickenbacker and other early makers.) The resonator guitars were intended through mechanical means to produce a louder, more cutting sound than that of the normal acoustic instrument.

George Beauchamp had apparently been toying with another solution to the problem of making a guitar louder: electric amplification. In the very early 1930s he tried applying these theories to a working instrument and with Paul Barth, a nephew of John Dopyera who had worked for National, he put together an experimental electric steel guitar. The main result was an instrument with a long wooden neck and round wooden body in which was a large "horseshoe" pickup. Yet another ex-National man, Harry Watson, built the one-piece neck and body for Beauchamp. The guitar's most famous nickname, the "Frying Pan," reflects its shape.

Perry Botkin
The 1930s session guitarist is seen with Rickenbacker's short-lived Vibrola Spanish model. The stand is necessary, as the guitar was made heavy by on-board motorized pulleys. These moved the bridge to create a crude vibrato effect.

THE FRYING PAN

The first electro-magnetic pickup to be used on a guitar was mounted on the original Frying Pan: it had two large horseshoe magnets surrounding the strings, with a coil situated underneath.

The electro-magnetic pickup is based on a relatively simple principle. If a magnetic field is disturbed by the vibrations of a metal string, a current will be induced in a coil situated in that field. The coil generates a signal of electrical current as the strings are plucked and vibrated, and this signal is fed out of the guitar to the amplifier where it is boosted and fed to an accompanying loudspeaker.

The prototype Frying Pan electric steel guitar was adapted to a production instrument in 1932 by Ro-Pat-In, a company set up for that purpose by Beauchamp, Rickenbacker and Barth. It was now made from cast aluminum, and came in two versions – the A22 and the longer-scale A25.

During the early 1930s Ro-Pat-In changed its name to the Electro String Instrument Corporation, and the guitars began to bear the combined Rickenbacker Electro brand in 1934. Some early instruments had Rickenbacker spelt without the anglicized k – "Rickenbacher." The first batch of nameplates was simply misspelled, but used anyway, and these appeared on and off through the next few years.

At first the Frying Pan sold poorly, according to Richard Smith in his book *The Complete History of Rickenbacker Guitars*. The aluminum apparently caused problems with the stability of the guitar's tuning. The instrument appeared sporadically in Rickenbacker's catalogues until the late 1950s, but in the mid-1930s Rickenbacker had moved to a more immediately successful series of electric steel guitars. These had small bodies of a normal guitar shape and were made from sheet metal or from Bakelite (for examples, see page 50).

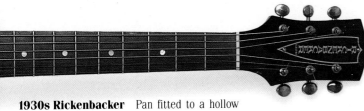

1930s Rickenbacker Electro Spanish
This was among Rickenbacker's earliest electric-acoustic guitars. The Electro Spanish model was made between about 1932 and 1935, and featured the horseshoe magnet of the Frying Pan fitted to a hollow body with f-holes (this body was probably made for Rickenbacker by the Harmony company of Chicago). Near the pickup are two attractive octagonal knobs for volume and tone, and the front-mounted jack socket.

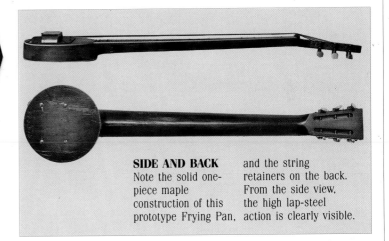

SIDE AND BACK
Note the solid one-piece maple construction of this prototype Frying Pan, and the string retainers on the back. From the side view, the high lap-steel action is clearly visible.

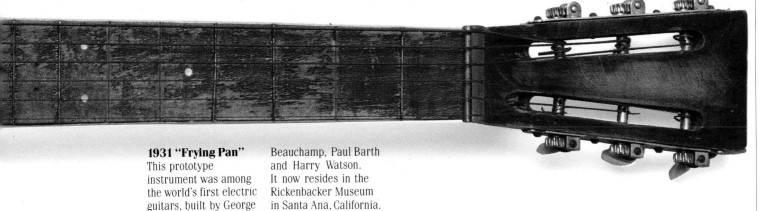

1931 "Frying Pan"
This prototype instrument was among the world's first electric guitars, built by George Beauchamp, Paul Barth and Harry Watson. It now resides in the Rickenbacker Museum in Santa Ana, California.

GIBSON'S FIRST ELECTRIC

In the 1930s some guitarists needed more volume. A number had even taken up the banjo, particularly in the studio where it cut through a loud band more effectively than a guitar. And so, despite the overwhelming popularity of high-action "lap steel" guitars in the USA, a number of makers began to test-market the avant-garde electric-acoustic guitar. This was a conventionally shaped acoustic guitar with normal action, but an electric pickup and associated controls built into the body. Rickenbacker put out their Electro Spanish electric-acoustic model in about 1932 (see page 55), but only a handful were sold. Other early examples came from Dobro and National (with pickups by Dobro man Victor Smith). Gibson stepped toward the new electric instruments with the launch in the mid-1930s of the ES150, the company's first "Electric Spanish" guitar.

1937 Gibson catalog
The cover (below right) notes Gibson's new "electrical" range. The spread from inside (below left) shows "another guitar miracle from Gibson," the electric ES150 and its accompanying amplifier, plus a number of electric steel players of the day. The steel guitar had a high action so that a steel bar could be slid across the strings to change pitch. It was usually played on the seated musician's lap.

Finish The ES150 came in brown, and had a sunburst top.

F-holes These are very long and thin on the ES150. Gibson first used f-holes on the 1920s L5.

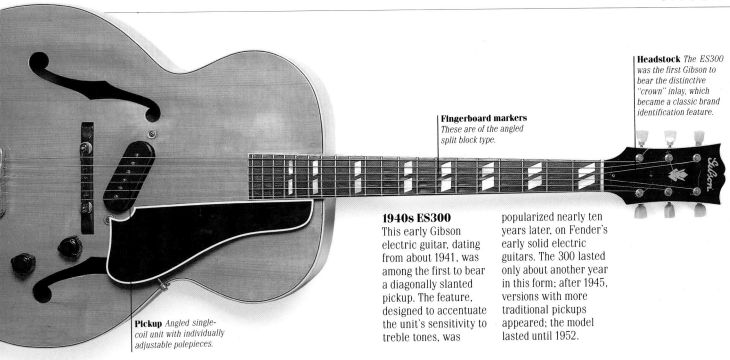

Headstock *The ES300 was the first Gibson to bear the distinctive "crown" inlay, which became a classic brand identification feature.*

Fingerboard markers *These are of the angled split block type.*

Pickup *Angled single-coil unit with individually adjustable polepieces.*

1940s ES300

This early Gibson electric guitar, dating from about 1941, was among the first to bear a diagonally slanted pickup. The feature, designed to accentuate the unit's sensitivity to treble tones, was popularized nearly ten years later, on Fender's early solid electric guitars. The 300 lasted only about another year in this form; after 1945, versions with more traditional pickups appeared; the model lasted until 1952.

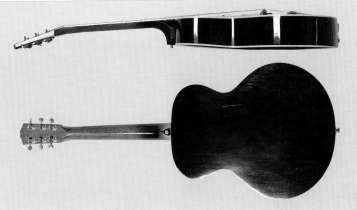

SIDE AND BACK

The rear view clearly shows the distinctly V-shaped back of the one-piece mahogany neck, a relatively common design feature at the time. The bulge visible below the strap button is the unusually positioned socket for the jack plug.

1937 ES150 (below left)

This is a fine example of Gibson's first electric model, which was introduced around 1936. The unadorned tailpiece and simple dot fingerboard inlays make for a plain appearance, inspired by Gibson's cheap L50 acoustic on which the ES150 was based. The bar pickup was replaced around 1940 by a rectangular unit of more standard appearance. Note the long pickguard, and the Bakelite volume and tone control knobs with arrow markers. When production re-started after World War II, the ES150 was offered with a larger body. The model was withdrawn in 1956.

Pickup *Known as the Charlie Christian type after the guitarist's use of the ES150, this "bar" pickup has two long magnets fixed under the body top with the three adjustment screws shown.*

Charlie Christian (1916-42)

With Benny Goodman, and jamming with early be-boppers, Christian created electric jazz-guitar playing.

Lloyd Loar at Gibson

Electric instruments were not completely without precedent at Gibson when they introduced the ES150. There is firm evidence that acoustic engineer Lloyd Loar experimented with pickups and amplification while employed by Gibson from 1919 to 1924. For example, in the company's self-published "Gibson Story" (1973) by employee Julius Bellson a photograph is shown of an electric double bass made by Loar at Gibson. Loar set up the short-lived Vivi-Tone company in 1933 for whom he devised some spectacularly peculiar guitars, including an early solid-body electric. None of the Vivi-Tone instruments seems to have sold in any significant quantity.

LES PAUL'S "LOG"

Les Paul's inventions changed the way that modern music sounds. Best known of these is the Gibson Les Paul solid electric guitar, launched in 1952 (see pages 63, 80-85), but his electric guitar experiments began much earlier.

Les first amplified a guitar when he was 12, working to entertain the customers at a local hamburger stand who had complained that they couldn't hear him. So he jabbed a record player pickup into his acoustic guitar, slid a telephone mouthpiece under the strings, and wired up both to his parents' radio which doubled as an amplifier.

That made Les start to think about a solid body electric guitar. What he had in mind was the production of an amplified tone that accurately reproduced and sustained the sound of the strings. To this end he would stuff rags into hollow-body guitars, and even had a company called Larsen Brothers in Chicago build him a guitar with two pickups and a solid maple top. Around 1939 Les started working on a prototype solid electric guitar, known as "The Log" after the block of wood that formed its body.

Les took The Log to Gibson in 1941. "They laughed at the idea," he remembered in 1989 of Gibson's initial reaction more than 45 years before. "They called it the kid with the broomstick with the pickups on."

Center section *This is a 10×10cm (4×4in) piece of solid pine, the "log" of the guitar's nickname.*

Sides *These were commandeered from an Epiphone guitar and cosmetically added to the center section.*

Controls *Here are volume and tone, but no-one can remember what went in the "hole."*

Vibrato *A crudely made brass unit, added some time after 1942.*

Pickups *The covers were made from old clock parts, painted to match the center section.*

Screw holes *These remain from a time when Les Paul covered the center section with plastic.*

SIDE AND BACK
Note the black-painted wooden block that serves to join the center section to the neck. The spruce top and the sides are from an Epiphone guitar, and a plywood back was unceremoniously screwed on. Visible from the side is the fact that the bridge is made from a steel dowel.

Les Paul: musician and inventor
Lester William Polfus, whose inventions have had a lasting effect on modern electric guitars and on the methods adopted in today's recording studios, was born in 1916 in Waukesha, about 20 miles from Milwaukee, Wisconsin.

As a teenager Lester called himself "Rhubarb Red" and "The Wizard from Waukesha," pseudonyms for the young guitarist who was

Les Paul & Mary Ford

already playing country music and rhythm 'n' blues. "Red" moved to Springfield, Missouri, then to Chicago, and on to New York, where by late 1938 his trio was appearing on the Fred Waring radio show. "Red" had by this time adopted a new name, Les Paul, and the Les Paul trio toured coast-to-coast for several years.

During World War II Les was in the armed forces radio service, playing with his various groups. His friend from that time, Bing Crosby, helped get him signed to Decca Records in 1945. A couple of years later Les Paul went to Capitol Records, for whom he made many of his most influential and innovative recordings between 1947 and 1959, both instrumental and with the vocals of his girlfriend Mary Ford, whom he married in 1949.

Les came up with a recording method now called sound-on-sound. This involved recording on to one machine, and then transferring the first recording to another machine while adding a new part. Les sometimes varied the speed of the recording to create impossibly high, fast guitar passages. The process was repeated until multiple layers of sound were built up.

At first Les used disc recorders to make his guitar "multiples," as he called the recordings (such as *Lover*, 1948) but quickly moved to tape recorders (the first to use tape was *How High The Moon*, 1951). Another of his very important inventions was the multitrack tape recorder — the basis of all modern recording — which he eventually persuaded Ampex to produce in 1953.

Gibson had laughed at his first attempt in the early 1940s to interest them in his solid electric "Log" guitar, which he'd put together at weekends at Epi Stathopoulo's Epiphone factory in New Jersey. About this time Les moved to California, where he continued to play The Log.

There were other players and inventors dabbling with the idea of the solid electric guitar, and three of them were then in California: country musician Merle Travis, mechanical expert Paul A Bigsby, and radio repairman Leo Fender. When Fender started his revolutionary mass-production of solid electric guitars around 1950, Gibson decided that they might now need "the kid with the broomstick with the pickups on it," as they'd described Les and his Log. (For the story of Gibson and the Les Paul guitar, see page 63.)

Neck *From a Gibson L-series guitar, this was joined to the centre section by a small block.*

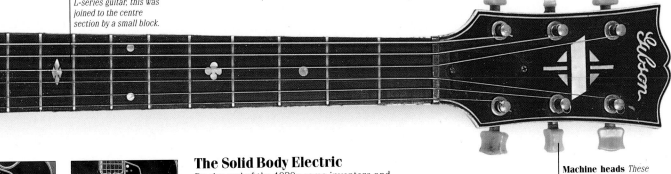

Machine heads *These were taken from an Epiphone guitar.*

The Solid Body Electric
By the end of the 1930s some inventors and musicians had the idea of a solid body electric guitar. Here was an opportunity to dispose of the involved construction of the acoustic guitar, and concentrate on a solid base to support the strings and pickups that would create a clear amplified tone.

Back at Rickenbacker, for example, the "normal" guitar version of their Bakelite steel, the Model B, was launched in 1935, effectively one of the earliest solid-body electric guitars. Their Vibrola Spanish Guitar from 1937 was a deeper-bodied variant of the Model B, designed by Clayton Orr ("Doc") Kauffman and featuring a novel motorized vibrato system. But the guitar was so heavy it had to be supported on a stand attached to its amplifier (see page 55). Experiments continued in the US, but it wasn't until 1950 that a commercial solid body electric guitar appeared.

Floating pickups
During the 1930s and 1940s pickups and controls built into pickguards began to appear. Added to existing guitars, they "floated" free of the surface to avoid compromising inherent tonality. The popular DeArmond unit (left) with sliding pickup was joined later by the Gibson "Ted McCarty" (right), designed by the company president and patented in 1948.

1939-41 The Log
This is Les Paul's prototype solid electric guitar, now in the Country Music Hall of Fame in Nashville. It was the instrument which Paul took to Gibson in the early 1940s in an initially unsuccessful attempt to have them build a solid electric guitar. "The Log" is the solid pine block used in the center of the body.

THE BIGSBY – TRAVIS GUITAR

Paul A. Bigsby's guitar, designed by Merle Travis and built in 1947 or 1948, never succeeded commercially on anything like the scale of the later Fender solid electric guitars (see pages 62-3). But the Bigsby/Travis guitar is very significant historically: it looks closer to the modern idea of a solid electric guitar than anything that had been made before.

Country musician Travis and the mechanically adept Bigsby put their heads together and came up with an astonishingly fresh design. Writing in *Guitar World* in 1980, Travis explained that he wanted an instrument with machine heads along one side of the headstock, because "reaching down to change the first, second and third [strings] bugged me. I wished somebody would build a guitar with all the tuning pegs on the top." More importantly, Merle insisted that the body should be "thin and solid. That way it'll keep ringing like a steel."

"Short-plate" I
Without tension bar.

"Short-plate" II
With tension bar.

"Horseshoe"
A number of variations of the basic Bigsby vibrato design are shown here. This "horseshoe" type is intended for fixing to solid guitars.

"Gretsch by Bigsby"
Exclusive to Gretsch.

"Long-plate"
Without tension bar.

Bigsby Vibratos
Paul Bigsby designed his first vibrato unit in the 1940s. The Bigsby works by "wobbling" the string retainer with a spring-loaded handle, and is often a later fitting to an existing guitar. Around 1950 Gibson were the first to offer Bigsby units as factory options on some guitars. Gretsch also began to use specially-made "Gretsch by Bigsby" vibratos around this time. The occasional use of the extra "bar" pulls the strings down to help maintain their tension at the bridge.

Decoration *This was described by designer Merle Travis as "a cosmetic armrest."*

Pickup. *Handmade by Bigsby, with a single magnetic "blade."*

Body *This and the through-neck are made from attractive bird's-eye maple.*

Through-neck *The maple neck section travels right through the body.*

Pickguard *This is added here in mother-of-pearl. These darker wood fittings are of walnut.*

Bridge *This is made from cast aluminum, as on Bigsby's vibratos.*

Merle Travis and Paul Bigsby

Merle Travis (1917-1983) was a country singer and guitarist. He developed a damped-picking style of guitar playing which inspired Chet Atkins, among others. Merle was also a successful country songwriter — probably his best known song is *Sixteen Tons*.

Less is known of Paul A. Bigsby, but guitarists will be most familiar with Bigsby's name through his vibrato unit, the prototype of which was built, like their solid electric guitar, after a suggestion by Travis.

Bigsby also had some success in the late 1940s and after with electric pedal steel guitars, used by some of the leading steel players of the day such as Bud Isaacs and Speedy West. Bigsby's pedal steels were among the first to range the pedals in a line, rather than in a fan shape as on Gibson's earlier Electraharp model.

But Bigsby's more lasting contribution to the electric guitar came through his vibrato system which, despite many modern "improved" vibrato units, is still seen on numerous guitars. Paul A. Bigsby died in 1968. He had sold the company three years earlier to Ted McCarty, recently departed from his job as president of Gibson.

CHRONOLOGY

The history of the early electric guitar started with Rickenbacker's "Frying Pan" lap-steel of 1931 and culminated with the Gibson Les Paul "Gold Top" model in 1952. This chart catalogues the key events during this crucial period of the instrument's development. The dates are approximate.

1931
Rickenbacker's "Frying Pan" prototype, among the world's first electric steel guitars, is built by George Beauchamp, Paul Barth and Harry Watson in California.

1932
Rickenbacker market production versions of the Frying Pan, and launch one of the earliest electric acoustic guitars, the Electro Spanish. Similar models are produced elsewhere in the US at this time by National, Dobro, and Vivi-Tone.

1935
The Rickenbacker Model B appears, an electric steel guitar with a solid Bakelite body. Few solid-body guitars pre-date this instrument.

1936
Gibson's first electric guitar, the "Electric Spanish" ES150, goes into production at their factory in Michigan. Its bar pickup is later nicknamed the "Charlie Christian" type.

1939-41
Guitarist and inventor Les Paul builds in New Jersey a prototype solid electric guitar, "The Log". He fails initially to interest Gibson in the future of the idea.

1947-48
Country musician Merle Travis designs an early solid-body electric guitar. Travis collaborates with Paul Bigsby in California who builds a guitar, the "Bigsby/Travis," based on the design.

1950
Leo Fender and George Fullerton design and build in California the world's first commercially successful solid electric guitar, the Fender Broadcaster (quickly renamed the Telecaster).

1951-52
In 1951 Gibson reacts to Fender's launch by contacting Les Paul again. In the following year they market their first solid electric, the Gibson Les Paul "Gold Top" model.

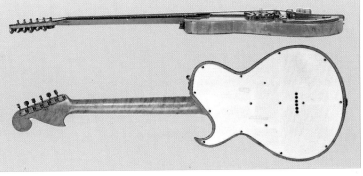

SIDE AND BACK
A large plastic plate covers the back of the guitar. Note also on the back the six ferrules for anchoring the strings, which feed through the body. There is evidence of some damage around the back of the headstock.

Late 1940s Bigsby/Travis guitar
This was a very early solid-body electric guitar, designed by Merle Travis, a country musician. It was built by Paul Bigsby, better known for his widely used vibrato system. While the Bigsby/Travis pre-dates Fender's first solid-body electric by some years, it was produced in very small numbers. As with Bigsby's various electric pedal steels, the standard solid could be bought with custom parts. Fortunately the Bigsby/Travis guitar is on public display at the Country Music Hall of Fame in Nashville, Tennessee.

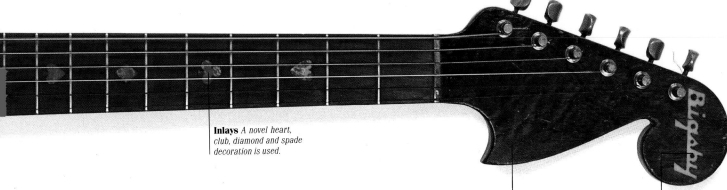

Inlays A novel heart, club, diamond and spade decoration is used.

Headstock Compare this design with that of the European-influenced Martin on pages 26-7.

Logo This is the same style as that used on Bigsby's vibrato units.

The Bigsby/Travis collaboration

Pattern-maker Paul A. Bigsby was keen on both racing and fixing motorcycles, reported Merle Travis, writing in *Guitar World* in 1980 about the story of his collaboration with Bigsby during the 1940s. So Travis asked Bigsby to apply his mechanical skills to the vibrola on a Gibson L10, which was always putting the strings out of tune. Instead, Bigsby built his own-design vibrato unit which worked much better.

Travis then set a much more adventurous task for Bigsby — building a solid electric guitar (shown above) — and in his *Guitar World* piece

Travis estimated that Bigsby made about a dozen similar guitars for later customers. It is clear that the Bigsby/Travis guitar was ahead of its time not only in its assembly: the neck extended right through the body, a method that became fashionable more than 20 years later.

There was some dispute, mainly provoked by comments from Merle Travis in the 1970s, as to whether the Bigsby/Travis guitar directly influenced the later and far more successful solid electric guitars of Fender. If anything, the shape of the Bigsby/Travis headstock may have influenced that of Fender's 1954 Stratocaster.

Bridge *Each pair of strings shares a single brass bridge saddle.*

Pickups *This angled bridge unit heightens treble response, while the front pickup offers more bassy tones.*

Pickguard *This is made from Bakelite and on Broadcasters is always black.*

Selector *On the Broadcaster and earliest Telecasters this gave back, front or bass-boosted front pickup.*

Body *The clear "blonde" finish was applied to solid ash.*

THE FENDER BROADCASTER

The Fender Broadcaster, launched around 1950, was the world's first commercially available electric guitar with a solid wooden body and bolt-on neck. Leo Fender's whole design was geared to mass production and to a simple, effective electric instrument, and as such has been a great and long-lasting success.

After engineer George Fullerton joined Leo's Fender Electric Instrument company in 1948, the two men set about devising their production solid-bodied electric guitar, the Fender Broadcaster. Leo later explained to *Guitar Player* his design criteria for the Broadcaster: "On an acoustic-electric guitar you have a string fastened to a diaphragm top, and that top does not have one specific frequency. If you play a note the top will respond to it and also to a lot of adjoining notes. A solid guitar body doesn't have that, you're dealing with just a single note at a time."

This seems in line with Les Paul's theory that the principal advantage of the solid body is to deliver a clean, amplified version of the string's inherent tone. Clearly many clever people were thinking along similar lines, and this collective inspiration led inexorably to the solid-body electric guitar.

Even if Leo Fender had only made the Broadcaster (soon renamed the Telecaster) his company's place in the history of the electric guitar would be assured. And yet a year afterwards, Fender invented the electric bass guitar (see page 160), and four years after their Telecaster had defined the mass-production solid-body electric guitar the Fender company introduced the stylish Stratocaster solid electric (pages 72-75).

There can be little doubt that the Telecaster, the Precision and the Stratocaster designs will be around in various guises for many years to come, a testament to the quiet genius of Leo Fender.

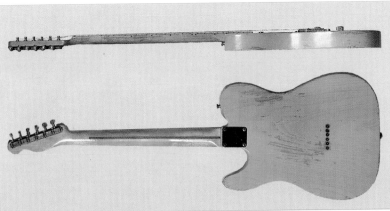

SIDE AND BACK
The contrasting dark walnut stripe is added once the truss rod has been fitted inside its channel in the maple neck. A few of the very earliest Broadcasters had neither truss rods nor stripes.

1950 Fender Broadcaster (below left)
This was the instrument that established the idea of the modern, mass-produced, solid body electric guitar. The

Californian Fender company's revolutionary Broadcaster of 1950 was soon renamed Telecaster, and as such was still in production 40 years after its introduction.

Logo *The Broadcaster introduced the classic Fender "spaghetti" logo, used until the mid-1960s.*

Neck *This was made from solid maple, and was bolted to the body.*

Leo Fender

Clarence Leo Fender was born in Anaheim, California in 1909. As a teenager his hobby was fiddling with radios, and that led to an interest in amplifiers and electronic gadgets in general.

Leo began to formulate the idea of a solid body guitar, and built a one-off instrument in 1943 or 1944 which proved popular when hired out to local musicians. In the mid 1940s he established the K&F company with "Doc" Kauffman, who had helped design some of Rickenbacker Electro's electric guitars. K&F produced chiefly electric steel guitars and amplifiers, and lasted until 1946, when Leo formed the Fender Electric Instrument Company in nearby Fullerton, continuing the K&F lines.

George Fullerton joined Fender in 1948 and the two men devised the solid electric Broadcaster together. Fender quickly changed the name Broadcaster to Telecaster (see pages 68 to 71) when Gretsch pointed out their prior use. Some rare transitional models, known as "No-casters", have no name at all on the headstock.

After more guitar innovations, Leo Fender became ill and the company was sold to CBS in 1965 for $13 million. Leo's health improved and he rejoined CBS/Fender briefly before resigning in 1970. He went on to make instruments for Music Man and G&L, and died in March 1991.

Leo Fender

The founder of the Fender company is pictured by a punch press in his Fullerton, California factory, probably during 1954. By this time the Broadcaster had become the Telecaster (see pages 68-71) and the new Stratocaster model (see pages 72-75) had just been launched.

1952 Gibson Les Paul "Gold Top"
This example from the launch year is probably among the first 50 made. Nicknamed the "Gold Top" after its distinctive finish, the model was replaced by the sunburst Standard in 1958. The "Gold Top" was re-issued by Gibson in 1968, 1982 and 1987.

1950s catalog
Gibson's Les Paul model appeared in 1952. This late 1950s brochure describes the Les Paul Custom as "the fretless wonder," thanks to its easy playability.

THE GIBSON LES PAUL

Les Paul's prototype solid electric "Log" had been rejected by Gibson in the early 1940s. He is quite certain what it was that eventually made Gibson warm to the idea of producing a solid electric guitar. "Leo Fender started to make one," he told this author in 1989. "When Gibson heard about that, they said: 'Find that guy with the broomstick with the pickups on it!' They came to me in '51."

Gibson wanted to manufacture a guitar to Les's design, but were initially reluctant to put their company name on it. "And I said, why don't you call it the Les Paul guitar? They said will you put that in writing? And I says, course!"

The first Les Paul guitars, launched by Gibson in 1952, had a stunning gold finish. This model, now generally referred to as the "Gold Top," was joined by the solid-color Custom models in 1954 and replaced in 1958 by the more traditional sunburst Standard (see page 82).

Gibson drastically redesigned the Les Paul in 1961, but a huge surge of popularity later in that decade for the originals meant Gibson had little commercial choice but to relaunch them in 1968.

The Gibson Les Paul model is still made in various forms today and, together with Leo Fender's designs, it created the blueprints from which the vast majority of solid electric guitar makers still draw their inspiration.

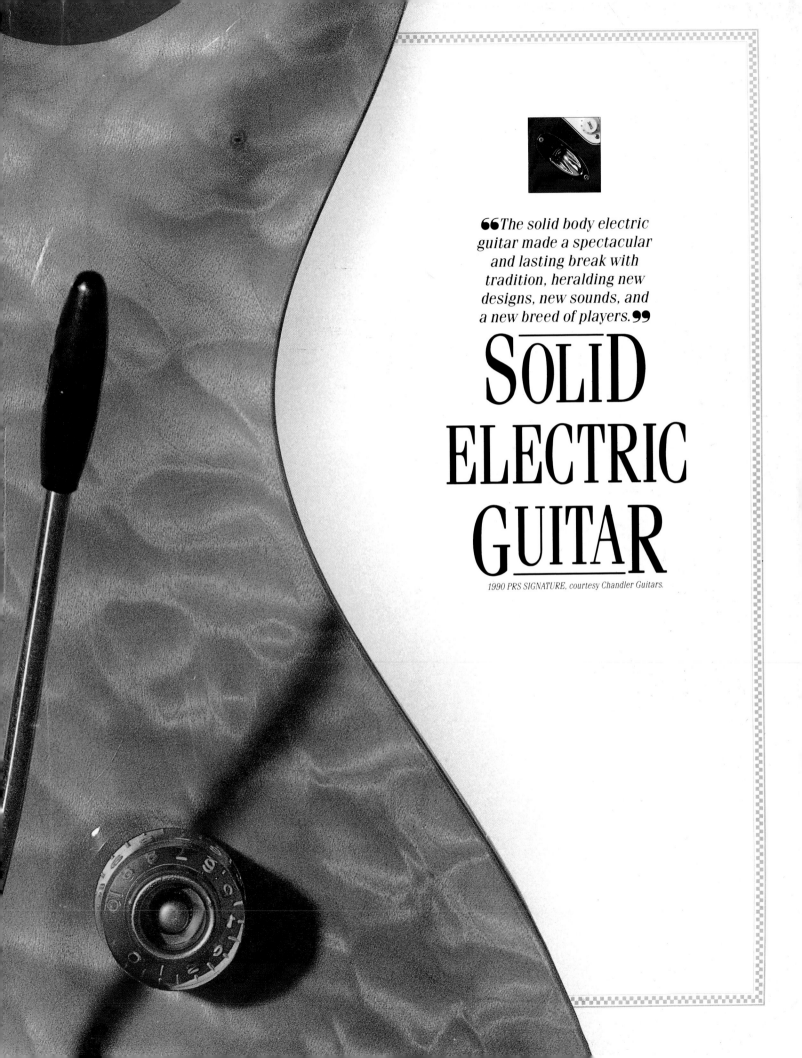

66_The solid body electric guitar made a spectacular and lasting break with tradition, heralding new designs, new sounds, and a new breed of players._**99**

SOLID ELECTRIC GUITAR

1990 PRS SIGNATURE, courtesy Chandler Guitars.

SOLID ELECTRIC ANATOMY

The solid body electric guitar is a relatively recent invention, and many contemporary makers now take advantage of modern mass production methods in their factories, enabling them to produce a precisely tooled and cost-effective instrument.

The Fender company, with 1950s innovations like the Telecaster and the Stratocaster (pages 68-75), did more than any other to foster these production systems. Their guitars, and those of many major makers, are based on the idea of modular construction: necks and bodies can be made separately and bolted together; controls, pickups and wiring are fitted to a pickguard, which is then screwed to a body with routed channels to allow for these components; and other hardware, including the bridge, machine heads and jack socket, is screwed to the body.

Other methods

There are, of course, exceptions and variations. Glued-in necks are a traditional alternative to the bolt-on type, primarily on guitars made by or in the style of the Gibson company. Another method has the neck made from a single or laminated piece of wood which travels the whole length of the guitar; wooden "wings" are then added to complete the body shape. This "through-neck" design was visible on some natural-finished guitars popular during the 1970s, but now is often hidden under colored finishes.

However, the classic wooden Stratocaster design (page 72) remains a blueprint for a stylish, modern, mass-produced electric guitar, despite many makers' experiments with different shapes and materials.

Fretting the neck
This is another view of Gibson's Nashville factory. It shows a worker preparing the fret slots on the neck. Accurate work at this stage is critical to well-seated frets.

Metal frets *Edges must be carefully smoothed or bound to protect the player's hand.*

Neck *Fender-style solids have a separate neck bolted to the body which simplifies construction and can facilitate later repairs or customization.*

Body shaping *The classic Stratocaster design popularized the inclusion of a gentle "contouring" of the back of the body. This makes the guitar more comfortable to play.*

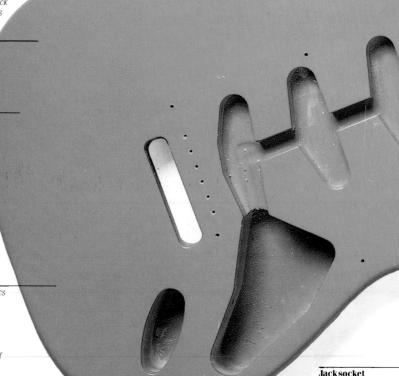

Body *Solid electrics are usually made from various hardwoods. Maple, mahogany, alder, ash, and related types are all popular, each subtly affecting tone.*

Gibson factory
A workman at Gibson's Nashville plant is seen here shaping a neck, which will eventually be glued to a body. The Nashville factory is where Gibson's electric guitars are made; acoustics are built at their Montana works.

Finish *Modern electrics come in a variety of finishes: natural; sunburst; solid or metallic colors; even wild graphic designs. After numerous coats of paint, the surface is buffed to a high gloss.*

Jack socket

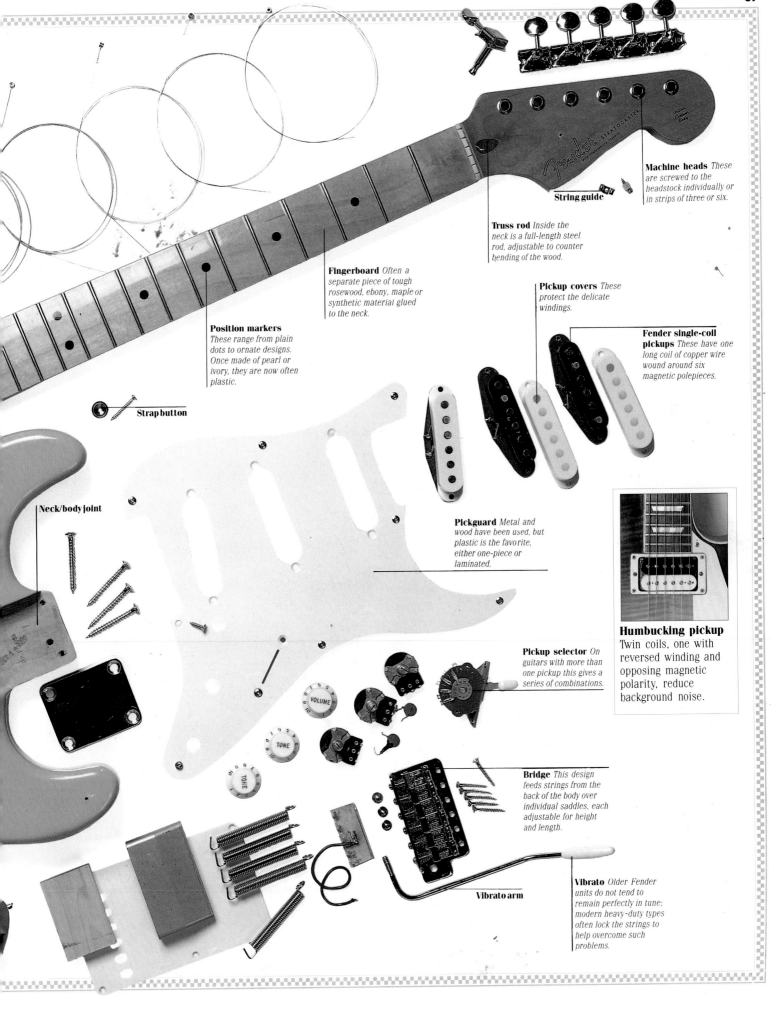

Machine heads *These are screwed to the headstock individually or in strips of three or six.*

String guide

Truss rod *Inside the neck is a full-length steel rod, adjustable to counter bending of the wood.*

Fingerboard *Often a separate piece of tough rosewood, ebony, maple or synthetic material glued to the neck.*

Pickup covers *These protect the delicate windings.*

Fender single-coil pickups *These have one long coil of copper wire wound around six magnetic polepieces.*

Position markers *These range from plain dots to ornate designs. Once made of pearl or ivory, they are now often plastic.*

Strap button

Neck/body joint

Pickguard *Metal and wood have been used, but plastic is the favorite, either one-piece or laminated.*

Humbucking pickup
Twin coils, one with reversed winding and opposing magnetic polarity, reduce background noise.

Pickup selector *On guitars with more than one pickup this gives a series of combinations.*

VOLUME

TONE

TONE

Bridge *This design feeds strings from the back of the body over individual saddles, each adjustable for height and length.*

Vibrato arm

Vibrato *Older Fender units do not tend to remain perfectly in tune; modern heavy-duty types often lock the strings to help overcome such problems.*

THE FENDER TELECASTER

The Fender Telecaster is the longest-running solid electric guitar still in production, a brilliantly simple piece of design which works as well today as it did when introduced in 1951.

In fact, the Telecaster was Fender's original Broadcaster electric (see page 62) under a new title, the company being forced to change it when Gretsch claimed prior rights to the name. But Leo Fender and his small workforce in Fullerton, California must have been delighted with the new Telecaster name, its thoroughly modern reference to the emerging medium of television just right for an equally innovative device like the Telecaster, the first commercially marketed solid electric guitar.

The Telecaster – usually abbreviated in discussion or print to the suitably simple "Tele" – is known for its bright, cutting tone and its straightforward, no-nonsense operation. For these reasons it has been used throughout its long history by players from all kinds of musical backgrounds. However, it is with country musicians that the instrument has seen most consistent service, players from this area particularly valuing the Tele's ability, in talented hands, to emulate steel guitar sounds.

The secret of the Tele's sound centers on the bridge. The strings pass through the body and are anchored at the back by six ferrules, giving solidity and sustain to the resulting sound. A slanting-back pickup is incorporated into the bridge, enhancing the guitar's natural treble tone.

Whatever its cause, the distinctive sound of the Telecaster looks set to ensure the instrument's survival for at least another 40 years among guitarists who value simplicity, effectiveness, and versatility.

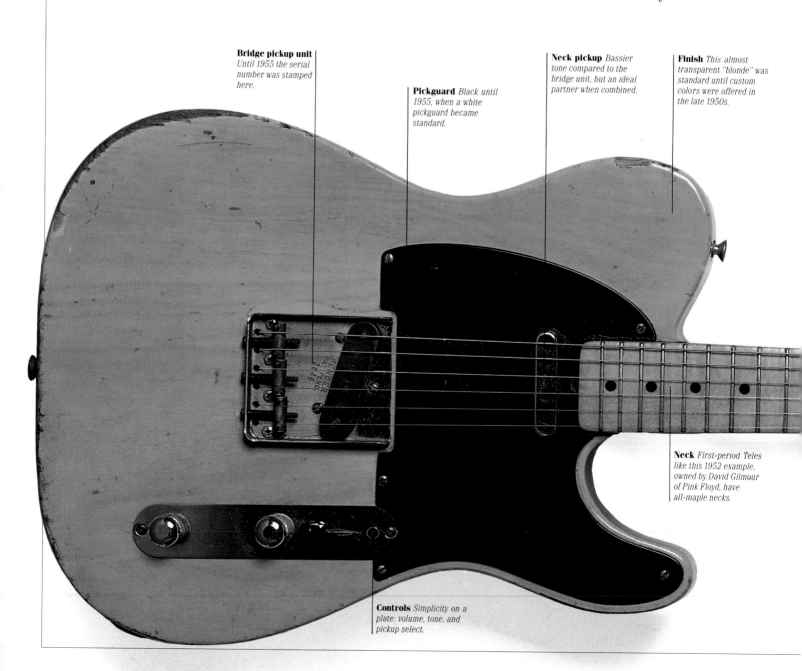

Bridge pickup unit *Until 1955 the serial number was stamped here.*

Pickguard *Black until 1955, when a white pickguard became standard.*

Neck pickup *Bassier tone compared to the bridge unit, but an ideal partner when combined.*

Finish *This almost transparent "blonde" was standard until custom colors were offered in the late 1950s.*

Neck *First-period Teles like this 1952 example, owned by David Gilmour of Pink Floyd, have all-maple necks.*

Controls *Simplicity on a plate: volume, tone, and pickup select.*

BACK AND SIDE
Clearly a slab of solid timber, the Tele exhibits none of the contouring found on Fender's later guitars like the Stratocaster. A dark walnut neck strip, known as the "skunk stripe," is seen on the back of Fenders without separate fingerboards.

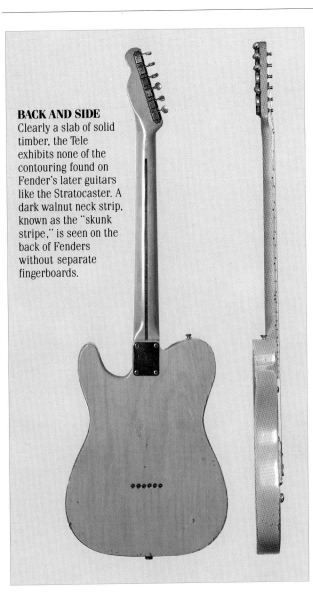

Fender promotion
The company's early literature accentuated features and style in much the same way as automobile brochures of the period. Shown here are Telecasters in catalogues from 1963-64 (right) and 1968 (below right), and a stylized Telecaster among other Fenders on the cover of the 1955 catalogue (top right).

Country comfort
A number of add-on gadgets have been developed for the Telecaster which take further its inherent ability to make sounds suited for country music. One of the earliest of such devices was called the B-Bender, invented in the late 1960s by two guitarists from country-rock group The Byrds, Gram Parsons and Clarence White. The Parsons/White B-Bender employs a system of levers inside the body (the close-up picture, right, shows the back of a Bender-equipped Tele with covers removed). The B-Bender's levers connect the bridge to the top strap button. When the player "pulls" on the strap the levers raise the pitch of the B-string, giving bends within chords to emulate sounds associated with the pedal steel guitar.

The Bigsby Palm Pedal was simpler. Pushing one of two levers behind the bridge raised the pitch of the B- or G-strings for similar effects. A refinement of this idea is the modern Hipshot, and with the addition of its optional knee-levers it is virtually a bolt-on pedal steel for a Tele.

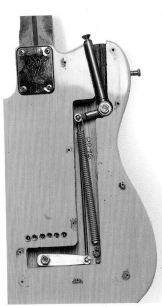

Esquire (right)
Produced between 1951 and 1970 this was essentially a one-pickup version of the normal Tele, minus the neck pickup (though Fender used Tele bodies for the Esquire with all the pickup routing). Control layout looked identical, but the selector provided three versatile settings.

1952 Fender Telecaster (above)
This early example sums up the elegant simplicity that lives on in today's Telecaster.

Headstock *A round string-retainer is found on the earliest Fenders.*

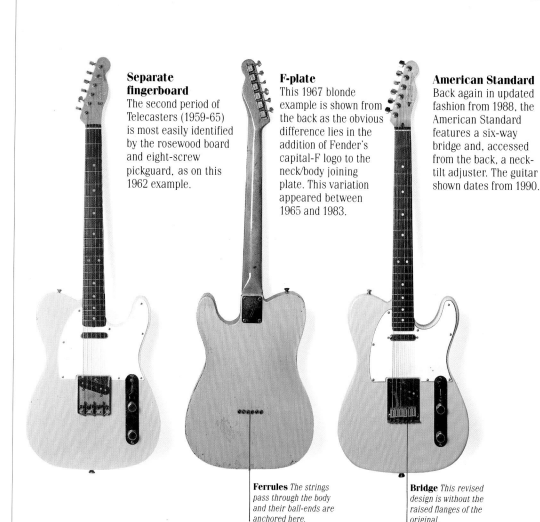

Separate fingerboard
The second period of Telecasters (1959-65) is most easily identified by the rosewood board and eight-screw pickguard, as on this 1962 example.

F-plate
This 1967 blonde example is shown from the back as the obvious difference lies in the addition of Fender's capital-F logo to the neck/body joining plate. This variation appeared between 1965 and 1983.

American Standard
Back again in updated fashion from 1988, the American Standard features a six-way bridge and, accessed from the back, a neck-tilt adjuster. The guitar shown dates from 1990.

1989 40th Anniversary
This guitar is number 221 of 300 in a limited edition of 40th Anniversary Telecasters. The special issue was based on the American Standard model (see left), but with several deluxe features. These included a bound body faced with attractive tiger-striped maple and fitted with gold hardware. By choosing to release this commemorative model in 1989 Fender seem to have decided that the Tele's birthdate was 1949.

Ferrules *The strings pass through the body and their ball-ends are anchored here.*

Bridge *This revised design is without the raised flanges of the original.*

Neck *Made from a single piece of flame maple, with pearl position dots.*

TELECASTER DEVELOPMENT

The Telecaster has had very little modification during its 40-year history. Few guitars that have been around even half as long as the Tele have survived without some interference. But Fender evidently realized very soon that a large part of the Telecaster's success was due to its unencumbered simplicity. Above, we chart the timing of the three official minor alterations made to the original Telecaster, which was characterized by its all-maple neck, blonde natural finish and contrasting black pickguard (see page 68).

Not that Fender has left the Tele entirely alone. In addition to the exceptions shown on the right, we can mention the Custom version of the Telecaster, which was made between 1959 and 1970, featuring a sunburst finish and a bound-edge body. This should not be confused with the later Telecaster Custom model (third from right, opposite page), easily identified by its humbucking pickup.

In the 1980s, cost-cutting produced the short-lived Standard, differing most noticeably in its lack of through-body stringing, which instantly diminished the Tele sound. Gold hardware made fleeting appearances in the 1980s on the black-finish Black & Gold Tele and the Gold version of the Elite Telecaster.

Thinline (left)
The semi-hollow Thinline (note the f-hole) first appeared in 1968 sporting conventional Tele hardware and a new "pearloid" pickguard. From 1972-80 it gained two humbuckers and a six-way bridge (as shown).

1976 Custom (right)
From 1972 this title applied to a new model featuring a humbucker at the neck along with a revised four-control layout on a newly designed pickguard. Production of this Custom ceased in 1982.

Telecaster Elite
This distinctly different Tele was introduced in 1983. It featured new pickups, circuitry and hardware. However, its up-market image met with little success, and it was withdrawn in 1985.

Deluxe
Available from 1973 to 1982, this model had a Strat-like headstock, contoured body and two humbuckers. This mid-1970s example is one of a very small number that came with a Strat-style vibrato.

1990 Jerry Donahue
In the late 1980s Fender started to make guitars endorsed by well-known players. This prototype for a proposed Jerry Donahue model couples the familiar Tele feel with custom wiring that offers Strat-like tones as well as Tele sounds.

Toting the Tele
Jimmy Bryant (center) plays a Telecaster in Fender's brochure for 1955, the same year he made a fine country LP with steel man Speedy West. Ten years later, British magazine *Beat Instrumental* shows Jeff Beck with a Telecaster (right). A press ad from 1966 (left) pronounces the Tele "the most wanted guitar in Britain."

STRATOCASTER VARIATIONS

The Fender Stratocaster is arguably the most popular and most emulated solid electric guitar ever. Launched in early 1954, it was designed by Leo Fender together with his colleague Freddie Tavares. The two were also helped by the contributions of country musician Bill Carson.

The Fender Musical Instrument Company of Fullerton, California had already pioneered the solid electric with their Telecaster. The stylish Stratocaster, epitome of 1950s tailfin-flash design, built upon Fender's idea of a guitar engineered for mass-production rather than hand-crafted for individual players.

It had three pickups where most electrics had one or two, there was a vibrato arm to bend the pitch of the strings and return them more or less to accurate tuning, adjustment of all six strings at the bridge, a dramatically contoured body for player comfort, and a jack-plug socket recessed into the front of the body. Musicians were amazed, and have been ever since – testament to the genius of Fender in the 1950s.

Richard Thompson
A prime exponent of the battered Strat, proof that a great player doesn't necessarily need a glossy guitar: note the missing volume knob and loose pickup.

Blonde Strat
A rarity for the period, this 1957 model is in the "blonde" finish more often seen on Telecasters.

Three pickups *Placed in optimum positions for maximum tonal variation, these do much to create the classic Strat sounds.*

Scratchplate *First period Strats have a single-layer, white pickguard fixed with eight screws.*

VOLUME

TONE

TONE

Vibrato *The first combination bridge-vibrato unit.*

Rosewood fingerboard (1959-1965)

The separate rosewood fingerboard is glued to the maple neck. The pickguard, fixed with 11 screws, is three-layer laminated white/black/white plastic, the top of which often fades to a so-called "snot-green" tinge. The above is a rare left-handed example from 1962.

Wide headstock (1965-1971)

This 1966 model shows the new larger headstock and four-screw neck/body joining plate with large F (below). CBS bought Fender in 1965, hence the term "pre-CBS."

Bullet headstock (1971-1981)

A chrome "bullet" is added to the wide headstock for truss rod adjustment (formerly carried out at the body-end of the neck). The neck/body plate now has three screws and an added neck-tilt feature. This is a Lake Placid Blue example from 1973.

Small headstock (1981-1983)

The last classic Strats made at Fender's Fullerton, California plant return to a narrow headstock and four-screw neck/body plate. Truss-rod adjustment is back at the neck's body-end. This example is autographed on the pickguard by Shadows guitarist Hank Marvin.

Two controls (1983-1985)

A transitional instrument issued at a time of financial cutbacks for Fender and lacking classic Strat features – note, for example, only two controls, the socket mounted flush to the pickguard, and the restyled vibrato. This is a left-handed example.

American Standard (started 1987)

Back at last in classic but updated style, the American Standard Strat came from a revitalized Fender company under new ownership and committed to make some Fenders in its new factory at Brea, California, despite the start in 1982 of production in the Far East.

Maple neck *Strats from 1954-59 have a one-piece neck with no separate fingerboard, as on this superb 1957 example.*

Headstock *This carries the original "spaghetti" logo and post-1956 "wing"-type string guide.*

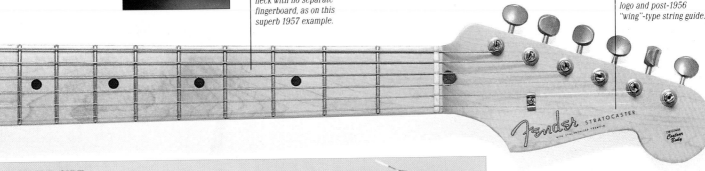

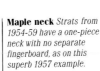

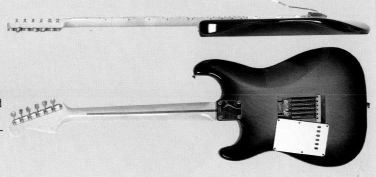

BACK AND SIDE

A good side view shows the Strat's original contoured body, a new idea in the 1950s. At the back is the plain four-screw neck/body joining plate. A removed plastic plate reveals vibrato springs, tension-adjustable to balance the pull of the strings.

1957 Stratocaster

This guitar, which is in superb original condition, is from the first period of the model's production. A Strat made between 1954 and 1959 can be distinguished by its maple neck into which the frets are set directly, and single-layer white plastic pickguard held by eight fixing screws. The Strat first came in this black and yellow "two-tone" sunburst; by 1958 red was added to give a "three-tone" burst (but the red often fades from early examples).

THE FENDER STRATOCASTER

The Stratocaster has survived for more than 35 years with very few changes, proof that Fender's original design was uncannily right. It has lent itself to every conceivable style of music, and even Leo Fender could surely not have guessed how great the demand for his Strat would become. It peaked in popularity during the 1960s, and then again in the 1980s when its clean, cutting sound could compete with the newly popular synthesizers. Even the most recent challenger to the Strat's world-dominating status, the so-called "superstrat" (see page 96), borrows heavily from the original.

It wasn't until the 1980s that Fender made alterations to the classic Stratocaster, and then the variations were subtle. There was the distinctly heavy all-walnut Strat early in the decade, along with the Gold Strat's glittering finish and hardware. Later on came the Elite models, with pushbuttons to select the plain-cover pickups, and most recently the Strat Ultra with an extra single-coil at the bridge. Fender is faced with a tricky choice over their modern Stratocaster. The company is keen to innovate and update the model, but it seems musicians want the basic, classic Strat – and probably always will.

Strat Number 0001 (below)
Despite its serial number, this Stratocaster, owned by David Gilmour of Pink Floyd, is not the very first one that was made. It bears a neck-date of June 1954, some months after the instrument began production.

Headstock *Fender used a single, roller-type string guide here.*

25th Anniversary (left)
To celebrate 25 years of Strat production, this 1979 model has an Anniversary body logo and deluxe machine heads. The first 500 came in white, but severe cracking meant a change to a more appropriate special silver finish. Supposedly a limited edition, around 10,000 were made up to 1980.

Finish *The silver color often tarnishes, as on this example.*

Pickguard *This guitar is fitted with a gold anodized aluminum type.*

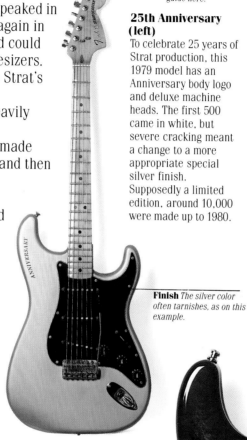

Vintage Reissues
The continuing popularity of vintage Stratocasters gave Fender the idea for a smart marketing move in the 1980s – making their own "new" versions of vintage-specification guitars. From 1982 to 1985, and again from 1987, Fender USA produced two Vintage Reissue models, the 57 (left) and the 62, based on a maple fingerboard 1957 model and a rosewood board 1962 Strat. Quality was high but accuracy was not 100 per cent, ignoring points like placement of position dots.

35th Anniversary (right)
This genuinely limited-edition anniversary model from 1989 combines quality timbers and active electronics. The ebony fingerboard is unusual for a Strat.

Controls *The switch selects an active circuit, giving extra boost from the lowest knob and added range to the middle control.*

Woods *The beautiful maple top on this 35th Anniversary's ash body has a superb grain pattern that creates the kind of effect described as "quilted."*

Headstock *This wider type was used on Strats from 1965 to 1981.*

Rhinestone Strat
This is one of only seven Strats with a body made of cold-cast bronze encrusted with rhinestones, specially built by sculptor Jon Douglas for Fender's UK agent in 1975.

Body *The cold-cast bronze makes this rare guitar very heavy.*

1961 Stratocaster
The ultimate battered Strat, as owned and well-used by Rory Gallagher. The body, originally sunburst, is down to bare wood almost all over, and the much-refretted neck bears wide Gibson frets.

Clapton Strat
Based on Eric Clapton's taste in new Fenders, this "signature" version of the American Standard Deluxe was issued in 1988 with active electronics and Eric's favored blocked-off 1950s-style vibrato.

1959 Stratocaster
The Strat was officially unavailable in Britain until 1960. This is the first one brought in direct, for Hank Marvin of The Shadows, and the Fender is now restored to its former glory by owner Bruce Welch.

Headstock *The guitar is from the 1954-59 period, with attractive one-piece maple neck.*

Five-way selector
From the beginning, Strats were issued with a three-way pickup selector switch mounted in front of the three rotary controls, giving a choice of front, middle or back pickup. But musicians quickly discovered that excellent hollow-sounding tones could be obtained by lodging the selector midway between these positions, giving combinations of front-and-middle pickup, and middle-and-back. Fender took a while to respond to this trend, and their five-way selector did not appear as a standard fitting until 1977.

Oddities
There have been a number of one-of-a-kind Stratocasters built over the years, and Fender now has a custom shop where musicians with the money and inclination can have virtually any requirements built into a new guitar. Before that, there were such unique instruments as a paisley-finish Strat, a see-through plexiglass model, and a semi-acoustic Strat along the same lines as the Thinline Telecaster. Built in greater quantity were the Alex Gregory seven-string Strat, the reversed-neck Hendrix model, and Yngwie Malmsteen's scalloped-fingerboard version.

COLORS
Guitarists in the 1950s were mostly a conservative lot: by and large guitars had sunburst finishes, and that was what the players expected. But the Stratocaster design called for more – and got it.

The tailfin-flash design of the Strat was clearly influenced by American automobiles of the 1950s, so it was hardly surprising that when Fender started to offer custom colors later in the decade they chose DuPont paints, originally designed for use on cars.

In the 1970s fashion swung back. Noticing that many players were stripping down guitar bodies to the wood, Fender offered a range of natural finishes to meet this demand. More recently there has been a move again to outlandish colors and Fender obliges with Purple Frosts and Crimson Bursts.

Collector's items
Some early custom-color Strats have become highly prized by collectors, mainly because relatively few survive in good, original condition. Some of the most alluring colors have equally romantic names, such as Lake Placid Blue, Burgundy Mist, Shoreline Gold, Surf Green or Fiesta Red. No collection is complete without one.

Daphne Blue 1963 Strat

Fiesta Red 1962 Strat

GALLERY OF FENDER SOLIDS

Fender's other electric guitars tend to be overshadowed by the spectacular success of the Stratocaster and the hardly less impressive achievements of the Telecaster. Yet from the 1950s to the 1990s Fender issued over a dozen different models in addition to their celebrated duo, some of which are excellent and each one of which gives its own unique sounds. A selection of Fender's wide range is featured here.

In 1965, the huge CBS corporation paid $13 million for the Fender companies, and Leo Fender departed to form CLF Research (which later manufactured Music Man guitars). Once Leo's association with the Fender brand ended, there was little innovation in design, and there was an apparent loss of quality.

A new outlook came eventually in 1985 when the existing Fender management, headed by Bill Schultz and Dan Smith, bought the company from CBS and successfully set about returning Fender to consistent quality production, both in the USA and the Far East.

Fender serial numbers
These are found on bridge plates, neck/body joint plates, or headstocks. As a rough guide:
0-0600 means pre-1956;
0601-9999 pre-1960;
00001-20000 1954-57;
20001 to 50000 1957-61;
50001-99999 1959-63 (some five-figure numbers are prefixed with 0 or –);
L00001 to L99999 1962-65;
100000 to 199999 1965-67;
200000 to 399999 1966-73;
400000 to 599999 1966-75;
600000 to 999999 1972-82;
seven digits 1976-82;
S plus six digits 1976-82;
E, F, or G plus five or six digits 1980 onward;
V plus six digits 1982 onward.

Neck dates
Some Fenders have dates stamped or penciled on the end of the neck.

Headstock logos (above)
Top to bottom: original "spaghetti" (to mid-1960s); "Transitional" (mid to late 1960s); "CBS" (late 1960s to early 1980s). "Modern" (from early 1980s).

Jazzmaster
This misleadingly named guitar was Fender's top-of-the-line solid when introduced in 1957 with a new offset-waist body and a richer, deeper sound from the wide coils of the steel-guitar-like pickups. Yet another long-running Fender model, it remained virtually unchanged until dropped in 1980.

Fingerboard *This is an early 1960s dot-neck. Binding was introduced in late 1965, followed by block inlays in 1966.*

Lead /rhythm switch *This selects between two circuits: a secondary circuit acts on the neck pickup only, and is controlled by the two nearby rollers which govern volume and tone.*

Controls *These adjust the volume and tone of the main circuit.*

Jaguar
This has the same styling as the Jazzmaster but with a shorter-scale 22-fret neck, and switches for pickup on/off and tonal variation. The Jaguar (1961-75) was Fender's most expensive solid, but never a huge success.

Vibrato *A new design, a single-spring unit with separate rocker bridge.*

Maverick
This was a rarer version of the Custom, a hybrid designed to use up leftover parts (modified Electric XII bodies and necks and Mustang hardware) and produced between 1969 and 1972.

Swinger
Also known unofficially as the Arrow, or Musiclander, this model came from a shortlived and small 1969 production run, using surplus cut-down Musicmaster bodies, necks and hardware.

1957 Musicmaster (above)
Fender catered for the cheaper end of the market too, and in 1956 launched its first economy models, the Musicmaster and Duo-Sonic. These continued until 1980 and 1970, undergoing various design changes, and were later joined by the Mustang (1964-81) and the Bronco (1967-80). These were in turn succeeded by the medium-priced Lead in 1979, and the original Bullet models in 1981.

Fender Japan

In the face of increasing oriental competition, mainly in the form of well-produced copies, CBS set up Fender Japan in 1982. Initial production concentrated, naturally, on high-quality copies of the most popular Fender vintage originals, alongside cheaper versions marketed under the Squier brandname (taken from the name of a string-making company bought by Fender in the 1960s). An expanded mid-1980s range boasted new models and updated design ideas and hardware.

More copies appeared, reproducing the majority of the Fender USA range and spanning all price brackets. Fender Japan then seemed to tire of copying and tried its first original designs, the Master series of 1984. But these were unusually conventional and quite different from Fender's usual style, as was the quirky but equally shortlived Katana from 1985. These were followed in the same year by the angular Performer, but it also proved unpopular and lasted only until 1986.

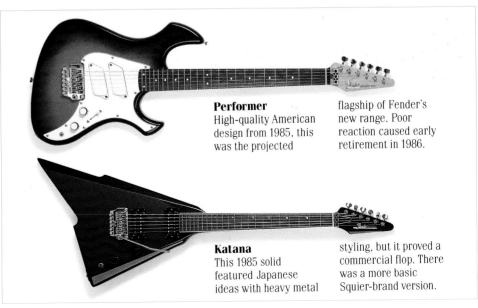

Performer
High-quality American design from 1985, this was the projected flagship of Fender's new range. Poor reaction caused early retirement in 1986.

Katana
This 1985 solid featured Japanese ideas with heavy metal styling, but it proved a commercial flop. There was a more basic Squier-brand version.

FENDER AFTER FENDER

Despite selling the Fender companies to CBS in 1965, Leo Fender stayed on as a consultant, contributing new ideas and designs (such as the Mustang Bass) until 1970. He then became a partner and major shareholder in Music Man, which had been set up in 1970 by former Fender men Forrest White and Tom Walker. Leo provided two new guitars for them, made by his own company, CLF Research. First was the StingRay, soon followed by the Sabre.

Leo Fender
Thirty years after defining the modern electric guitar, Leo Fender founded G&L Music Sales in 1980 with his long-standing associate George Fullerton. This 1980s flyer pictures Mr Fender among a brace of G&Ls in the company's factory in Fullerton. It also carries in small print the line: "Leo Fender is not associated or affiliated with Fender Musical Instruments in any way."

Body *In addition to this walnut, finishes included black, white, natural and sunburst.*

Music Man StingRay
This versatile Leo Fender design was produced between 1976 and 1980, but never matched the success of his earlier guitars. Humbucking pickups replaced the usual Fender single-coil trademark. In keeping with 1970s trends there was no vibrato.

Chromed control panel *Treble, bass, and master volume controls, plus four-way rotary selector switch.*

BACK AND SIDE
Note that the neck/body joint is secured by three bolts, a method used on Fender guitars of the same period. There is also a row of six string-retainers sunk into the back of the body; this was another distinctive feature of Fender instruments.

Truss rod slot *Maple-necked models continued the tradition of a "skunk-stripe" cover.*

MUSIC MAN AND ERNIE BALL

In 1984 Music Man was acquired by the Ernie Ball company, probably best known for their guitar strings. Demand from players meant that the Music Man basses (see page 169) were the first to be revived. The first guitar was launched in 1987.

The first Ernie Ball/Music Man guitar was the Silhouette, an all-new model designed by Dudley Gimpel and developed with the help of country guitarist Albert Lee. The Fender tradition was still apparent, but there were a number of refinements, including a 24-fret neck giving the player a full two octaves per string, a six-bolt neck/body fixing, a small body, interchangeable pickup/pickguard assemblies in various formats, and a distinctive, compact four-and-two headstock. Still in production at the start of the 1990s, this model has enjoyed increasing popularity.

In 1987 the Silhouette was joined by the Steve Morse model. This incorporated a multiple pickup layout along with other individual features requested by this respected guitarist.

Albert Lee
A refined country guitarist, Lee replaced James Burton in Emmylou Harris's band in 1977. The British guitarist has also played with The Everly Brothers, among others.

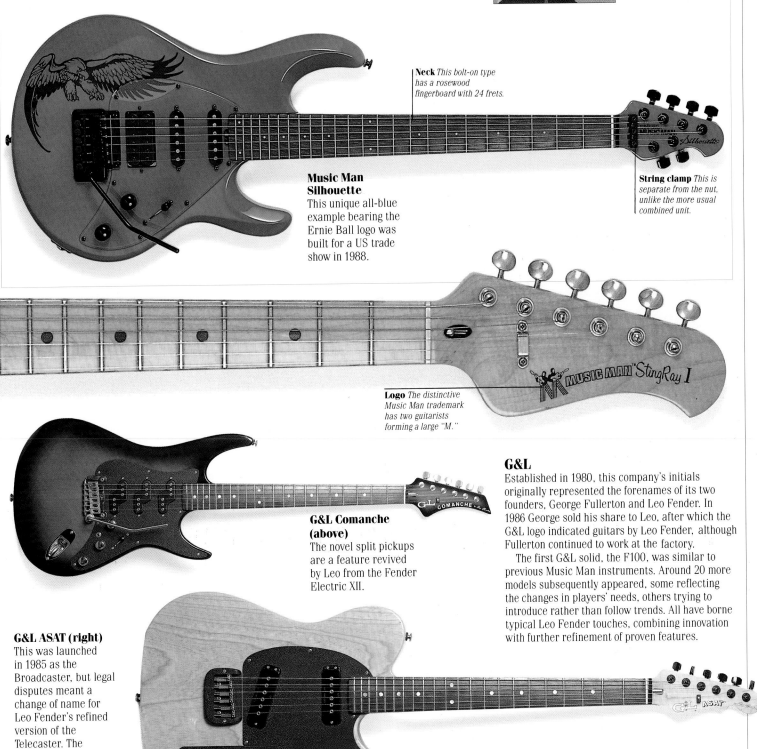

Neck *This bolt-on type has a rosewood fingerboard with 24 frets.*

Music Man Silhouette
This unique all-blue example bearing the Ernie Ball logo was built for a US trade show in 1988.

String clamp *This is separate from the nut, unlike the more usual combined unit.*

Logo *The distinctive Music Man trademark has two guitarists forming a large "M."*

G&L Comanche (above)
The novel split pickups are a feature revived by Leo from the Fender Electric XII.

G&L
Established in 1980, this company's initials originally represented the forenames of its two founders, George Fullerton and Leo Fender. In 1986 George sold his share to Leo, after which the G&L logo indicated guitars by Leo Fender, although Fullerton continued to work at the factory.

The first G&L solid, the F100, was similar to previous Music Man instruments. Around 20 more models subsequently appeared, some reflecting the changes in players' needs, others trying to introduce rather than follow trends. All have borne typical Leo Fender touches, combining innovation with further refinement of proven features.

G&L ASAT (right)
This was launched in 1985 as the Broadcaster, but legal disputes meant a change of name for Leo Fender's refined version of the Telecaster. The example shown is a recent version.

GIBSON LES PAUL "GOLD TOP"

In the early 1950s, the very traditional Gibson company recognized the growing popularity of the revolutionary Fender solid body electric guitar. They decided to collaborate with Les Paul, a leading guitarist of the time and a very keen inventor (see pages 58-59). The resulting instrument bore his own name and many of his ideas, the first version appearing in 1952.

The styling was pure Gibson: the heavily carved top and classic symmetrical headstock were borrowed from their established archtop guitars, as was the scaled-down yet much heavier solid body. These aspects of the Les Paul guitar's design, together with features such as the glued-in neck and ornate fingerboard inlays, conveyed Gibson's craftsmanship, almost certainly intended to contrast with Fender's slab-bodied instruments and mass-production approach.

Gibson's Les Paul started life as the company's first tentative step toward a modern solid body instrument, yet the design has remained virtually unchanged throughout its 40-year history. Together with Fender's Telecaster and Stratocaster designs, the Les Paul is among the most popular and emulated electric guitars ever made.

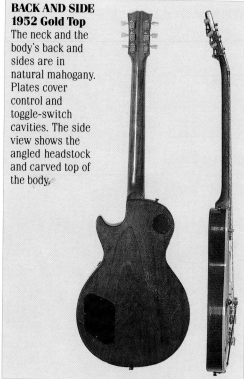

BACK AND SIDE 1952 Gold Top
The neck and the body's back and sides are in natural mahogany. Plates cover control and toggle-switch cavities. The side view shows the angled headstock and carved top of the body.

Tailpiece *"Trapeze" type with combined bridge.*

Finish *The nickname "Gold Top" derives from the finish of the body face.*

Toggle switch *This selects neck (rhythm), bridge (treble), or both pickups.*

P90 pickups *Single-coil units with adjustable polepiece screws.*

Controls *Volume and tone for each pickup.*

FRONT, BACK AND SIDE
1955 All-Gold
A rare variation, completely finished in gold. Gibson had already used this idea on their ES295 model.

Bridge/tailpiece *A combination unit fitted from 1953 to 1955.*

Pickups *Two mini-humbuckers, as used on Epiphone guitars.*

Deluxe
This Les Paul was made between 1970 and 1984; the distinctive pickups gave the instrument a brighter sound than the normal humbuckers.

Humbuckers *This current version has two; a three-pickup model was reissued between 1977 and 1984.*

1990 Custom
This model is still in production in this format. Reintroduced in 1968 but now with two humbuckers, it has proved the most popular layout, because the third, middle pickup on the 1960s Custom impeded playing.

Neck pickup *Single-coil with six oblong alnico magnets.*

Headstock *The Custom has a split-diamond pearl inlay.*

1956 Custom (left)
The "Black Beauty" nickname derives from the all-black finish.

Fingerboard *Block pearl inlays set into ebony.*

Headstock *This model has a split-diamond pearl inlay.*

Fingerboard *Crown inlays in rosewood.*

1960 Custom (below)
From 1957, three humbuckers replaced the two single-coil pickups.

1952 "Gold Top" (above)
The lack of binding on the fingerboard and the "joined dot" logo identify this as an early example, estimated to be among the first 50 Les Pauls produced. The "trapeze" bridge/tailpiece proved impractical.

Finish *This is an example of the rare wine red finish; most were black.*

GIBSON LES PAUL STANDARD

In 1958 Gibson replaced the Les Paul Gold Top with the Standard model, an identical guitar except for its more conservative three-tone sunburst finish; at last the maple top could be seen, sometimes to stunning effect. Demand for the Les Paul had dwindled, so perhaps Gibson was trying to attract customers with more traditional tastes who had been deterred by the earlier model's garish gold paint.

Gibson gave up on this model in 1961, and launched the SG style instead (see pages 84 and 88). However, later in the decade, players discovered that a Les Paul at high volume produced a desirably thick, sustaining sound, ideal for blues-based music. This renewed interest led to the reintroduction of some Les Paul models in 1968, but surprisingly the Standard didn't appear again until 1975, since when it has remained in continuous production at Gibson.

1959 Standard
The factory-fitted Bigsby vibrato tailpiece is a rare feature on any Les Paul model.

1960 Standard
Another good example of a "flame top"; compare its narrow grain to the wider "tiger stripes" of the Standard below.

Pickups *These are humbucking type. The bridge unit has the protective metal cover removed, exposing the twin coils.*

Tune-O-Matic bridge
In this design, strings are anchored at the separate tailpiece and then pass over the bridge, which has six individual saddles allowing accurate intonation.

Sunburst *The nickname derives from the shaded three-color finish of the body face.*

1960 Standard

Owned in the late 1960s by Paul Kossoff while in the group Black Cat Bones. The guitarist, who later joined Free, wrote his London address on the inside of the control backplate (below).

Pickups *The covers on both units are absent, revealing contrasting black and white bobbins, known among collectors as "zebra" types.*

The Les Paul sound

The sound of the Les Paul Standard depends to a great extent on the timbers used in its construction. The original concept was for a mahogany body to provide depth of tone, with a maple front adding brightness. The combination offered good sustain without being too heavy, and these woods have remained consistent throughout the Standard's production history.

The glued neck and the large humbucking pickups also contribute to the guitar's natural sustain and wide tonal range, elements that meet Les Paul's own original requirements and are responsible for the instrument's continuing and wide-ranging popularity.

The Les Paul price

In the hands of a few players such as Eric Clapton in Britain and Mike Bloomfield in the United States, the Les Paul Standard reached unprecedented levels of popularity in the late 1960s. The Les Paul's thick, sustained sound featured by Clapton on John Mayall's "Blues Breakers" album (1966) and later by Bloomfield on Paul Butterfield's "East-West" (1966) was a big influence on contemporary players.

These sought-after Standards were made between 1958 and 1961, but only about 2000 were produced during this period. Demand has, therefore, always far outstripped supply. Prices shot up during the Les Paul boom of the late 1960s and have consequently reached such high levels that, ironically, mere musicians are now rarely able to afford these instruments, many of which have ended up locked away in bank vaults as financial investments.

1990 Classic

This vintage reissue is intended to combine the appearance of a matured 30-year-old Standard with the relatively low price of a new guitar.

Pickguard *The "1960" logo emphasizes the supposed vintage of this new guitar.*

1960 Standard (above)

This is an excellent example of a "flame top" Standard, a lurid description of the vividly striped maple front. Not all Standards of the period display this desirable effect.

1958 Standard

This guitar shows how the red element of the three-tone sunburst finish can fade, leaving a duller, single-color effect overall that is sometimes amusingly described as an "unburst" finish.

LES PAUL VARIATIONS

The guitarist's imagination has been captured by the Les Paul Standards, Customs, and Gold Tops, but that hasn't stopped Gibson applying this famous name to a bewildering array of models. Not all of these have been successful, and certainly none has made such a lasting impact as the celebrated trio.

For example, Gibson has produced an assortment of reissues, which began in 1968 with a revitalized Gold Top. Others include the Heritage Standard (1980-82), Pro Deluxe (1977-83), 54 Limited Edition Custom (1972-73), 57 Gold Top (from 1987), and 58 Standard (from 1985). The company also celebrated three production birthdays with limited edition guitars, the first being the 20th Anniversary Custom in 1974, followed by the special 25/50 five years later, and the 30th Anniversary Gold Top in 1982. Then there were the more unusual Les Paul variations which Gibson marketed from time to time, such as the Recording (1971-79) with complex circuitry for studio use, the battery-power Artist (1980-81), and the LP XR2 (1981-82) which came minus a pickguard and with unusual pickups.

1978 Artisan
There was an unusual amount of decoration on this short-lived version (1977-80) from Gibson: note the work on fingerboard and headstock.

1979 25/50 Anniversary
The model marked Les Paul's "25-year association with Gibson and fiftieth year in the music business."

1990 Studio
This carved-top model without binding appeared in 1983.

Promotion
A picture from an early 1960s Gibson catalogue shows a three-humbucker SG/Les Paul Custom version.

Logo *Les Paul's name appears on SG models dated up to 1962.*

SG/Les Paul Standard
Gibson restyled the Les Paul range in 1961, introducing a new and more adventurous body shape on all models. The end result was not to Les Paul's liking, however, and his signature-logo was not used on the headstock from 1962. Since then the shape has simply been known as the SG.

Inlays *Of the early SGs, only the two-humbucker Standard had these "crown" markers.*

Cutaways *The new, heavily beveled, twin-cutaway design gave more access to higher frets, the neck joining the body at the last fret.*

Body *This is of all-mahogany construction, much lighter than earlier Les Paul models.*

Sideways vibrola *An alternative to the widely used Bigsby unit, this short-lived Gibson design altered pitch by moving the vibrato arm sideways instead of in the normal up-and-down action.*

Les Paul Junior
This 1954 example, a slab-bodied budget version with basic hardware and single P90 pickup, is from the first year of production. The single-cutaway type lasted until 1958.

Les Paul Special
Another down-market mahogany-bodied solid, but with two P90s, this 1955 version is in Gibson's "TV" finish, designed to stand out on contemporary black-and-white television.

Les Paul Junior
In 1958 the Junior's body shape was changed to a twin-cutaway style, which was a first for Gibson. The guitar shown is from 1958, with a TV finish.

Les Paul Special
Originally introduced in 1955 as a single-cutaway guitar, the Special also adopted the new double-cutaway style in 1958. This 1961 example is from the last year of production.

Toggle switch *Normal Les Paul location; moved next to controls on double-cutaway Special.*

Body *The revised styling and the new neck joint allowed easier access to higher frets.*

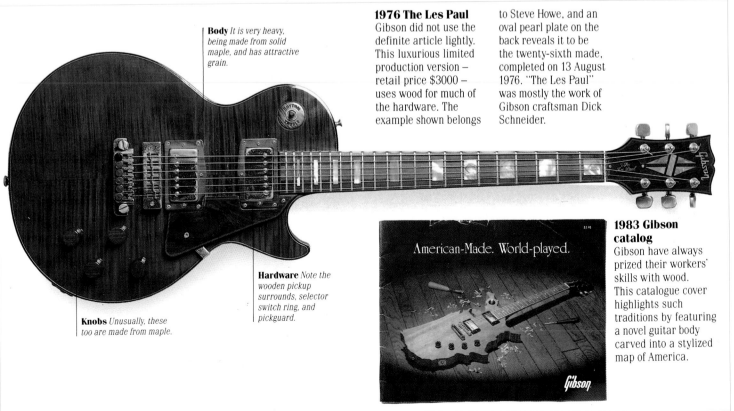

Body *It is very heavy, being made from solid maple, and has attractive grain.*

1976 The Les Paul
Gibson did not use the definite article lightly. This luxurious limited production version – retail price $3000 – uses wood for much of the hardware. The example shown belongs to Steve Howe, and an oval pearl plate on the back reveals it to be the twenty-sixth made, completed on 13 August 1976. "The Les Paul" was mostly the work of Gibson craftsman Dick Schneider.

Hardware *Note the wooden pickup surrounds, selector switch ring, and pickguard.*

Knobs *Unusually, these too are made from maple.*

American-Made. World-played.

1983 Gibson catalog
Gibson have always prized their workers' skills with wood. This catalogue cover highlights such traditions by featuring a novel guitar body carved into a stylized map of America.

ODD-SHAPED GIBSONS

Until the late 1950s, Gibson's solid body guitar designs had been very traditional. All that changed with what the company called its "modernistic" guitars: the Flying V, the Explorer and the Moderne. Before these designs, solid electric guitars had reflected established acoustic guitar styling: a waisted body with smaller top bout balancing a larger bottom. But Gibson's oddball trio featured totally original, boldly adventurous styling.

Gibson president Ted McCarty came up with the new shapes by using "modern" straight lines rather than "traditional" curves – a very radical move for the time. So radical, in fact, that the response from both retailers and players was negative. Despite Gibson's high hopes, none of these unusual guitars sold well and production stopped within two years.

Many years later these rare guitars became very desirable, and the renewed interest led to other makers adopting the Flying V and Explorer styling. Gibson itself has also managed to offer simple reissues, as well as updates based on the shapes of the Explorer and Flying V designs, proving that these innovative guitars were well ahead of their time.

BACK AND SIDE
Note the V-shaped string anchor on the back of this original 1958 Flying V.

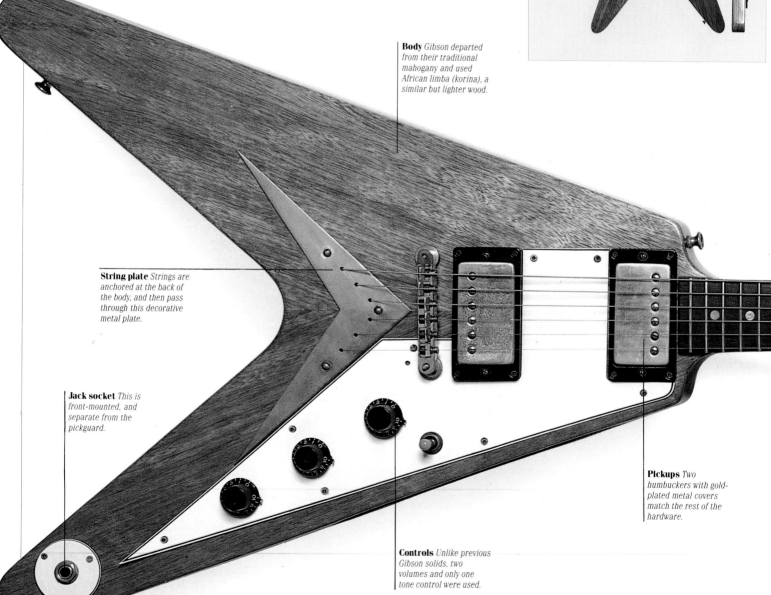

Body *Gibson departed from their traditional mahogany and used African limba (korina), a similar but lighter wood.*

String plate *Strings are anchored at the back of the body, and then pass through this decorative metal plate.*

Jack socket *This is front-mounted, and separate from the pickguard.*

Controls *Unlike previous Gibson solids, two volumes and only one tone control were used.*

Pickups *Two humbuckers with gold-plated metal covers match the rest of the hardware.*

"Reverse" Firebird (1963-65)

In 1963 Gibson launched the first series of Firebird models, devised with the help of car designer Ray Dietrich and clearly intended to compete with Fender. The four models – I, III, V, and VII – used specially designed humbuckers and all but the I featured a vibrato tailpiece.

These were Gibson's first through-neck guitars, using a one-piece body center and neck, with added body wings to complete the shape.

Sales were disappointing, and the design was drastically revised in 1965.

"Non-reverse" style (1965-69)

Gibson played safe with the new Firebirds, disposing of that innovative back-to-front look. A conventional glued neck replaced the more expensive through-neck construction of the originals, machine heads reverted to normal side-mounted types, and stock P90 single-coil pickups were fitted to models I and III.

Despite the changes and the longer production run, these Firebirds were unpopular, although the "reverse" versions have enjoyed later success, prompting copies and Gibson reissues.

Reverse headstock *This echoed the body styling, and was fitted with banjo-style back-mounted machine heads.*

1980 Explorer

Launched in 1958, the Explorer's odd styling took some time to catch on. This is a prototype of the 1983 model.

Reverse body
Phil Manzanera's 1960s VII: three humbuckers, gold hardware, and custom red finish.

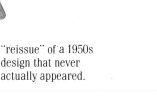

Non-reverse body
1966 III with three P90s and the standard slide select switch, owned by XTC's Dave Gregory.

Headstock This shows the original Gibson Prototype stamp, and special low serial number.

1980 Moderne
This was a prototype for Gibson's 1983 "reissue" of a 1950s design that never actually appeared.

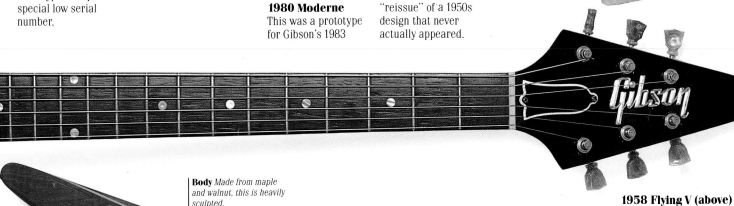

Body *Made from maple and walnut, this is heavily sculpted.*

Tailpiece *This repeats the "boomerang" shape of the pickups.*

Pickups *The V2 had two of Gibson's specially designed gold-plated Boomerang units.*

1981 V2
Gibson's variation on the V theme, made from 1979 to 1982.

1958 Flying V (above)
This first version is rare, as only around 100 were made before production ceased in 1959, and is highly sought-after. It was replaced by a revised version (1967-79) with a different control layout and normal hardware. An authentic Gibson reissue appeared in 1983.

GALLERY OF GIBSON SOLIDS

In the early 1960s more and more teenagers began to buy electric guitars, but Gibson's rather staid instruments proved unattractive to these youthful guitarists. Even the new SG guitars suffered in comparison to Fender's flashy, colorful Jazzmasters, Jaguars, and Stratocasters.

Later in the 1960s serious musicians emerging from the teenage pop scene began to rediscover Gibson instruments, and so the pendulum of fashion swung back in Gibson's favor over the next ten years, as described for the Les Paul Standard (page 82).

The Stratocaster-dominated early 1980s proved to be a lean time for Gibson: their traditional thick sounding, humbucker-equipped guitars didn't mesh with the new synthesizer-based music. Even the normally Gibson-toting heavy metallers were playing Fenders. Given historical precedent, Gibson must have expected fashion to swing back in their favor. But in the mid-1980s came a new trend, the Fender-inspired "superstrat," and again Gibson lost out. At the start of the musically diverse 1990s, Gibson found more success by returning to their classic designs.

1964 Melody Maker
This was Gibson's first economy solid, launched in 1959 as a single-cutaway design with one or two pickups, altered to an equal cutaway type in 1961. This example has the optional short-scale neck, another feature aimed at beginners. In 1966 the Melody Maker adopted SG body styling, which lasted until its demise in 1971.

Headstock *A simple, plain, budget design for Gibson.*

Neck *Shorter scale for beginners and players with small hands.*

Body *The slim, slab-style body was cheap to produce.*

Pickups *Simple single-coil type, similar to cheaper Fender designs.*

SG Custom 1990
The three-pickup SG Custom replaced the Les Paul logo version in 1962, and remained in production until 1979 undergoing various cosmetic and hardware changes. The original 1960s style was reissued in 1986, and this example shows how Gibson recaptured the vintage character.

1963 SG Special
The SG body style replaced the earlier Special in 1961. This P90-equipped model was produced until 1971.

DATING GIBSONS

As with many brands, Gibson serial numbers sometimes offer only a rough indication of the production period of a particular guitar. Often it becomes necessary to examine specific construction and hardware to pinpoint more accurately the date of a guitar, requiring specialist knowledge and experience.

Gibson serial numbers

From 1953 to 1961 solids can be dated by the first number of the five- or six-digit serial, eg 5 8274 = 1955, 910857 = 1959, 0 0195 = 1960, 1 2602 = 1961, and so on.

From 1961 to 1975 there was no specific chronological scheme, but much confusion and duplication. As a very rough guide:

100-99999	= 1961-3
000001-099999	= 1967
100000-199999	= 1963-67
200000-299999	= 1964-65
300000-599999	= 1965-69
600000-999999	= 1966-69

Confusingly, numbers 000001-999999 were used again between 1970 and 1975.

Six digits prefixed with C, D, E or F were used from 1974 to 1975; then came an eight-digit system where the first two numbers were coded to indicate the date (99 = 1975; 00 = 1976; 06 = 1977).

From 1977 onwards a simple system was at last adopted, where first and fifth numbers indicate the year, eg 87684832 equals 1984.

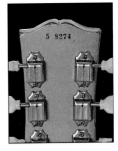

1955 Les Paul
The serial number stamped on the rear of this headstock shows the early dating system.

1990 Firebird
The number on the back of this headstock employs Gibson's logical post-1977 dating system.

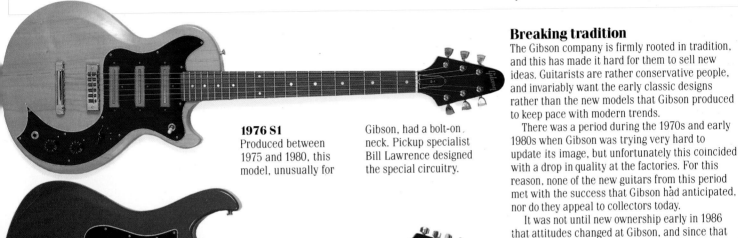

1976 S1
Produced between 1975 and 1980, this model, unusually for Gibson, had a bolt-on neck. Pickup specialist Bill Lawrence designed the special circuitry.

1982 Victory MVX
In 1981 Gibson reacted to Fender's renewed popularity by producing this solid, so clearly influenced by their Californian competitor. However, Gibson combined traditional humbuckers with a central single-coil in an attempt to create a guitar for all reasons.

1983 Corvus III
This model with its can-opener-shaped body escaped in 1983. Quite what was the market Gibson was aiming at remains a mystery; the Corvus sank without trace two years later.

1978 Artist RD
This series, launched in 1977 after collaboration with the synthesizer company Moog, incorporated complex active circuits. An unhappy marriage of traditional and modern design.

Breaking tradition

The Gibson company is firmly rooted in tradition, and this has made it hard for them to sell new ideas. Guitarists are rather conservative people, and invariably want the early classic designs rather than the new models that Gibson produced to keep pace with modern trends.

There was a period during the 1970s and early 1980s when Gibson was trying very hard to update its image, but unfortunately this coincided with a drop in quality at the factories. For this reason, none of the new guitars from this period met with the success that Gibson had anticipated, nor do they appeal to collectors today.

It was not until new ownership early in 1986 that attitudes changed at Gibson, and since that time Gibson has capitalized on the need for affordable "new oldies" by sensibly reissuing its classics and mostly avoiding fashionable or oddball designs. It seems to have learned the lessons of previous decades, and now acknowledge its past in a commercially successful manner.

Carlos Santana
This 1973 Gibson flyer shows Santana with the new L6S, an all-maple solid that remained in production until 1982.

AMERICA: THE FIFTIES AND SIXTIES

Now we look beyond Fender and Gibson to other American makers who started producing solid instruments in the 1950s and 1960s. They range from better known names like Epiphone, Rickenbacker and Gretsch, to smaller companies such as Hallmark, Premier and Micro-Frets.

Many other manufacturers flourished during this period, meeting the huge demand for guitars. Harmony and Kay were both Chicago-based concerns producing a wide range of instruments under a variety of additional brandnames, such as Silvertone, Regal, Airline, and Old Kraftsman.

Of the brands illustrated here, three survived into the 1990s and of those only Rickenbacker had not succumbed to moving some production to the Far East.

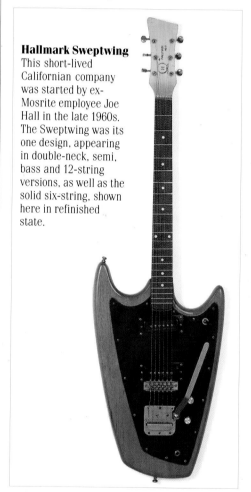

Hallmark Sweptwing
This short-lived Californian company was started by ex-Mosrite employee Joe Hall in the late 1960s. The Sweptwing was its one design, appearing in double-neck, semi, bass and 12-string versions, as well as the solid six-string, shown here in refinished state.

Epiphone
Gibson bought the Epiphone company in 1957 and soon produced an Epiphone equivalent of its own Melody Maker model, the Olympic Special. A new design solid was later added (right), with features roughly corresponding to Gibson's SG series. USA production of Epiphones ceased in 1970; solids made since then originated from Japan and, later, Korea. From 1989 some Epiphone solids have been produced once again in America.

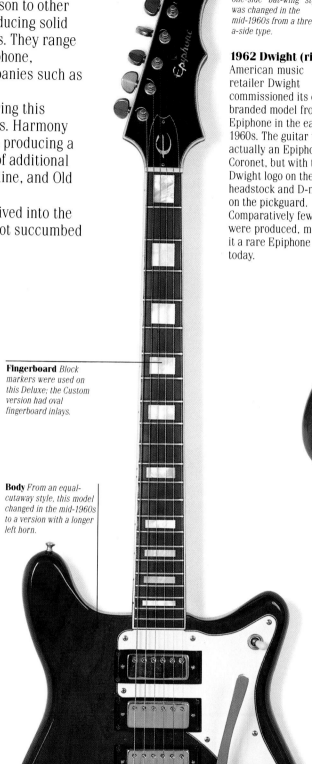

Fingerboard *Block markers were used on this Deluxe; the Custom version had oval fingerboard inlays.*

Body *From an equal-cutaway style, this model changed in the mid-1960s to a version with a longer left horn.*

Headstock *This six-on-one-side "bat-wing" style was changed in the mid-1960s from a three-a-side type.*

1962 Dwight (right)
American music retailer Dwight commissioned its own branded model from Epiphone in the early 1960s. The guitar was actually an Epiphone Coronet, but with the Dwight logo on the headstock and D-motif on the pickguard. Comparatively few were produced, making it a rare Epiphone today.

1966 Epiphone Crestwood Deluxe
In the early 1960s Epiphone launched a range of solids sharing one body style. Top of this line was the Crestwood Deluxe, followed by the Crestwood Custom, Wilshire, Coronet and Olympic models. They were made until 1970.

Pickups *The Deluxe has three mini-humbuckers; the Custom version had two.*

Vibrato *This is Epiphone's own Trem-o-tone unit.*

Premier

This was a brandname of the Multivox company of New York. Premier solids of the 1950s and 1960s had a distinctive scroll-shaped left horn. Others, such as the model shown, sported crushed-plastic pickguards bearing a large array of controls. Later Premier solids featured a six-on-one side headstock, imported hardware, and plastic finished bodies.

Micro-Frets Golden Melody

The Micro-Frets company, based in Maryland, produced guitars in the 1960s and 1970s. It specialized in innovative hardware, such as the Micro-nut and the Calibrato vibrato unit, both seen on this Golden Melody, aimed at improving intonation. Another feature of some models was a built-in radio transmitter, an idea well ahead of its time.

1957 Rickenbacker Combo 800

The Combo series, Rickenbacker's first modern electric guitars, appeared in 1954. There were two basic versions, the Combo 600 bearing a single pickup. Early Combo 800s, like that shown, also appear to have one "horseshoe" pickup, but this is in fact a twin-coil unit. Later versions have two separate pickups. The Combos lasted until the late 1960s.

Rickenbacker solids

The Californian company is best known for its electric acoustics (see pages 148-149), but its first solid electrics predated these. It has produced numerous solid guitar models, only a few of which have succeeded in capturing the best of the Rickenbacker character and image, albeit in a more manageable package than the bulkier electric acoustics. Most successful in this respect has been the 600 series, produced since 1962. These models share the "hooked" body shape of the 400 series, made between 1958 and 1984.

1957 Gretsch 6129 Silver Jet

In 1955 Gretsch launched their Jet models, featuring three colored tops: the black Duo Jet, silver-sparkle Silver Jet, and red Jet Firebird. Later versions came in other sparkle colors.

Inlays *These "hump" blocks succeeded the original plain blocks and were replaced with "thumbnails" during 1957.*

Body *Single-cutaway style, replaced by double cutaways in 1962.*

Gretsch

A number of Gretsch solids were made in the 1950s and 1960s, and collectors avidly seek these guitars. They include the 6121 Chet Atkins and its G-brand relative the 6130 Round Up, the very rare 6134 White Penguin, and the 6132 Corvette with its pastel partner, the 6106 Princess. Later Gretsch solids do not share this appeal; consequently it was the 1950s solids which Gretsch chose for their Japan-made reissues at the end of the 1980s.

Gretsch Astro Jet (below)

This peculiarly shaped solid appeared in 1965, Gretsch's first real departure from tradition. It has an unusual four-and-two machine head layout.

AMERICA: FROM THE SEVENTIES

During the 1970s, the number of electric guitar producers in the USA mushroomed. Even established acoustic-makers entered the market, alongside a multitude of new brandnames from companies of all sizes. The increased competition meant that makers had to establish their own identities, leading to the appearance of many original designs. But most failed to make any significant impact on players' tastes, and many brands disappeared. This lack of success for originality prompted most US designers to play safe in the 1980s and 1990s. The majority chose to follow trends like the so-called "superstrat" (see page 96).

Headstock *Locking machine heads improve tuning stability.*

Veillette-Citron Shark Baritone Guitar (right)

Joe Veillette and Harvey Citron started instrument production in the late 1970s, making a range of Alembic-styled guitars. This Baritone model comes from their S Series of the early 1980s, styled after Guild's Thunderbird solid. It used a very long 73cm (28¾in) scale and was tuned below normal guitar pitch, aimed to fill the gap between guitar and bass.

1990 Paul Reed Smith EG4

A relatively major change for PRS, the EG adds a pickguard with two optional pickup layouts to the classic shape, plus a 22-fret bolt-on neck. This launch-year example was the first into the UK of the more Fender-influenced PRS.

Inlays *The dots have contrasting sections that give a "crescent moon" effect.*

Construction *This guitar has a maple through-neck, with maple body "wings."*

Body *The insides of the cutaways are chamfered.*

Controls *Master volume, rotary selector, and "sweet" switch.*

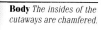

Paul Reed Smith

This Maryland-based maker's design became one of the most influential of the late 1980s. Smith began building guitars in an attic in 1975, and by 1982 had arrived at his now-famous design. It combines in a modern package the best of Fender and Gibson traditions, blending their style, construction, and sounds into a "new vintage" guitar. In 1985 Smith set up his own factory, and continued to produce a range of subtle variations on his successful design.

1986 Paul Reed Smith

This was the first PRS guitar to be imported into the UK, production having commenced in the USA late in the previous year. The design has remained unchanged since then, including features such as the simple yet effective vibrato.

1980 Martin EM18

Martin is much better known for its acoustic flat-tops, but has flirted occasionally with electric guitars. Its first solids appeared in 1979, and this example clearly shows its laminated body style. A second series came in 1980, featuring a carved-top body and an active circuit. The models were not a success, and Martin stopped making solid electrics in 1983.

Body *Despite the appearance of a through-neck, it is of glued neck construction.*

1975 Ovation Breadwinner

Also better known for their acoustics (and electro-acoustics), Ovation's first solid electric was the Breadwinner, launched in 1971. The unusual design limited the popularity of this and the deluxe Deacon of 1972. Ovation came up with other, more conventional solids such as the Preacher and the Viper (both 1975). None was successful, and Ovation abandoned solids in the mid-1980s.

Body *The extra cutaway here was designed to improve guitar balance when played seated.*

1979 Guild S70D

Guild's earliest solids were the 1960s Polara, Thunderbird and Jet-Star models. These were followed by the Gibson-influenced "M" and "S" ranges of the 1970s. The model shown comes from the third generation of Guild solids, launched in 1977 and featuring novel but apparently uncommercial styling. More models appeared, all proving unsuccessful, and Guild dropped its solid lines in 1989.

American Catalogs

Dean (started 1979), Hamer (1975), and B C Rich (1979) are all best known for their early odd-shaped solids.

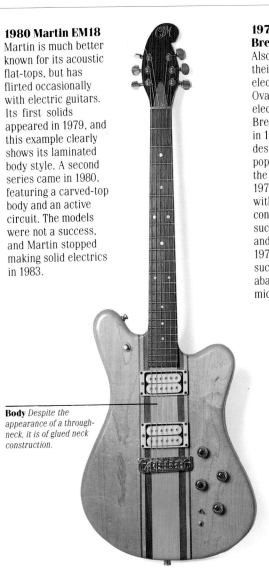

1988 Mosrite Model 88 (below)

Semie Moseley founded his Mosrite company in the 1950s, and enjoyed great success in the following decade with the classic "lop-sided" Ventures model. Business waned, but Moseley attempted many comebacks, one of which provided this 1988 update.

1979 Peavey T60 (below)

Hartley Peavey started Peavey Electronics in 1966, soon making a wide range of amplification, with guitars following in 1978. The company was among the first to use computer-controlled mass-production methods. Many models have since been added, all well built and dependable.

LOOKING FOR NEW MATERIALS

Guitars have traditionally been made from wood, but makers have occasionally tried out alternative materials. Sometimes this has been for economic reasons, sometimes to improve the guitar's sound, strength, or appearance.

Metals and plastics have been tried since the 1920s for their apparent improvement of rigidity and sustain. Some plastics also offered potentially faster production. But working these materials often presented new problems to the makers, and some players found that metals felt cold and plastics appeared cheap. It wasn't until the 1980s, and new materials such as "graphite" (see page 174), that musicians eventually accepted more alternatives to good old wood.

1977 Travis Bean TB1000 Standard (left)
To combat the instability of wooden necks, Travis Bean developed his aluminum alternative in California in 1974. Despite increasing volume and sustain, the neck's cold feel made Bean's expensive, high-quality guitars unpopular. Production ceased in 1979.

Catalogue
The cover shows a TB chassis in full flight.

Kramer's neck design
This detail from the catalogue shows a cross-section drawing.

1977 Kramer 450G
Gary Kramer, previously a partner of Travis Bean, started his own company in New Jersey in 1975. Guitars appeared from 1976 as Kramer continued and refined the idea of the aluminum neck. In 1985 Kramer guitars changed completely to normal wooden necks, and met with more success.

Nut *This metal type was unusual for the period, but was another common Dano feature.*

Fingerboard *The Guitarlin normally had 31 frets. This example is fitted with 32.*

Pickups *The guitar is equipped with two of Danelectro's unusual single-coils, nicknamed "lipstick" units.*

1966 Danelectro Guitarlin
This New Jersey company was founded by Nathan Daniel in the late 1940s to make amplification. Guitars were made between 1956 and 1968, and all offered a lot for very little. This was achieved by using cheap materials and construction in a simple and effective way. Bodies were of hardboard (masonite) on a wooden frame, fitted with basic hardware and pickups made from lipstick cases. The combination worked surprisingly well, and many budget Danos now sell for high prices.

Veleno (left)
John Veleno built his unusual guitars in Florida in the early 1970s. They were made almost entirely from aluminum, including the body, neck and fingerboard. There were pickup and finish options, and the peculiar headstock was inlaid with a ruby.

Headstock *Supro versions pointed to the left; Nationals to the right.*

Body *Valco called its fiberglass "Res-o-glas", described as "polyester resins with threads of pure glass".*

Pickups *These Vista-Power units are designed to prevent "string fade-out".*

Selector *This switches between pickups.*

Volume controls *These adjust volume for each of the three pickups.*

1964 National Glenwood 95 (right)
Valco owned the National name in the 1960s and made a range of fiberglass-bodied models, intended for speedy, cost-effective production; but these ended up more expensive than planned. There were also Newport fiberglass guitars, and similarly styled but wooden-bodied Westwood models, plus a range of slightly cheaper and less ornate Supro-branded versions.

1969 Ampeg Dan Armstrong
Armstrong designed this model for Ampeg, using clear plastic to improve sustain, hence its common "see-through" nickname. It was made between 1969 and 1971.

1969 Kalamazoo KG2A
Gibson countered price competition from the orient by building this guitar from cheap chipboard. They revived their old down-market brandname, Kalamazoo, for the occasion.

1980 Ovation UKII
Ovation were no strangers to the use of synthetic materials. This short-lived solid electric had a plastic body mounted on an aluminum frame.

From wood to plastics
In the future guitar makers will be forced to find more alternatives to wood. Quality timbers are already scarce, and the use of certain woods in quantity is out of step with modern ecological thinking. Some woods have already been embargoed, while other rare types are too costly for mass-produced guitars. Cheaper varieties including basswood are now in common use. The trend today is to combine woods with synthetic materials, such as ebonol plastic (fingerboards) and carbon graphite (necks).

Tone controls *These three knobs adjust the tone of the three pickups.*

Bridge *This Silver-Sound unit has a contact pickup built in.*

SUPERSTRATS

Grover Jackson's California-based company can lay claim to the invention of the so-called "superstrat," which refined and updated Fender's Stratocaster design (see page 72). The Strat's 21 frets were expanded to 24, increasing the playing range, and cutaways were deepened to allow access to these extra frets, giving the body longer horns.

Up-market superstrats use a through-neck rather than Fender's bolt-on type with its bulky joint, also facilitating top-fret access. The superstrat added the power of a humbucker to the Strat's pickup layout, and the simple Fender vibrato gave way to a heavy-duty locking system.

The first Jackson superstrat was the Soloist, introduced in 1980. It embodied all these improvements, together with a newly designed "droopy" pointed headstock. Since then, Jackson has added US-built variations, plus oriental lines under their Jackson Pro, Charvel, and Charvette brandnames. The success of these designs has led virtually every other guitar manufacturer in the world to copy the superstrat.

1988 Jackson Custom Shop Soloist Note the Soloist's angled-back headstock, for correct string tension. Custom Shop Jacksons are made to players' specs, as with the four mini-switches of this example.

Top-fret access *This is helped by the scalloping here, a result of the through-neck construction.*

Pickups *Standard superstrat layout: two single-coils and a humbucker at the rear.*

Body *Other graphic designs included "skull graveyard", "psychedelic checkerboard" and "eerie dess."*

Vibrato *Heavy duty Floyd Rose locking type.*

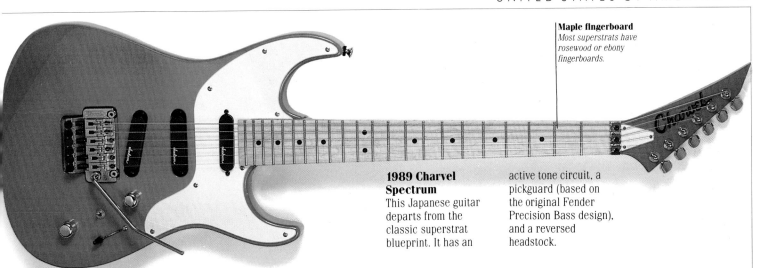

Maple fingerboard
Most superstrats have rosewood or ebony fingerboards.

1989 Charvel Spectrum
This Japanese guitar departs from the classic superstrat blueprint. It has an active tone circuit, a pickguard (based on the original Fender Precision Bass design), and a reversed headstock.

Pickup layout
Guitarists have often wished their Strats – and particularly the bridge pickups – would give more powerful, Gibson-like sounds. The superstrat caters for this need by replacing the bridge single-coil with a humbucker. A further refinement provides this pickup with a coil-tap facility, switching out ("tapping") one coil of the two in the humbucker. This approximates the single-coil sound, and a superstrat so equipped can deliver all the classic Fender tones, plus the thicker, louder humbucker sounds, and in any combination.

Locking vibrato

Early vibratos such as the Fender and the Bigsby systems were designed for gentle, expressive use, and ideally only for lowering the strings' pitch. But players began to demand greater pitch variation, which highlighted the limitations inherent in the design of these units. The main problem that musicians encountered with these early designs involved tuning stability: they found that such vibratos did not always return to accurate pitch after they had been used.

The solution that emerged in the late 1970s was to lock the strings – if they couldn't move, they couldn't go out of tune. New Zealander Dave Storey clamped them at the nut on his design, which was marketed by the US Kahler company. American Floyd Rose took this further: he added bridge clamps for each string. Both systems used bridge-mounted fine-tuners so that tuning could be adjusted once the strings had been clamped.

The popularity of the heavy-duty locking vibrato grew as a new breed of fast-fingered, high-volume guitarists emerged. The efficiency of the new systems enabled these players to drag from the guitar sounds way beyond its normal range. The Floyd Rose design now dominates the market, and virtually every superstrat comes fitted with this unit, or one of its many licensed versions.

1990 Jackson Custom Shop Soloist (right)
This attractive sunburst example has a flamed maple top and gold hardware. From 1990, the original shaded Jackson logo was reserved for Custom Shop models.

1990 Jackson USA Soloist (below)
An example of Jackson's graphic-finish front, available as a standard option on their USA production models. This particular design is "Californian Sunset."

Fingerboard *The "shark-fin" position inlays are a Jackson trademark.*

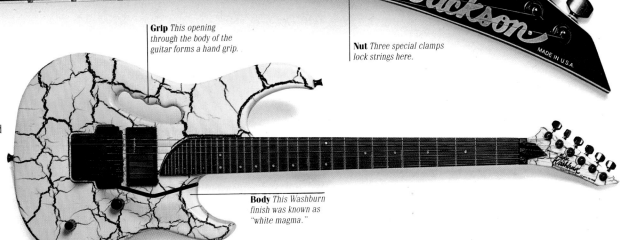

1988 Washburn EC36 (right)
This Japanese superstrat featured the Washburn "Stephens Extended Cutaway." It provided access to all 36 frets, unprecedented on a production electric solid. The companion EC29 had a mere 29 frets, but gained an extra single-coil pickup.

Grip *This opening through the body of the guitar forms a hand grip.*

Nut *Three special clamps lock strings here.*

Body *This Washburn finish was known as "white magma."*

BRITAIN: JIM BURNS

From small beginnings as Burns-Weill in 1959, Jim Burns's company became the most successful British guitar-making organization at its peak in the 1960s, exporting high-quality instruments throughout the world and making some important contributions to the evolution of the electric guitar.

In 1965 the American Baldwin company bought out the Burns companies, having been beaten by CBS in their attempt to acquire Fender. This signaled a change in fortune, and by 1970 all guitar production ceased. But the Burns name was not dead and after a brief flirtation in 1969 with the British Hayman company, the new Burns UK outfit was launched in 1974 with an odd-looking assortment of solid electrics. This lasted until 1977, but the guitars were not well received.

Two years later Jim Burns made another comeback with a new company and a new range of guitars, mixing reissues with yet more oddball designs. Again, reaction from players was less than enthusiastic and this, combined with poor management, led to the final collapse of Burns in 1983.

Jim Burns Scorpion
The model name refers to the peculiar body shape of this 1979 guitar.

Burns Vibra-Artiste
This was the first Burns production solid (1960-62), with short-scale neck and complex controls.

1977 Burns UK Flyte
This design was apparently inspired by the Concorde aircraft.

Pickups Three Ormston Burns Ultra-Sonic single-coil units.

Colour This 1964 example has the rare red finish instead of the normal black.

Controls These are (left to right) volume; tone; two-way circuit selector; and four-way pickup selector offering Bass, Treble, Wild Dog, and Split Sound.

BACK AND SIDE
The back view shows a bolt-on neck, which replaced the glued-in type of the first version. Note on the side how the body horns curve forward.

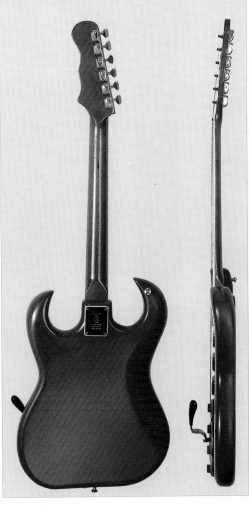

Burns firsts
Jim Burns and his team were never short of original ideas, which were often later claimed as firsts by other companies.

The 1960 Artist had a heel-less glued-in neck with 24-fret fingerboard. The 1961 Bison had a truss-rod gear box for effective neck adjustment, and low-impedance pickups for greater clarity. The 1963 Burns TR2 was the first guitar with tone-boosting active circuitry. The 1964 Marvin used a knife-edge vibrato, and the 1965 Virginian had a stacked-coil pickup.

Scroll headstock
This design idea was suggested by Hank Marvin for the Burns Marvin.

Collector's items
The 1960s Marvin is the most sought-after Burns guitar. Demand is high, mainly due to the Shadows connection, and far exceeds supply, as only around 350 were made. The various Bison models come next on the Burns collector's list, while most of the many remaining Burns instruments are much less desirable. But many of these 1960s models have strong nostalgic appeal for older British guitarists, who may have started their playing careers on instruments such as the Sonic, Jazz Split Sound, the Vibraslim, or the Vista Sonic.

Literature
Burns promotional material often indulged in colorful and enthusiastic prose, boasting of the "cushioned impact of the unique Burns circuitry" and a "trigger-touch action."

Baldwin Baby Bison (right)
In 1965 Burns designed a cheaper, smaller version of the Bison for export only, though most carried the Baldwin name. A later type appeared with a different headstock.

Bison (above left)
This second type (1962-64) replaced the earlier four-pickup version (1961-62) and was succeeded by the restyled scroll-head Bison (1964-65).

GALLERY OF BRITISH MAKERS

There is an interesting contrast between the huge impact of British music throughout the world over the past 30 years and the rather low-key nature of the UK guitar-making scene. During the 1960s only a handful of British guitar brands made any significant impact on their home market. Most guitarists seemed to prefer the imported competition.

Although UK-made guitars have often offered better value and quality, they apparently lack the mystique of leading USA instruments. The discovery of the caliber of British guitars seems limited mostly to beginners or British enthusiasts. Only Burns and Vox had any noticeable success with the exporting of guitars, and the majority of UK-made models were destined for home consumption.

Competition

The subsequent influx of competing instruments, mainly from the orient, has led to the demise of all quantity makers in the UK. These have been replaced by numerous small-scale operations building limited numbers of mostly hand-made, up-market guitars. A few brave makers have produced models with original designs, trying to compete by offering something different.

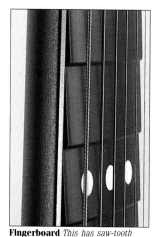

Fingerboard *This has saw-tooth stepped ridges instead of normal frets.*

Display *Illuminated digital display shows control levels and pickup phasing.*

Bond
This graphite guitar with control read-outs and stepped fingerboard was the brainchild of Scottish maker Andrew Bond. An impressive launch in early 1984 was followed by a series of production hiccups, and an ever-increasing retail price effectively negated the initial promise. Despite considerable financial investment, the company folded in 1986, having sold very few production instruments.

Materials *One-piece neck and body made from molded carbon fiber.*

Ned Callan Cody
Ned Callan is a pseudonym for custom-maker Peter Cook. The distinctive styling of the Hombre and the Cody (right) earned these mid-1970s mass-produced solids the nickname "Nobbly Neds."

Karnak Isis II
Between 1985 and 1987 Scottish makers Maurice Bellando and James Cannell produced a range with novel styling and appropriately Egyptian names.

Controls *Push pickup selectors illuminated volu treble and bass switches.*

Vox

As one of the few big UK guitar names of the 1960s, Vox produced some models that have since become classics of the period. Best known are probably the coffin-shaped Phantom models, and the Mk series, such as the Mk VI (right), nicknamed "teardrops." Vox were not limited to one price bracket, and their large, ever changing range included many original designs and features.

Vox instruments came from various sources, the name first appearing on imported models during the early 1960s. British-made guitars followed, and later in the decade production moved to Italy.

Shergold

Ex-Burns man Jack Golder established his company in the late 1960s, supplying instruments and parts for British brands like Hayman, Burns UK and Ned Callan. Jack's own Shergold range of the 1970s and early 1980s included the Meteor, Modulator, Cavalier, and Activator. Shergold was the last company to make guitars in quantity in the UK. Golder, regarded as the godfather of the British electric guitar, now concentrates on custom work.

Shergold Custom Masquerader (above)
An unusual color combination of apple-green sunburst body with black hardware.

Hayman White Cloud (right)
The first Hayman models appeared in 1970, developed with help from Jim Burns and with woodwork by Shergold. Hayman lasted until 1975, and the White Cloud was one of the last models produced.

Catalogs

Unlike the colorful literature of many American and other European makers, most UK material from the past 30 years has been uniformly dull,

with products treated in typically stiff fashion. Even today UK makers shrink from promoting their products in the crass but commercial manner employed by much of the competition.

Vox Apache
Some Vox models were made in very limited quantities, like this rare 1960s Apache. Cheap and oddly shaped, it had typically basic Vox materials, hardware and construction.

Fenton-Weill Triplemaster (left)
Henry Weill's company started in 1959, producing many distinctive solids and semis until stopping guitar manufacture in the mid-1960s. This example is from 1962.

Wilson Sapphire III (right)
Wilson evolved from Watkins, a well-known 1960s name catering mainly for beginners. Production lasted until 1982.

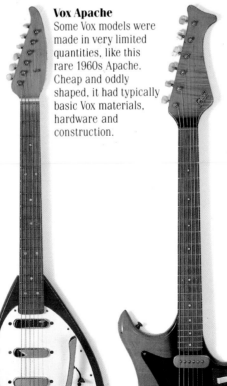

GALLERY OF GERMAN MAKERS

The influence of rock 'n' roll was felt in West Germany earlier than in other parts of Europe, thanks mainly to the American armed forces stationed there who brought their music with them. USA instruments were either unobtainable or unaffordable, and so domestic guitar-makers were faced with an increasing demand in the late 1950s from German guitarists who wanted to produce the sounds they were hearing on American rock 'n' roll records. This gave German companies a significant head start over other European makers and they were soon exporting guitars to many other countries – including, ironically, the United States.

Most of the major German makers – Hofner, Framus, Klira, and Hoyer – were concentrated in the Bubenreuth and Erlangen areas, and overall production continued to expand to match the demand generated by the thousands of groups active in the beat boom of the 1960s.

After that peak came the era of the copy guitar, a 1970s phase when virtually every guitar-maker produced versions of famous Fender and Gibson originals. Because of dwindling demand for homegrown products, over the next decade some major names disappeared. Currently German companies still produce high-quality guitars but in smaller quantities, finding it hard to compete with American and oriental competition.

Hofner 175 (right)
A special version of this model had a vinyl-covered body and red pearloid pickguard. In the 1960s, demand for guitars was so great that some companies speeded production by using vinyl instead of time-consuming paint.

Inlays *Hofner's distinctive triple-bar position markers.*

Controls *Unusually this set-up has no knobs, only rollers and slide switches to select pickups and tonal variations.*

Hofner 176 Galaxie
European players who couldn't afford real Fenders were attracted to Hofner's 1960s solids, which offered the visuals if not the sounds of the American originals. The Galaxie was a classic mix of Hofner features and Fender influence.

Early electrics
Designs such as the Roger 54 (right) and the distinctly Les Paul-like Framus Hollywood 3 were clearly Gibson influenced. Both of these semi-solid guitars were made around 1960.

Framus Nashville

Framus, started in 1946, made many Fender-based solids in the 1960s. Later original designs included the Jan Akkerman and this 1975 Nashville, which was aimed at Gretsch fans.

Hopf Telstar Standard

One of the longest-running instrument makers, established in 1669 and lasting until the 1980s, Hopf produced many good quality solids during the 1960s and 70s. This Telstar model is from 1963.

Huttl Star

The Star model of 1982 was one of the stranger-looking solids from this lesser known maker. The quality of Huttl guitars was certainly inferior compared to the major German brands.

Fingerboard *The off-center marker dots are unusual for this period.*

Klira Tornado

Klira is the brandname of maker Johannes Klier, who set up the company in 1887. During the 1960s there were numerous original, Fender-inspired solids, including this Tornado from 1966. Klira have since concentrated on copies.

Rockinger Lady

Started in 1978, Rockinger make high-quality spares and complete guitars.

Catalogs

German guitar companies tried to emulate modern American electric guitar designs, but their catalogs had a somewhat old-fashioned image.

Roger Rossmeisl

Most German guitar-makers were content to work within their native country and one such craftsman was Wenzel Rossmeisl, an established maker who named his company after his son, Roger.

But Roger Rossmeisl (1927-79) decided he was an exception to the rule, and in the 1950s took his skills to America, initially working for Gibson in Michigan. He soon moved to Rickenbacker in California, and while employed there was responsible for making many custom designs, as well as production models such as the Capri and Combo. He left Rickenbacker in 1962 to join Fender, developing their first acoustic range plus the later Montego and LTD archtop electrics.

Rossmeisl's work was a major influence on Semie Moseley, an apprentice to Rossmeisl at Rickenbacker who later founded his own Mosrite company of California.

The Rossmeisl trademark was the "German carve" originally used by his father, a carved, indented "lip" following the outline of the guitar's body. This feature was adopted by many other makers, particularly in Japan – where Mosrite enjoyed great popularity.

Quite why such an influential craftsmen never set up his own guitar-making company remains a mystery. Instead, Roger Rossmeisl brought the benefits of German guitar craft to some very important American instrument manufacturers.

GALLERY OF ITALIAN MAKERS

Like every European country, Italy experienced the pop music boom of the 1960s, and this led to a great demand for electric guitars. Many Italian models were supplied by accordion makers who combined aspects of this established instrument with their own ideas about electric guitar design – and the end result was unlike anything being produced elsewhere.

Later, instruments began to reflect American design influences. By the 1970s much of the accordion flavor had disappeared and, as in most countries, copies of famous brands became commonplace.

FINISHES

Two more examples of Italian plastic whackiness from the 1960s, these come courtesy of Bartolini (right) and Crucianelli, the latter bearing the Elite brandname. Both have the accordion-style heat-molded plastic covering so typical of the period. Other features influenced by the accordion include the row of pushbutton selectors and the generally colorful presentation.

Pushbuttons *These offer preset tones, such as "Twang," "Take Off," and "Jazz."*

Pickups *Four dou... polarity Alnico V ur...*

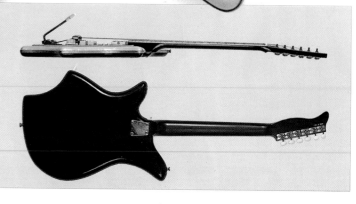

BACK AND SIDE
These views show the guitar's plastic covering in contrasting colors. Note the gold dividing strip on the side of the body.

Eko 700 4V

The triple-cutaway 1964 model is from the major Italian maker Oliviero Pigini & Co of Recanati, who exported their Eko brand to 28 countries. It was the top of Eko's range of plastic-covered solids. Eko's literature proclaimed "necks made from warp proof Jong-Kong wood from Thailand," and "5-ply proxylin guardplate."

Wandre
A novel feature of this 1960s brand was the "Duraluminum" metal neck and headstock, predating the American trend by several years. The hardware is reminiscent of motor-bike parts.

Galanti Grand Prix
Unusually, this 1960s solid came with a genuine wooden body – no plastic in sight. But the maker could not resist that typical bank of pushbuttons, this time on a lightning-bolt pickguard.

Stonehenge II
This novel instrument with a tubular metal body frame was designed and built in 1984 by Alfredo Bugari of Castelfidardo. The model name derives from his theories about the sound properties of the ancient English stone circle.

Melody Blue Sage
Made in 1982 by a decidedly more conservative company, this model is of much higher quality than most Melody guitars. It has a wooden-covered humbucker and a piezo pickup in the bridge.

Gemelli 195/4/V
This brand was made by Benito & Umberto Cingolani in Recanati. According to their catalogue the 195 features "volume and tone plunger commands" giving functions such as "Acute," "Bass Acute," and "Closed."

Catalogs
These were sometimes even more outlandish than the instruments they were selling – no mean achievement. The literature promoted a lighthearted, glitzy image, perfectly suiting these fun guitars.

EUROPEAN GALLERY

Many European guitar-making companies started in the early 1960s boom. Often one domestic brand per country was enough to cater for the demand, offering cheaper alternatives to the imported competition.

Naturally, many of these guitars have been based on the big name American brands, but some European makers added distinctive features of their own that lent some local character – and avoided the copying so widely practiced by oriental companies in the 1970s.

Even in eastern Europe the solid electric guitar made an early impression. Although there were far fewer makers than in the west, large numbers of instruments were produced, and many were exported.

European instruments have never enjoyed the same level of worldwide success as the American originators, but some brandnames did enjoy limited success and a reasonable lifespan. Circumstances changed again as standardized products from the USA and the orient supplanted most of the local varieties. Smaller makers that have survived usually offer small runs of high-quality guitars, which sell to a select and often elite minority of relatively well-off players.

Europa Cristal
This model comes from a range of up-market solids made in France in the 1980s. It features a carbon graphite neck, synthetic fingerboard, German pickups, and American vibrato unit.

Egmond 3
Dutch-built Egmond instruments produced from 1960 to the mid-1970s were aimed at beginners – with quality and construction to match. This vinyl-covered 3 from 1965 carries the brandname of UK importer Rosetti.

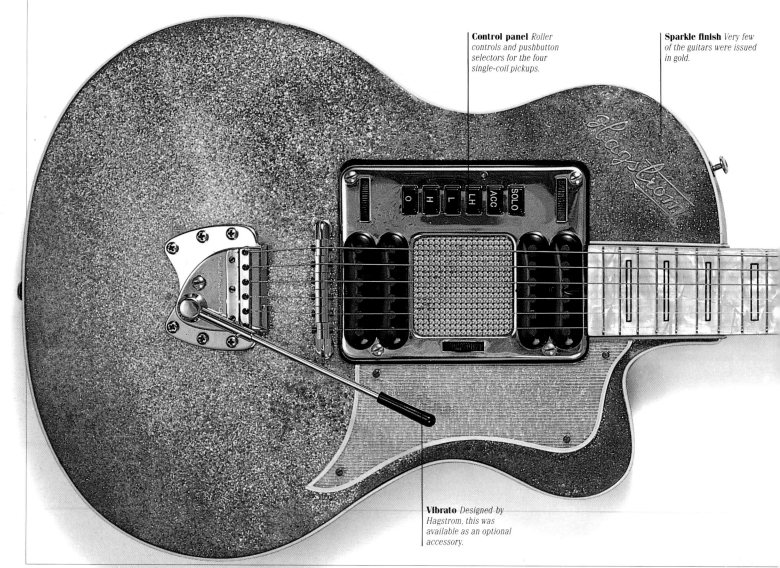

Control panel *Roller controls and pushbutton selectors for the four single-coil pickups.*

Sparkle finish *Very few of the guitars were issued in gold.*

Vibrato *Designed by Hagstrom, this was available as an optional accessory.*

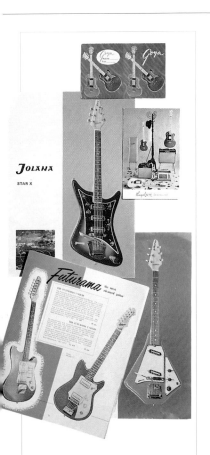

Catalogs
The four makers represented in this selection are Jolana and Futurama (both from Czechoslovakia), and Hagstrom and Goya (Sweden). Futurama and Goya were foreign importers' brandnames.

Special 64
The three-pickup solid electric shown here was built in the mid-1960s by the Muzicka Naklada company, based in Yugoslavia. Although it is crudely made and of poor quality, there is no mistaking the Fender inspiration.

Futurama 3 (above)
This was the brandname of UK importer Selmer, first appearing on these Czech-made solids of the late 1950s and early 1960s.

Musima Eterna Deluxe (below)
An East German company making electric guitars in the late 1950s. This model is the 1982 version of the Eterna Deluxe.

Fingerboard *Frets are set into clear plastic over white pearl.*

Hagstrom P46 Deluxe (above)
This was the first solid from Hagstrom, a Swedish company operating between the late 1950s and early 1980s. A two-pickup version was offered along with the four-pickup model shown here, in various colorful plastic finishes.

Defil Jola 2
The only company mass-producing guitars in Poland, Defil is long-established and responsible for a wide range of solids and semis. This example shown is from the mid-1970s.

Logo *Yamaha's trademark of crossed tuning forks appears on many of their musical instruments.*

1959 Guyatone LG30 Guitar-makers since 1933, Guyatone introduced original design solid electrics in the late 1950s. These were imported into the UK under brandnames such as Star, Guyatone, and Antoria (as used by Hank Marvin in his early pre-Strat-days).

1967 Yamaha SG5A Yamaha have been making musical instruments for over 100 years. Their first solid electric guitars were launched in 1966, a range of models with strong American character. The guitar shown is from their highly original second series, and like all early Yamahas has a degree of quality far above that of the contemporary competition.

Pickguard *The three-way split design was borrowed from some British Burns guitars.*

1965 Ibanez This is the main brandname to emerge from the prolific Fuji Gen-Gakki factory, based in Matsumoto. Original-design Ibanez solid electrics first appeared from Fuji in the early 1960s. In the USA they bore a Goldentone logo.

Controls *The pickguard carries selector, volume, tone, and balancer.*

1968 Tokai Humming Bird This early original-design solid electric from the Hamamatsu-based Tokai company was strongly influenced by Mosrite. The huge Japanese success of the Mosrite-toting Ventures had made this US maker very popular in Japan during the 1960s.

JAPAN: ORIGINALS AND COPIES

The Japanese began to produce solid electric guitars in the late 1950s. Looking at the instruments of that period and of the early 1960s, one can see that the oriental makers had absorbed western influences, incorporating them into their own relatively original designs. These early instruments are significant, because it is often wrongly assumed that the Japanese guitar industry was founded on the production of copies.

The copy era actually came later, starting around 1970, and the Japanese took to the exercise with great enthusiasm. The principal targets were the best known US models, such as the Gibson Les Paul and the Fender Stratocaster, but virtually every original was flattered by an oriental imitation. Lack of technical knowledge meant that the early efforts were often of poor quality, making "Japanese copy" a derogatory description. But as expertise and understanding improved, so did their product, eventually presenting the established western makers with a very real challenge.

Headstock *A good attempt at the Mosrite logo but omitting the all-important ". . . of California" underline.*

1975 Ibanez 2364
Ibanez became one of the leading copyists in the 1970s, often emulating general appearance rather than fine detail. This example copies the Ampeg Dan Armstrong (see page 95), although it replaces the original's single slide-in pickup with two fixed units.

1978 Clearsound "Strat"
This was not an exact copy of any specific Fender. Instead, it featured a Strat-style body of see-through plastic, which was thinner than normal to cut down weight. The neck and hardware were also based on the much-copied Stratocaster.

Pickups *Faithful copies of Mosrite's originals, even down to the logo.*

1985 Tokai TST50
Some Japanese companies became so good at copying US originals that the Americans began consulting their lawyers. Fender USA decided to start their own oriental production in 1982 because of the increased competition, typified by this Tokai.

1979 "Mosrite" copy (right)
An example of the copyist turning pirate. This unauthorized "Mosrite" attempts to pass itself off as the real thing, even borrowing the name.

Catalogs
Early original designs from Yamaha and Ibanez, "Les Pauls" from Tokai, and a Mosrite bootleg.

JAPAN: FROM THE SEVENTIES

With the great success of their copies, many of the well-established Japanese makers felt confident enough to produce original designs once again. Western influences were still there, but during the 1970s a distinct Japanese visual style emerged. Some designs were radical, and in the 1980s a number of makers experimented with synthetic materials. The Japanese popularized several construction methods during this period, including the laminated through-neck style, which made a distinctive striped center-section on the body.

Increasing US production costs in the early 1980s encouraged various American makers to have some of their guitars built in Japan, most significantly Fender. The Stratocaster design and its modern "superstrat" derivatives became the dominant guitar styles of the 1980s. Oriental companies were quick to follow these trends.

The Japanese, too, were hit by an increase in production costs, and major guitar companies began to put production out to other eastern countries to maintain their cheaper lines. Modern Japanese-built guitars now sell for prices similar to those of their American competitors.

1990 Jackson Professional Warrior (above)
This Japanese-built Jackson is a radical departure from the US company's well-known superstrat style.

1982 Aria Urchin Deluxe
Aria is a brandname of the Arai company. Many of their best models, like this Urchin, were made at the Matsumoku factory between 1977 and 1987. The Urchin was the first odd-shaped guitar from Aria, and its sales did not match those of their popular, more traditional instruments.

1982 Aria catalogue
This details the models in the Urchin series.

1984 Tokai Talbo A80D
Original thinking is evident in the design of the Talbo (Tokai ALuminum BOdy). The material was chosen for its sustaining and tonal properties. Tokai added a pair of subtle Blazing Fire humbuckers to complete the Talbo's rich, ringing sound.

1985 Tokai MAT M602
This guitar was part of Tokai's "Most Advanced Technology" series. These Fender-influenced models were available with graphite or fiberglass necks or bodies, in any combination. The example shown is all-fiberglass and features active circuitry.

Body This is made from ash, with a flamed-maple top and back.

1981 Yamaha SC400 (right)

Despite the success of the traditional SG range, especially the 2000 (below), Yamaha decided to revive and revise one of their early odd shapes in the SC400. It featured the popular Strat pickup layout, and construction quality was high. But the unusual styling put off most players; the SC400 was made for only a couple of years.

Yamaha SG2000S (below)

More than any other guitar, the SG2000 convinced musicians that the Japanese could produce an instrument comparable to the best from the west. This model was from Yamaha's third SG series, and in the mid-1970s it combined modern performance with vintage character. These SGs were Yamaha's longest-running solids, built from 1973 to 1988.

Markers *Yamaha's distinctive "arrow-head" inlays are used on up-market models.*

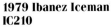

1979 Ibanez Iceman IC210

The first weirdly shaped guitar from Ibanez, with hints of Rickenbacker and the Gibson Firebird. The unusual-looking pickup was controlled by the black four-way rotary tone selector, plus normal volume and tone knobs. Other Icemen from this period came with two humbuckers, or a single sliding pickup.

Pickup *This extra-large unit contains three coils instead of the usual two, and thus provides different sounds.*

1989 Ibanez Maxxas MX3

Despite coming from the age of the superstrat, this design evoked a 1950s rocket ship, with its sleek body lines, "Dan Dare" knobs, and the special Ibanez "Black Hole" finish. American DiMarzio pickups were mounted on a body with acoustic cavities. The Maxxas was a brave but unsuccessful departure from contemporary style.

Endorsing the Japanese

In the 1970s, poor-quality copies meant that most pros would not be seen dead with a Japanese guitar. But that was reversed from the mid-1970s into the 1980s: quality improved dramatically and Japanese guitars became hip, as these Ibanez ads show.

KOREA AND TAIWAN

Guitar players seem unwilling to spend the amount of money on their instruments that keyboardists and even bassists now take for granted. So when the cost of producing guitars in the United States and Japan began to climb during the early 1980s, the major makers in those countries had to look elsewhere for cheaper manufacturing sources. A few chose Taiwan, but the more suitable climate in Korea made it the most popular option.

The prime requirement from the Korean maker is a guitar built down to a price, and almost inevitably this causes compromises in the materials used. The result is often a guitar where fashionable features and a good paint job take precedence over quality and durability. However, the technical knowledge involved is much higher than on earlier oriental efforts, thanks to expertise provided from both the USA and Japan. Standards are gradually rising but so are prices – ironically, companies are again looking for cheaper production bases.

Yamaha Pacifica
Some Yamaha models have been designed in the west. The 1989 MSG series was created by Martyn Booth at Yamaha UK, and in 1990 the Les Paul-like Weddington design and this Fender-derived Pacifica came from Yamaha USA.

Neck *This through-type is fitted with a 24-fret ebony fingerboard.*

Hohner G3T
This 1990 headless guitar shows that oriental makers still like to copy. It is clearly based on the very expensive USA-made Steinberger of 1983, which prompted many subsequent copies; this model is one of the few survivors. It uses wood rather than the carbon graphite of the original, providing a much cheaper alternative.

Yamaha RGX Custom (left)
Yamaha's guitars were originally made in Japan, but in the early 1980s all production moved to Taiwan. Yamaha maintained quality by building its own, new factory in Taiwan. This 1989 RGX Custom, based on the popular superstrat style, was top of the range although it has since been superseded.

Position markers *The RGX Custom and Standard had these diamond-shaped inlays.*

Pickups *These Select types are designed by EMG in the USA.*

Vibrato *A Steinberger USA licensed design.*

Controls *These include a "Blend-Sound" tone circuit, designed by Claim Guitars, Germany.*

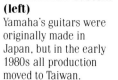

Pickups *This is a less common superstrat layout: two humbuckers and central single-coil.*

Vibrato *The Yamaha RM-Pro unit is based on the Floyd Rose principle, locking strings at nut and bridge.*

Gretsch Traveling Wilburys

Essentially this was a late 1980s gimmick to capitalize on the popularity of the Traveling Wilburys (see below), and loosely based on the group's old Danelectro guitars. The various models are all designed by Gretsch in the USA and built in Korea. Despite the decorative finish, the materials used are cheap and the construction is primitive. The guitars' main appeal lies in what Gretsch call the "original graphics."

Marlin Masterclass

Marlin, a UK importer's brandname, first appeared on Korean guitars in the late 1980s. The majority of Marlins were low-priced copies aimed at beginners, but this up-market, original-design Masterclass model came with a rechargeable active circuit.

Encore SE1

The Korean-made Encore brand has always been a source of budget copies. This 1989 model shows the company keeping up with modern trends by borrowing the style of one of the hottest USA makers, Paul Reed Smith. But the good finish covers a plywood body.

Onyx 1030

This Australian importer's brandname appears on a range of Korean-built guitars. The late 1980s 1030 combined strong influences from Semie Moseley's US-made Mosrite instruments of the 1960s with modern hardware and circuitry.

Starforce 8007

These Korean-made guitars promote a distinctively American image, with many models based on Fender and superstrat originals. However, the 8007 features less derivative styling, and includes some heavenly fingerboard inlays.

The Traveling Wilburys

The Wilburys are a fictional family "supergroup," formed for fun in the late 1980s by George Harrison ("Nelson"), Jeff Lynne ("Otis"), Bob Dylan ("Lucky"), Tom Petty ("Charlie T Jr"), and Roy Orbison ("Lefty").

Also from Korea

Many other well-known companies have used Korean sources for their cheaper brands: for example, Harmony, Gibson's Epiphone and Fender's Squier all now originate in Korea. Some American companies such as Kramer and B C Rich adopted a three-tier system, making their most expensive models in the USA, mid-price guitars in Japan, and the cheapest instruments in Korea.

Leading Japanese names such as Washburn, Westone, Aria, and Hondo have not missed out on the move to Korea. Recently Korean companies have entered the market with their own brandnames, including Fenix.

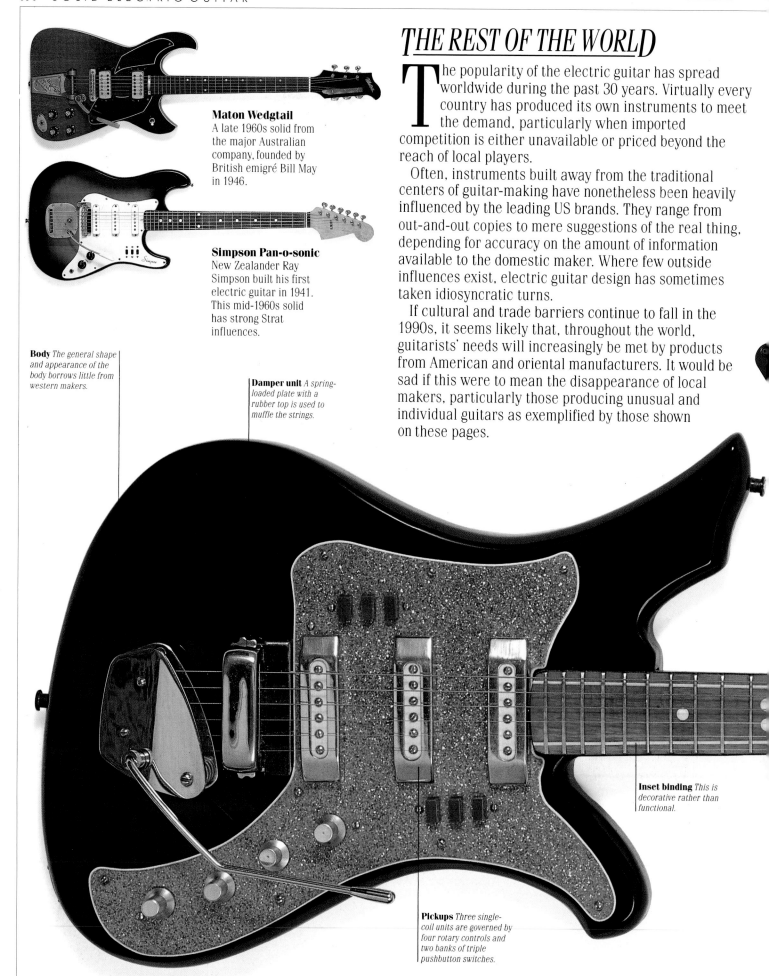

Maton Wedgtail
A late 1960s solid from
the major Australian
company, founded by
British emigré Bill May
in 1946.

Simpson Pan-o-sonic
New Zealander Ray
Simpson built his first
electric guitar in 1941.
This mid-1960s solid
has strong Strat
influences.

Body *The general shape
and appearance of the
body borrows little from
western makers.*

Damper unit *A spring-
loaded plate with a
rubber top is used to
muffle the strings.*

Inset binding *This is
decorative rather than
functional.*

Pickups *Three single-
coil units are governed by
four rotary controls and
two banks of triple
pushbutton switches.*

THE REST OF THE WORLD

The popularity of the electric guitar has spread
worldwide during the past 30 years. Virtually every
country has produced its own instruments to meet
the demand, particularly when imported
competition is either unavailable or priced beyond the
reach of local players.

Often, instruments built away from the traditional
centers of guitar-making have nonetheless been heavily
influenced by the leading US brands. They range from
out-and-out copies to mere suggestions of the real thing,
depending for accuracy on the amount of information
available to the domestic maker. Where few outside
influences exist, electric guitar design has sometimes
taken idiosyncratic turns.

If cultural and trade barriers continue to fall in the
1990s, it seems likely that, throughout the world,
guitarists' needs will increasingly be met by products
from American and oriental manufacturers. It would be
sad if this were to mean the disappearance of local
makers, particularly those producing unusual and
individual guitars as exemplified by those shown
on these pages.

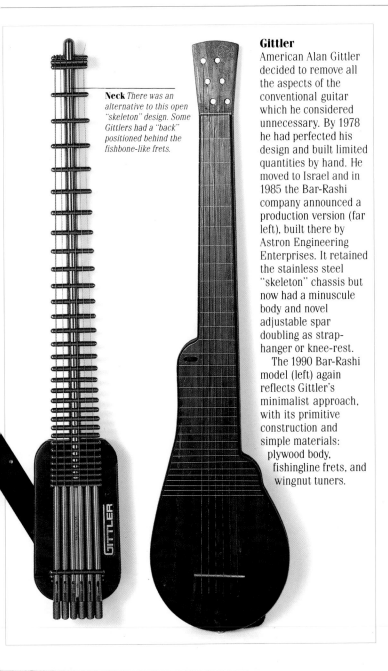

Neck *There was an alternative to this open "skeleton" design. Some Gittlers had a "back" positioned behind the fishbone-like frets.*

Gittler

American Alan Gittler decided to remove all the aspects of the conventional guitar which he considered unnecessary. By 1978 he had perfected his design and built limited quantities by hand. He moved to Israel and in 1985 the Bar-Rashi company announced a production version (far left), built there by Astron Engineering Enterprises. It retained the stainless steel "skeleton" chassis but now had a minuscule body and novel adjustable spar doubling as strap-hanger or knee-rest.

The 1990 Bar-Rashi model (left) again reflects Gittler's minimalist approach, with its primitive construction and simple materials: plywood body, fishingline frets, and wingnut tuners.

Sunn Mustang (right)

Best known for amplification, Sunn is now owned by Fender. This 1990 budget Mustang was built in India and borrows a mid-1960s Fender model name.

Hang-Don (above)

Built in Vietnam during the mid-1970s, this model shows overall styling heavily influenced by Fender, though materials and construction are basic.

Logo *The Russian brandname can be anglicized to "Aelita".*

AK Admiral

Made in Leningrad in 1984, this model was part of a failed project to mass-produce good electrics in the USSR.

Aelita (above)

This Russian-built guitar is from a late-1970s range of solids built by the Rostov-on-Don accordion factory. To a western eye they are of unusual styling – note the odd looking hardware and controls – and despite their recent manufacture, they are primitive.

CUSTOM ORDERS

The wide variety of mass-produced electric guitars is more than enough for the majority of players. But some guitarists don't like buying off the peg, and the idea of a guitar made to one's own design can be attractive. The custom-builder provides such unique guitars, unbounded by the inflexibility of major producers. In theory, the custom-maker can provide any instrument built to any specifications, in any style, and with any features. Some are based on established designs; others cater for more peculiar tastes. Sometimes custom oddities are made for promotional purposes, where very often the visuals come first and playing considerations a clear second.

The custom-maker fills an important gap, generally offering high-quality alternatives and a welcome deviation from the safe course of mass production.

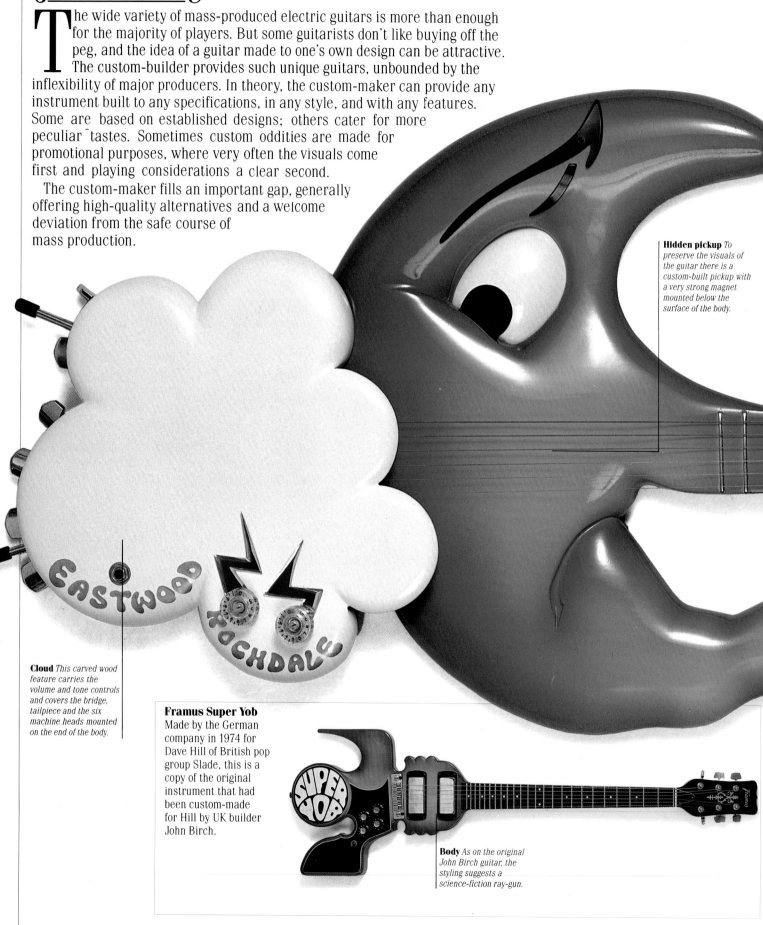

Hidden pickup *To preserve the visuals of the guitar there is a custom-built pickup with a very strong magnet mounted below the surface of the body.*

Cloud *This carved wood feature carries the volume and tone controls and covers the bridge, tailpiece and the six machine heads mounted on the end of the body.*

Framus Super Yob
Made by the German company in 1974 for Dave Hill of British pop group Slade, this is a copy of the original instrument that had been custom-made for Hill by UK builder John Birch.

Body *As on the original John Birch guitar, the styling suggests a science-fiction ray-gun.*

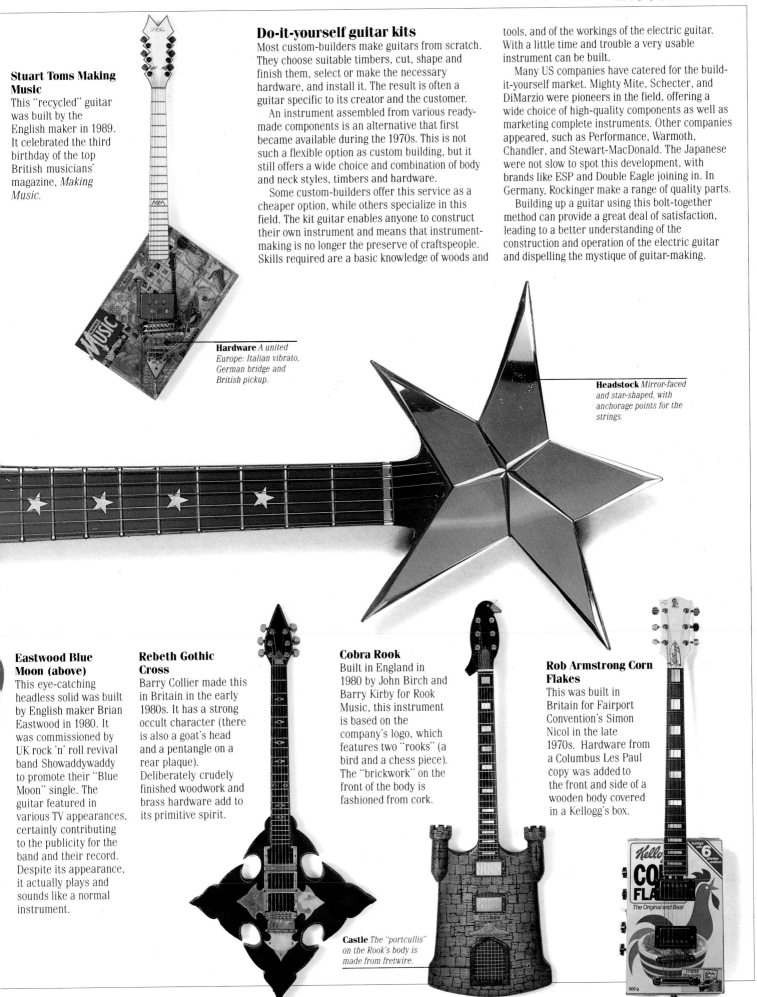

Stuart Toms Making Music
This "recycled" guitar was built by the English maker in 1989. It celebrated the third birthday of the top British musicians' magazine, *Making Music*.

Do-it-yourself guitar kits

Most custom-builders make guitars from scratch. They choose suitable timbers, cut, shape and finish them, select or make the necessary hardware, and install it. The result is often a guitar specific to its creator and the customer.

An instrument assembled from various ready-made components is an alternative that first became available during the 1970s. This is not such a flexible option as custom building, but it still offers a wide choice and combination of body and neck styles, timbers and hardware.

Some custom-builders offer this service as a cheaper option, while others specialize in this field. The kit guitar enables anyone to construct their own instrument and means that instrument-making is no longer the preserve of craftspeople. Skills required are a basic knowledge of woods and

tools, and of the workings of the electric guitar. With a little time and trouble a very usable instrument can be built.

Many US companies have catered for the build-it-yourself market. Mighty Mite, Schecter, and DiMarzio were pioneers in the field, offering a wide choice of high-quality components as well as marketing complete instruments. Other companies appeared, such as Performance, Warmoth, Chandler, and Stewart-MacDonald. The Japanese were not slow to spot this development, with brands like ESP and Double Eagle joining in. In Germany, Rockinger make a range of quality parts.

Building up a guitar using this bolt-together method can provide a great deal of satisfaction, leading to a better understanding of the construction and operation of the electric guitar and dispelling the mystique of guitar-making.

Hardware *A united Europe: Italian vibrato, German bridge and British pickup.*

Headstock *Mirror-faced and star-shaped, with anchorage points for the strings.*

Eastwood Blue Moon (above)
This eye-catching headless solid was built by English maker Brian Eastwood in 1980. It was commissioned by UK rock 'n' roll revival band Showaddywaddy to promote their "Blue Moon" single. The guitar featured in various TV appearances, certainly contributing to the publicity for the band and their record. Despite its appearance, it actually plays and sounds like a normal instrument.

Rebeth Gothic Cross
Barry Collier made this in Britain in the early 1980s. It has a strong occult character (there is also a goat's head and a pentangle on a rear plaque). Deliberately crudely finished woodwork and brass hardware add to its primitive spirit.

Cobra Rook
Built in England in 1980 by John Birch and Barry Kirby for Rook Music, this instrument is based on the company's logo, which features two "rooks" (a bird and a chess piece). The "brickwork" on the front of the body is fashioned from cork.

Castle *The "portcullis" on the Rook's body is made from fretwire.*

Rob Armstrong Corn Flakes
This was built in Britain for Fairport Convention's Simon Nicol in the late 1970s. Hardware from a Columbus Les Paul copy was added to the front and side of a wooden body covered in a Kellogg's box.

BEYOND SIX STRINGS

Most guitarists find six strings more than enough to cope with, but some brave players favor instruments with extra strings, usually added to the existing strings to form pairs, or "courses." The intention is to expand the range of the standard guitar, bolstering the sound with the additional higher-pitched strings and most effective for rhythm playing.

Sometimes for solo work single strings are added to the normal six. An early pioneer of this scheme was jazz guitarist George Van Eps whose 1960s Gretsch was based on his 1940s seven-string Epi Deluxe.

Ironically, using fewer strings than normal can provide new sounds, and probably the best-known exponent of this technique is Keith Richards. The Rolling Stones' guitarist often uses a five-string instrument, usually a six-string with the low E removed, for his powerful rhythm parts. David Bowie took the idea to its minimal conclusion on his 1990 tour by "playing" a one-string guitar.

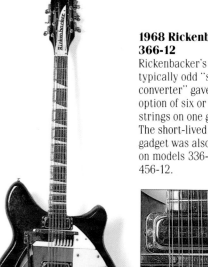

1968 Rickenbacker 366-12
Rickenbacker's typically odd "string converter" gave the option of six or twelve strings on one guitar. The short-lived 1966 gadget was also offered on models 336-12 and 456-12.

String converter
A hooked "comb" pulls down or reinstates the extra six strings.

Tailpiece *Plain version, soon replaced by one incorporating a large "R."*

Soundhole *This is slash-shaped, instead of the conventional f-hole.*

Inlays *These triangular position markers were unique to Rickenbacker.*

Pickguard
Rickenbacker's split-level two-piece type contains volume and tone for each pickup plus a mix control.

Fender Electric XII

Fender USA's first and only electric 12-string solid was launched in 1965. The distinctive "hockey stick" headstock was a typical Fender touch. Overall styling echoed its six-string Fender predecessors such as the Jazzmaster and Jaguar. In 1966 the Electric XII gained a bound fingerboard with block inlays. Production stopped in 1969.

Bridge *Fender was the first to feature a 12-saddle, fully adjustable type, offering improved intonation – vital on a 12-string.*

Headstock *This is in green sunburst to match the body. Later headstocks had a natural finish.*

Headstock *The unusual reversed styling is designed to accommodate the nine machine heads.*

Baldwin Double Six

British 12-string from 1965, successor to the Burns version.

Washburn A10/12

This 12-string has six of its tuners at the body base.

Twelve-stringing

On a 12-string guitar the normal six strings are doubled up. The lower four pairs each consist of a normally-tuned string plus a string an octave higher, while each of the top two pairs are tuned in unison. This strengthening of the guitar's sound through octave and unison doubling produces the classic 12-string jangling sound, almost as if two guitars were playing together.

The normal method for the octave pairs is to have the thinner string on top so that it sounds first when struck; however, Rickenbacker have their own, opposite method (see main picture).

Vox Starstream XII

A 12-string "teardrop" semi from the active electronic series of the late 1960s, made by Eko in Italy. This featured a built-in tuner, distortion, treble and bass boosts, repeat percussion and, behind the bridge, a novel hand-operated wah-wah.

1960s Framus Melodie nine-string

This mid-1960s 9-string solid from West Germany had an unusual arrangement of strings; the top three were doubled like a 12-string; the bottom three were standard singles. In theory this provided a 12-string type of sound without intonation problems.

Rickenbacker 360-12

This guitar was presented to George Harrison in early 1964, during the Beatles' American tour, and is reputedly the second Rickenbacker 12-string ever made. Its distinctive sound soon became a feature of many Beatles recordings.

BACK
This view shows Rickenbacker's brilliant solution to the problem of accommodating 12 machine heads: mounting the extra six in classical-style slots between and at right angles to the others.

TWIN-NECK GUITARS

Why use two guitars when one will do? That is the reasoning behind the twin-neck guitar, a design which incorporates two necks on one body. This provides instant changeover between two entirely different instruments, most commonly a six-string and a twelve-string.

However, there are drawbacks, the most obvious being the weight and general awkwardness of the resulting object. The body usually has to be larger than normal to accommodate the two necks, extra controls, pickups, and related hardware. Playing a twin-neck can be difficult – when one neck is in the ideal playing position, the other is invariably too high or too low. A twin-neck guitar is thus a compromise between comfort and convenience.

Rick Nielsen
In keeping with the Cheap Trick guitarist's whacky image, US maker Hamer built him this five-neck special in the early 1980s.

Gibson Double-Bass
Gibson's restyled twin-neck series (1962-70) added this guitar-and-bass model, with built-in "fuzztone" option.

BACK AND SIDE
The back view of the Double-12 shows a strap button positioned at the heel of each neck, allowing the guitarist a choice of playing heights.

Otwin Four/Six
This East German twin-neck was built specially for a music trade show in the early 1960s, to show off the abilities of the manufacturer, Musima. Note how the necks angle out from one another to assist access.

Fender 6/12
Made in Fender's custom shop, this recent twin-neck was built for exhibition purposes. It combines the looks of a vintage XII and Strat with modern Fender Lace pickups.

Twin-neck design

Many of the world's major guitar-makers have built twin-neck instruments since Gibson originally popularized the concept. Apart from the well-known examples illustrated, original designs have been offered by companies such as Danelectro, Mosrite, and Rickenbacker in the United States, Hofner, and Framus in Germany, Shergold in Britain, and Ibanez and Aria in Japan.

The relative popularity of Gibson's second series twin-necks led to several Japanese copies in the 1970s. Surprisingly, Fender never made a production twin-neck guitar, but this didn't stop the enterprising Japanese from inventing Fender-styled 4/6 and 12/6 models.

The idea of a guitar with more than one neck is more easily catered for by the smaller custom builder, who is used to fulfilling unusual orders. A good example was the triple-neck solid built by UK custom-maker Hugh Manson in the 1980s. Twin-neck guitars usually feature necks parallel to one another, but certain adventurous, ambidextrous artists have had instruments made with necks sprouting from either side of the body.

Gibson Double-12
A rare Gibson from the company's first twin-neck range of the late 1950s, this guitar combined six- and 12-string necks. It was offered alongside the Double Mandolin, which mated six-string and mandolin necks. Although production lasted until 1962, these models were built to custom order; examples are rarely seen.

Double-12 features
To avoid excessive weight, Gibson's first twin-necks had a carved spruce top on a maple body, although necks were mahogany. There were two humbuckers per neck, and the control layout offered volume, tone and three-way select for each neck, plus a master neck-selector above the 12-string bridge. Gibson's Tune-O-Matic bridges were fitted, but with special string anchors instead of the normal stop-bar tailpiece.

PORTABLE GUITARS

The solid electric guitar can be a heavy instrument to move about with, and needs to be amplified for its intended purpose. These two seemingly obvious factors can limit the normal instrument's use in some circumstances – on the tour bus, for example. So several manufacturers have made guitars which attempt to offer solutions.

The first are guitars which might be termed "travel minis." Some are effectively entire instruments scaled down in size, others have just the body made smaller. They are designed for convenience, to allow guitarists to practice wherever and whenever they want.

The second kind of go-as-you-please instrument is the "self-contained" guitar, which has a built-in, battery-powered amplifier plus loudspeaker. This provides the benefits of all-in portability, plus suitably amplified volume for practice purposes.

As can be seen on these pages, designing travel minis and self-contained guitars is not easy, and some results have been less elegant than others.

Pangborn
This mini-guitar was made for Phil Manzanera by British maker Ashley Pangborn.

Yamato
A 1980s oriental copy of US maker Mark Erlewine's Chiquita model.

Kay K45
This 1980s Korean model was known as the Austin Hatchet in the USA.

"Tongue" *The control panel and tailpiece are mounted on this extension of the aluminum neck.*

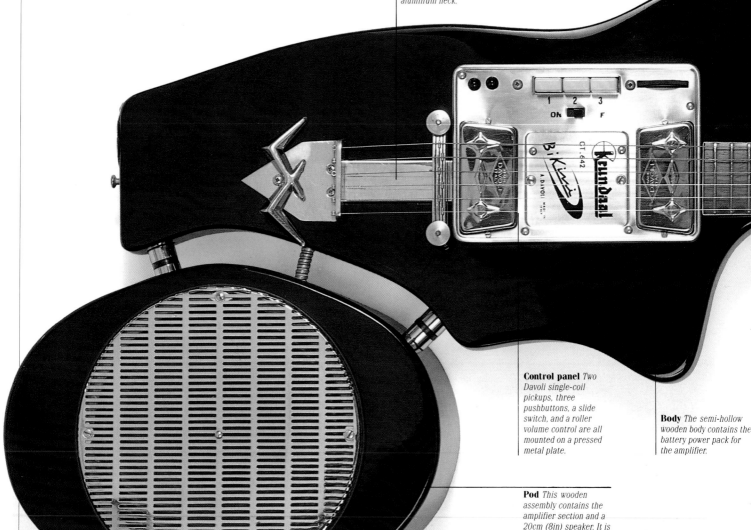

Control panel *Two Davoli single-coil pickups, three pushbuttons, a slide switch, and a roller volume control are all mounted on a pressed metal plate.*

Body *The semi-hollow wooden body contains the battery power pack for the amplifier.*

Pod *This wooden assembly contains the amplifier section and a 20cm (8in) speaker. It is attached to the body by two chromed spars.*

Silvertone
In the USA, the Sears mail-order company used Silvertone as a brandname. They had this particular model made in Japan by Teisco in the mid-1960s. It was similar to the Japanese maker's own version, which Teisco claimed was the world's first self-contained electric.

1982 Melody Blue Sage Nomad
The Italian Melody company usually made solids based on others' designs. But they launched their up-market Blue Sage series in 1982, including the Nomad with built-in amp and speaker. This model is a prototype.

1986 Kay Busker
This was a low-quality Korean-made model which offered a lot for very little money. The amp section even included electronic tremolo, an unusual feature at this budget price level.

1984 Maya 8029
This Japanese-made model appeared in the mid-1980s. In an unusually styled package, it combined the portability of the travel mini with the convenience of the self-contained guitar's built-in amp and speaker.

Rosewood fingerboard
This is fitted to a plastic-covered aluminum neck chassis.

Headstock *Machine heads are fitted to an aluminum frame over a wooden center section.*

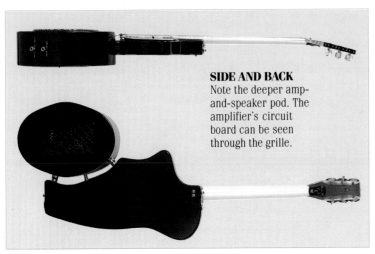

SIDE AND BACK
Note the deeper amp-and-speaker pod. The amplifier's circuit board can be seen through the grille.

The electric case

Many manufacturers have tried to make the electric guitar more portable. The innovative Hoyer Foldaxe from Germany came with a folding neck, remarkably maintaining normal string tension whether folded or unfolded. Hofner's Shorty travel mini came in a self-amplified version which combined the best of both portable worlds.

Another solution was to build an amp and speaker into the guitar case. Such models first appeared in the late 1950s from US companies such as Danelectro. Since then surprisingly few makers have adopted this idea, although in the early 1980s Peavey issued an "Electric Case" as an optional extra to their short-scale T15 and T30 solids. Despite the advantages of travel minis and self-contained guitars, none has proved successful and few makers produce them today.

Krundaal Bikini (above left)
This was probably the first self-contained electric guitar, made by the Italian Davoli company during the early 1960s. It uses the same novel construction features as some other Italian instruments from the period, but has a unique "ear"-shaped body and a "lobe" pod containing amplifier and speaker.

"*The electric acoustic
guitar delivers a fusion
of the warm, woody tone
of an acoustic body and
the cutting, electric sound
of pickups, using established
methods of construction.***"**

ELECTRIC ACOUSTIC GUITAR

1961 GIBSON ES355TD-SV, courtesy Guitar Gallery (UK).

ELECTRIC ACOUSTIC ANATOMY

The most accurate general term you can use for electric guitars with hollow bodies is "electric acoustic." An "archtop" electric is just that: the top is arched, traditionally by carving, or rather more easily by machine-pressing. Readily misused is the term "semi-acoustic" (or less frequently "semi-solid"), often applied to any electric acoustic. In fact it refers specifically to guitars like Gibson's ES335 (see page 138), with a solid block of wood running down the center of a thinline acoustic body. It is a semi-acoustic we illustrate here; this was being made in the workshop of English maker Chris Eccleshall. The workmen pictured separately are at the Rickenbacker factory in California.

Binding
A body is clamped at the Rickenbacker factory and a workman begins the application of binding.

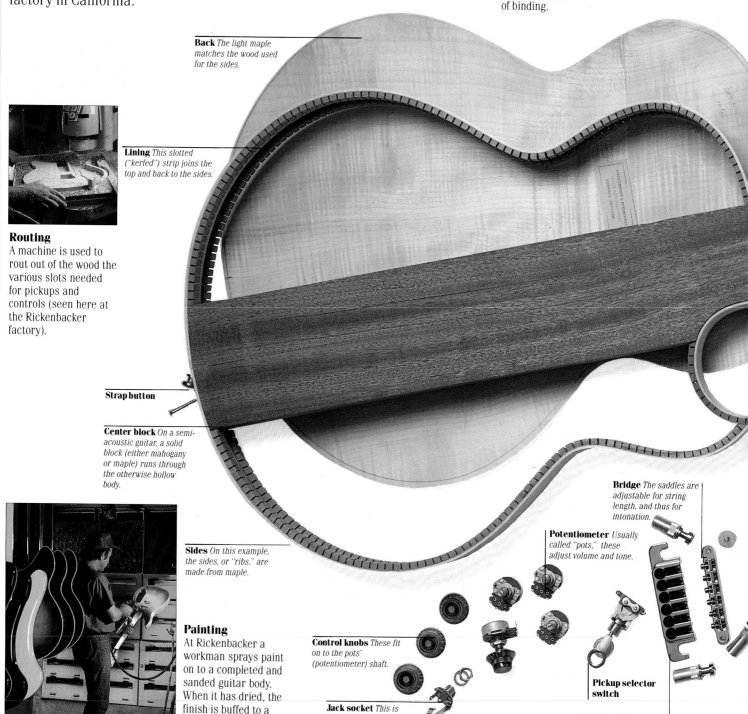

Back *The light maple matches the wood used for the sides.*

Lining *This slotted ("kerfed") strip joins the top and back to the sides.*

Routing
A machine is used to rout out of the wood the various slots needed for pickups and controls (seen here at the Rickenbacker factory).

Strap button

Center block *On a semi-acoustic guitar, a solid block (either mahogany or maple) runs through the otherwise hollow body.*

Sides *On this example, the sides, or "ribs," are made from maple.*

Painting
At Rickenbacker a workman sprays paint on to a completed and sanded guitar body. When it has dried, the finish is buffed to a high-gloss polish.

Control knobs *These fit on to the pots' (potentiometer) shaft.*

Jack socket *This is fitted to either front or side.*

Bridge *The saddles are adjustable for string length, and thus for intonation.*

Potentiometer *Usually called "pots," these adjust volume and tone.*

Pickup selector switch

Tailpiece *This anchors the strings.*

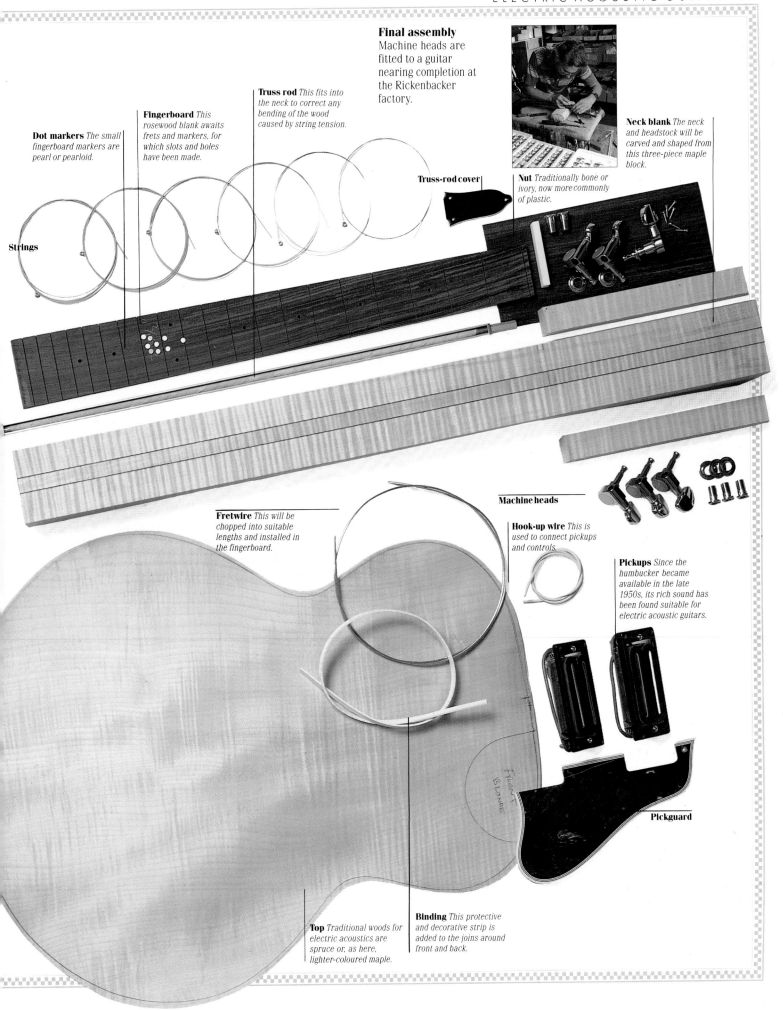

Final assembly
Machine heads are fitted to a guitar nearing completion at the Rickenbacker factory.

Dot markers *The small fingerboard markers are pearl or pearloid.*

Fingerboard *This rosewood blank awaits frets and markers, for which slots and holes have been made.*

Truss rod *This fits into the neck to correct any bending of the wood caused by string tension.*

Truss-rod cover

Nut *Traditionally bone or ivory, now more commonly of plastic.*

Neck blank *The neck and headstock will be carved and shaped from this three-piece maple block.*

Strings

Fretwire *This will be chopped into suitable lengths and installed in the fingerboard.*

Machine heads

Hook-up wire *This is used to connect pickups and controls.*

Pickups *Since the humbucker became available in the late 1950s, its rich sound has been found suitable for electric acoustic guitars.*

Pickguard

Top *Traditional woods for electric acoustics are spruce or, as here, lighter-coloured maple.*

Binding *This protective and decorative strip is added to the joins around front and back.*

THE GIBSON ES175

In the late 1940s, after some experiments earlier in the decade, Gibson at last began seriously to make production electric guitars. The important new guitars with fitted pickups – the ES350 (1947), ES175 (1949), and ES5 (1949) – were aimed at players prepared to commit themselves to fully electric instruments.

At the same time Gibson began to apply the body cutaway to electrics. There was little point in playing high up the neck on acoustic instruments, as the results were unlikely to be heard. But given an instrument equipped with a pickup and suitably amplified, a cutaway offered easier access to the now audible and musically useful upper fingerboard.

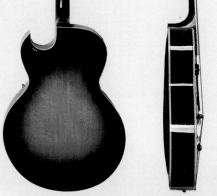

BACK AND SIDE
The unencumbered back highlights the elegant lines of the ES175. The sunburst finish was standard on the model, although a smaller number of natural (known as "blonde") examples were made as an option. The binding on this 1949 model has aged typically to a pleasing yellowish shade.

Pressed top *This is made from laminated maple, and gives a brighter tone than traditional carved-top jazz guitars.*

Controls *Single "hatbox" shaped knobs govern volume and tone.*

1949 ES175
This simple guitar was the first serious production electric from Gibson. It has become a classic jazz guitar, used by players from Joe Pass to Pat Metheny. The sharp cutaway, unusual for the time, was unique to the 175 for some years. The model also popularized the pressed, laminated maple top which contributed to the 175's distinctive sound.

1952 ES350
Launched in 1947, this was the first of the new-style Gibson electrics. It was also the first electric Gibson with a cutaway. The earliest ES350s had a single pickup, replaced by a two-pickup version with a volume control for each pickup on the lower body and a master tone knob by the cutaway, as on this 1952 example. Later in that year, the ES350 changed to the standard four-control layout. The model was dropped in 1956.

1951 ES5
This was the first electric guitar with three pickups, appearing in 1949. Like all Gibson's new electrics of the period, it had no pickup switching: each pickup had a separate volume knob, making it difficult to control. This blonde example is now owned by Mark Knopfler.

Round cutaway
This style first appeared on an electric (ES350) in 1947 and initially guitars with the feature were usually designated "Premier" models by Gibson and given a P suffix. From 1949 such models were simply called "Cutaway" types, with a C suffix.

Sharp cutaway
The ES175 of 1949 introduced this new pointed cutaway. It was not until the 1960s that Gibson applied it to many models which had previously sported the original rounded type. Both cutaway shapes give the player easier access to higher frets.

Headstock inlay *The standard Gibson "crown" shape.*

Position markers *These are angled split-block types.*

Finish *Around one in four of two-pickup 175s in 1960 were natural.*

1960 ES175DN
The 175 was offered with two pickups from 1953, and humbuckers replaced the original single-coil pickups in 1957. Note also the rarer "blonde" finish, different tailpiece, pickup selector, and labelled control knobs. Production of ES175 models continued into the 1990s.

GIBSON'S "CES" ELECTRICS

In 1951, two years after the launch of their innovative ES175 and ES5 electric guitars, Gibson decided to give the full electric treatment to its two big top-of-the-line acoustic jazz guitars, the L5 and the Super 400. The results were the CES (initially called SEC) versions of these classic guitars, at last with permanently installed pickups and controls. Both new instruments were issued with a rounded cutaway. Gibson also launched both guitars as twin-pickup models. Realizing that players needed a method to switch quickly and effectively between the two pickups, Gibson launched both the L5SEC and the Super 400SEC with a selector near the cutaway to choose both or either of the pickups.

50th Anniversary L5CES (above) and Super 400CES (below)
This mid-1980s pair have special 50th Anniversary inlays at the nineteenth fret.

Carved top Unlike the previous laminated-top electrics, the L5SEC and Super 400SEC kept traditional carved tops.

f-hole The label inside actually names this as an L5 "SEC" model, an unusual early variation.

Pickups Until about 1957 the SEC guitars featured single-coil units, either of the P90 (as here) or Alnico type.

Musicians

The Super 400CES and L5CES have long been seen as guitars for jazz players to aspire to, and over the years some of the great names in the music have used these big, impressive models. Best known of the jazz guitarists to play the L5CES was Wes Montgomery (1925-1968) who drew a mellow sound from it, thanks in part to his thumb-picking style. Jazz players of the Super 400CES have included Larry Coryell and Kenny Burrell.

Super 400CES

The electric version of the huge acoustic Super 400 guitar appeared, like the L5CES, in 1951. The two guitars did much to define the archtop electric acoustic guitar among other makers and, of course, players. The "Super 4" (as it is sometimes abbreviated) has always been less popular with guitarists than the L5CES because of its bulky body – nearly 11cm (4½in) deep and 45cm (18in) wide – and corresponding awkwardness.

Late 1960s Super 400CES

The Super 400CES followed the changes made to the L5CES in the 1960s. Humbuckers were fitted from about 1957. A sharp cutaway became standard around 1960, but was changed back to the rounded type later in the decade, as shown by this fine blonde example which dates from about 1968 or 1969. The model remained in limited production into the 1990s.

BACK AND SIDE This 1951 blonde example has beautifully grained wood. The side shows the L5 SEC's standard depth – 8.6cm (3⅜in) – common to archtops.

1950s Super 400CES This catalogue shot from the late 1950s shows the Super 400CES, introduced in 1951. Note the rounded cutaway.

Markers *The Super 400's distinctive "split-block" markers are inlaid into the ebony board.*

Body *This consists of a solid spruce top, with maple sides, back and neck. Only a quarter of the 228 Super 400CES models made during 1968 and 1969 were in this natural "blonde" finish.*

Tailpiece *The Super 400's distinctive "Y-in-V" unit is engraved with the model name.*

Fingerboard *The CES version keeps the acoustic Super 4's elegant point here.*

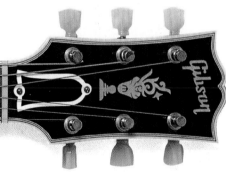

1951 L5SEC (above) The SEC shared the acoustic L5's deluxe features, such as the ornate silver and gold tailpiece with engraved name. This early example was specially made for a trade show in 1951.

Block inlays *The L5CES always features these rectangular markers, set in an ebony board.*

Cutaway *The sharp version came in around 1960. Toward the end of the 1960s the rounded cutaway returned.*

1960s L5CES Humbucking pickups began to appear from 1957, replacing the single-coil units. This attractive sunburst finish guitar dates from around 1967. Gibson continues limited L5CES production today.

GALLERY OF GIBSONS

Gibson has made a number of other electric archtop guitars. Quite clearly aimed at the beginner was the ES140, launched in 1950. This was a scaled-down version of the ES175 with small body and neck, referred to by Gibson as a "three-quarter size" model. The ES140 was later replaced by a thinline version.

Two of Gibson's oldest electric archtops, the ES150 and the ES125, were in effect combined into the ES135 during the mid-1950s, but this particular model was withdrawn later in the same decade.

One of Gibson's most luxurious electric archtops was the Citation, announced by them in 1969 as "the finest instrument of its kind in the world." It was available only to special order, and in 1971 cost $2500. By 1984 only 20 had been made.

In recent years Gibson has released very few genuinely new electric archtop models. The Super V BJB was issued at the very end of the 1970s, a floating pickup version of the V CES (right). At the end of the 1980s, Chet Atkins moved from endorsing Gretsch guitars to Gibson, and so a Gibson "refinement" of the Gretsch Country Gentleman (see page 146) was issued. The Gibson Country Gent had red-and-white fingerboard markers and displayed Chet's name on the truss-rod cover. At the same time, Gibson issued the L4CES as part of their "Historic Series." It was essentially a deluxe 175, with carved top, ebony fingerboard, and fancy tailpiece.

Gibson model code letters	T	Thinline (shallow body)
The model numbers of Gibson archtop and semi-solid guitars often feature prefix and/or suffix codes indicating various options as follows:	D	Double (two pickups)
	C	Cutaway (or sometimes means Cherry finish)
	3/4	Three-quarter size (and short scale)
ES Electric Spanish (hollow body, fixed pickup)	SV	Stereo and Varitone (wiring/control option)

1979 Kalamazoo Award (right)

Launched in 1978, this became the most expensive Gibson guitar available. By 1984 it was selling in the USA for $5350, nearly twice as much as the next most expensive guitar in their range. This is clearly a luxury model, reflected in the hand-carved top and the inlay liberally applied all over the instrument. This example is dated 11 September 1979 and is signed by Wilbur D. Fuller. The Award stayed in Gibson's guitar catalogue until 1985.

Super V CES (right)

This guitar was issued in the late 1970s, looking not unlike a Super 400CES. Its distinctive feature was the curious tailpiece, which enabled the strings to be individually tensioned. Each string passed through a pivoted "finger," at the base of which was a small adjustable screw to increase or decrease the angle of each "finger." The Super V CES lasted in production until 1987.

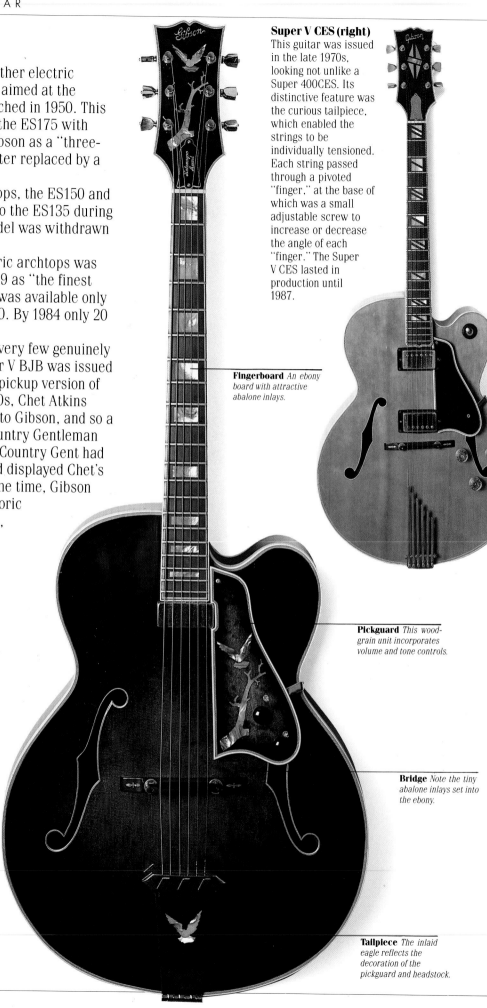

Fingerboard *An ebony board with attractive abalone inlays.*

Pickguard *This wood-grain unit incorporates volume and tone controls.*

Bridge *Note the tiny abalone inlays set into the ebony.*

Tailpiece *The inlaid eagle reflects the decoration of the pickguard and headstock.*

Gibson pickup types

P90

Gibson's prime single-coil, new in the 1940s, with adjustable pole-pieces. In black, cream, white, or chrome.

Alnico

Appeared early in the 1950s, made with magnets of iron plus ALuminum, NIckel and CObalt.

PAF

Early humbuckers had Patent Applied For labels on the base. Some insist these sound better.

Humbucker

Invented by Gibson in 1955, introduced in 1957, and patented in 1959. The two pictures show cover on (top), and with cover removed (below) revealing the twin coils which cut noise ("buck the hum").

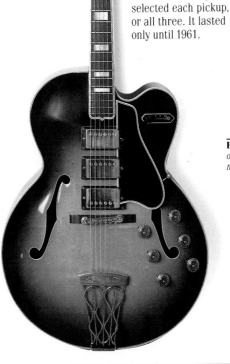

1958 ES5 Switchmaster

This new version of the ES5 (see page 129) appeared in 1955, now with a volume and tone control per pickup. The four-position switch near the cutaway selected each pickup, or all three. It lasted only until 1961.

1952 ES295

This was first seen in 1952, and is reminiscent of a hollow-body all-gold Les Paul (or a gold ES175). Note the early Les Paul-style "trapeze" tailpiece. Steve Howe's ES295 has new tuners. The model lasted until 1958, and was reissued in 1990.

Pickups The fixing lugs of these P90 types are nicknamed "dog-ears."

Serial numbers and factory order numbers

Most guitar-makers' serial number systems are not intended to date instruments, and until relatively recently Gibson was no exception. Here we offer a condensed, simplified version of the information available, intended as a very rough guide to dating acoustic and electric archtops and semi-solid guitars. (See page 37 for information on pre-1947 Gibson systems; page 89 for serial numbers on Gibson solid electrics.)

1947 to 1961 Serial numbers for this period are of three, four or five figures prefixed with an A, and are marked on a paper label (white until about 1954, subsequently orange) inside the upper f-hole. Overlaps occur, but this is a very rough guide:

A100-A9999   1947-52
A10000-20000 1952-55
A20000-30000 1955-59
A30000-36500 1959-61

In addition, between 1952 and 1961, a factory order number with a prefix letter plus several figures was sometimes stamped on to the wood inside the lower f-hole. Prefix letters run in reverse alphabetical order from Z to Q, where Z indicates 1952, Y 1953, and so on to R 1960 and Q 1961, though overlaps may occur.

1961 to 1977 From 1961 a new system began, and the serial number was stamped into the back of the headstock (and during the 1960s some guitars had serial numbers on both headstock and f-hole label). There was no specific chronological scheme, but much confusion and duplication. For a very rough guide to dating guitars from this period please see box below.

1977 to date Since 1977 a simple system has at last been used. The first and fifth numbers indicate the year; for example, 87684832 equals 1984.

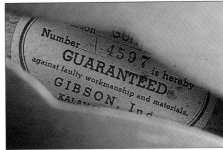

Serial numbers 1961 to 1977

100-99999   = 1961-3
000001-099999 = 1967
100000-199999 = 1963-67
200000-299999 = 1964-65
300000-599999 = 1965-69
600000-999999 = 1966-69

used again between 1970 and 1975.

Six digits prefixed with C, D, E or F were used from 1974 to 1975; then came an eight-digit system where the first two numbers were coded to indicate the date (99 = 1975; 00 = 1976; 06 = 1977).

Dating clues

A label bearing model details and a serial number is usually found inside the top f-hole of Gibson electric acoustics. It was white (above) until about 1954, and orange (center) after that time and continuing into the 1960s. A factory order number (left) is sometimes stamped on to the wood inside the lower f-hole.

GIBSON'S JAZZ GUITARISTS

As leaders in the field of archtop guitars, both acoustic and electric, Gibson has naturally come to be associated with many of the leading jazz guitarists. Consequently, some of its guitars have been named after musicians. Occasionally this results from collaboration between Gibson and the guitarist concerning the design of the instrument.

Of course, it is not just Gibson that has gained commercially from the association of famous jazz guitarists with their instruments. Epiphone, a brandname eventually related to Gibson (see page 142), was also very popular with jazz players, but relatively few "name" instruments were offered. An exception is the thinline Al Caiola model from the 1960s. Guild's Artist Award was originally called the Johnny Smith Award until he moved over to Gibson in the early 1960s, and in the late 1950s American maker Kay had also issued a range of Barney Kessel jazz models.

Gretsch bravely attempted to market the George Van Eps guitar, a strange seven-string instrument, around the beginning of the 1970s. Harmony had the Roy Smeck model (launched 1960), Framus the Attila Zoller model (1960), and Gretsch, again, the Sal Salvador (1958).

Recently it has been the turn of Japanese makers to offer endorsed jazz guitars. These include a trio from Ibanez — the Lee Ritenour (1977), George Benson, and Joe Pass (both 1981) — and two Aria models, the Ike Isaacs and the Herb Ellis (both 1979).

1964 Tal Farlow
Only 215 of these were made between 1962 and 1967. The immediately striking feature is the graceful scroll near the cutaway. The guitar would look cluttered if, as usual, the pickup selector switch had also been placed there, so the pickguard has been shaped to accommodate the switch's new site. Note also the relatively long 65cm (25½in) scale length, with ornate fretboard inlays.

Cutaway
The Tal Farlow's scroll-shaped styling was made by extending the binding onto the top of the body.

Tal Farlow
Born in North Carolina in 1921, Tal (short for Talmage) is best known for his fast, bebop-influenced work and his occasional use of a percussive finger-tapping style.

Serial number *During various periods Gibson guitars have included a serial number on the back of the headstock (see page 133).*

Machine head *This enclosed type was made by the Grover company, whose machines were used on many Gibson guitars.*

Tal Farlow headstock
The rear of the headstock of the 1964 Gibson Tal Farlow (right) has been autographed by Tal, giving this rare guitar even more appeal to collectors.

1961 Barney Kessel Custom

This model lasted ten years from 1961. The Custom version features gold hardware and "bow-tie" fingerboard markers, reflecting the contemporary jazz player's occasional need for formal stage dress. (The standard BKR model had nickel hardware and plain fretboard markers.) Note also the headstock decoration, and the symmetrical cutaways, rarely seen on a deep-bodied guitar.

Barney Kessel (above)

Born in Oklahoma in 1923, Barney has a blues-tinged style initially influenced by Charlie Christian's melodic lines. Kessel worked on many studio sessions for films and TV until the 1970s, and has toured with fellow jazz guitarists Herb Ellis and Charlie Byrd as "Great Guitars." He has played with Oscar Peterson, and makes many solo tours and records.

Johnny Smith (below)

Born in Alabama in 1922, Johnny's fame spread with his 1952 recording of *Moonlight In Vermont*. It featured his cool, floating chord style and precise ability with harmonics. Perhaps less well known is that Smith wrote *Walk Don't Run*, a pop hit when rearranged by American guitar group The Ventures. After 1960, Smith virtually retired.

1962 Johnny Smith

This guitar, with its cleanly attractive lines, was made by Gibson to "improve" on Smith's own D'Angelico "New Yorker" Special. The mini-humbucker pickup was designed especially for the Johnny Smith guitars. A two-pickup version, the JSD, joined the model shown, which was made between 1961 and 1988. In common with other Gibson archtops, fewer of the "blonde" natural-finish type were made, the majority being sunburst.

THE GIBSON BYRDLAND

In the years following Gibson's serious introduction of electric archtop jazz guitars, such as the ES175, L5CES and the Super 400CES, the company came to realize that one of the obstacles preventing the wider use of these particular instruments was their uncomfortably deep bodies.

In 1955 Gibson began the launch of a series of guitars in what they termed the new "thinline" style. The Byrdland and ES350T each possessed a body around 5 cm (2 in) deep, almost 4 cm (1½ in) shallower than the existing jazz guitars. These two new thinline guitars also featured a shorter scale-length of 60 cm (23½ in) and a shorter, narrower neck, which eased playing. These factors made them less cumbersome than their electric archtop predecessors.

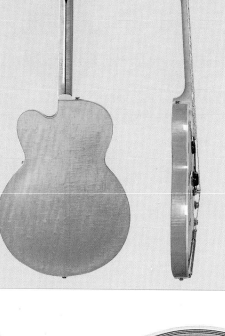

BACK AND SIDE
These views of the 1950s Byrdland show to good effect the attractive maple used to support the guitar's solid spruce top. This maple and spruce combination was used by Gibson on most of their better archtop electrics. The side view shows the relatively narrow thinline hollow body.

Woods *The Byrdland has a carved solid spruce top.*

Pickups *Single-coils were used until replaced by humbuckers in 1957.*

Cutaway *Until 1960 the Byrdland was made with a rounded cutaway.*

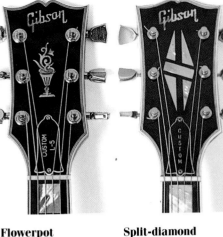

Crown headstock
An example of this headstock inlay.

Flowerpot headstock
Sometimes called a "torch" inlay.

Split-diamond headstock
This variety uses the most inlay.

Gibson headstock inlays
Some Gibson head-stocks, especially those on early models, display only the Gibson logo. But the company has often added one of its three principal styles of inlay (see left). The "crown" is used on almost all ES models, while the "flowerpot" is reserved for a few special guitars like the L5CES and the Byrdland. The "split diamond" usually indicates an up-market instrument, such as the Super 400CES or ES355.

1960s ES350T
The 350T did not last long after it moved to the sharp-cutaway style which Gibson imposed on its hollow-bodied electrics in about 1960. This blonde example was made just before the model "died" in 1963. A shortlived reincarnation occurred in 1977.

1957 ES350T
This was a cheaper maple-body version of the Byrdland, missing flourishes like the Byrdland's fingerboard "point" at the body. The earliest 350Ts had P90 single-coil pickups, but this 1957 model is equipped with the new humbucking types.

Thinline popularity

The thinline guitar appealed to players who found the bodies of normal jazz guitars bulky and cumbersome. But the new thinline instruments were, of course, still hollow-bodied. So they also found favor with guitarists who were worried by the heavy weight of the recent solid electric guitars, like Gibson's Les Paul models.

Other thinline models

There was a third thinline model launched around the same time as the Byrdland and ES350T, the ES225T. This had one of Gibson's long and awkward "trapeze" tailpieces, as on early Les Paul models and the ES295. In 1960 the 225T turned into the cherry ES125TC, which was fitted with a normal bridge and tailpiece.

A non-cutaway, single-pickup ES125T had been another early thinline model, joining the Gibson range in 1956. In 1957 a double-pickup version (ES125TD) and a small three-quarter-size variation (ES125T$3/4$) were added to the range.

Gibson had around this time issued another three-quarter-size thinline model, the ES140T$3/4$. This narrow-bodied version of the small ES140$3/4$ first appeared in 1956.

There have been other thinline versions of standard Gibson models, such as the ES120T which was made between 1962 and 1968, and even rare thinline editions of the classic ES175 and L5. But when Gibson issued the ES335 in 1958, combining thinline style with solid electric properties, they invented a new guitar, the semi-solid. Thinline guitars would never be the same again.

Frets *At the time, 22 frets were unusual for a hollow-body Gibson. The idea was borrowed from the Les Paul solid.*

Markers *Block inlays, as on the L5CES.*

1965 Byrdland (below)
This shows the model's middle-period style. It has two humbucking pickups, now in combination with the sharp cutaway introduced around 1960. In 1968 the rounded cutaway was back, and it remained into the 1990s.

1957 Byrdland (above)
Gibson named this model after two contemporary country guitarists, Billy Byrd and Hank Garland, who may have suggested some of its design features. While clearly based on the L5CES, the Byrdland has the new thinline body, a shorter neck, and a distinctive looped tailpiece inscribed with its name.

THE GIBSON ES335

In 1958 Gibson launched the ES335, a model that effectively combined a hollow-body guitar with a solid. While it appeared to have a thinline hollow body, it actually incorporated a solid block of wood running through the center of the otherwise hollow body. It also had, for the first time, a pair of symmetrical cutaways.

Guitarists were often plagued by screeching feedback when they tried to play ordinary hollow-body electric guitars at high volume. Feedback is caused by guitar pickups picking up their own sound from the loudspeakers and feeding it back to the system, creating an unpleasant "howlround."

The "semi-solid" 335 offered a depth of tone akin to hollow-body guitars but, thanks to the central body block, was much less prone to feedback at high volume. Many players took to this clever combination, including jazz-rock guitarists such as Larry Carlton and Allan Holdsworth, who found that the 335's fusion of the qualities of hollow jazz guitars and solid rock guitars fell in with their musical aims.

BACK AND SIDE
Exquisite maple was used for the back of this ES335TN, and its charm has lasted for more than 30 years. The sides, too, are maple, as is the solid block used inside the body. A single piece of mahogany is used for the neck.

Hardware *The center block allowed fitment of a stud tailpiece, as used on solids.*

Pickups *The 335 was from the start fitted with two humbucking types.*

Pickguard *Until 1960 the 335 was fitted with a long unit, stretching beyond the bridge.*

1958 ES335T

This is one of the very first 335s made. Look where the fingerboard overlaps the body at the highest frets and you will see that it is without the usual white edge binding. (Compare it with the red 335 to the right, for example.) Only the earliest examples were without this binding. This guitar is reputed to have been used at one time by the superb British blues guitarist Peter Green, founder of Fleetwood Mac.

1961 ES335TDC

Red became *the* color for the 335 in the 1960s. This 1961 example is from the second year that cherry red was generally available. It shows a number of the hardware changes made in this period. The shorter pickguard, stretching only as far as the bridge, was adopted around 1961. The metal-capped, labeled control knobs had been introduced the previous year. In 1962 the dot fingerboard markers became small blocks.

1960s ES335 twelve-string

Gibson have produced very few 12-string guitars, unlike some of the other big American makers (see pages 118-119). This 12-string version of the ES335 was a rare exception, and production was limited during its short lifetime in the 1960s. This attractive example is owned by Searchers' bassist Frank Allen.

Fingerboard markers
Dot inlays were first used until 1962. 335s with this feature are termed "dot necks."

1960s ES335 (below)

In the mid-1960s a trapeze tailpiece replaced the original stud-mounted unit of the 335. Many players claim the stud type gives much of the 335's prized sustain. Some models that originally bore trapeze tailpieces have thus been modified to stud versions. This 335 also shows block fingerboard inlays. Dots returned again in 1981, at the same time as the trapeze tailpiece began to revert to a stud type.

1959 ES335TN (above)

Launched in 1958, the 335 is still made today, but players and collectors get most excited about 335s made between 1958 and 1962, arguing that these classics are better than any made since. This 1959 guitar's beautiful finish is indicated in its model number by the N suffix, standing for natural "blonde" finish. Blonde 335s were made for just three years during the 335's classic first period, only 209 of them from 1958 to 1960. This compares to the 1193 guitars made with the alternative sunburst finish (model number ES335T) which were made by Gibson during those three years.

THE GIBSON ES355

Around the same time as the new ES335 was launched in the late 1950s, with its effective combination of hollow body and solid electric guitar characteristics, Gibson added two similar instruments to their range, the ES345 and ES355. These partners to the ES335 featured its new and distinctive symmetrical-cutaway body shape. They also had within the body the centrally positioned solid block of wood that gave some of the qualities of a solid-bodied electric guitar to this otherwise light-bodied series of instruments.

Both the 345 and the 355 were offered with stereo wiring and an unusual six-way selector switch called the Vari-tone. This tone-altering circuit was developed by Gibson's pickup expert, Walt Fuller, but proved unpopular with players. Many 345s and 355s fitted with stereo and Vari-tone have since been converted to normal wiring.

1969 ES340 (above)
This model, available from 1969 to 1974, looked identical to a 335. But it had an unusually wired three-way pickup selector, giving pickups out-of-phase, both pickups on, and both pickups off.

1963 Gibson catalogue (right)
The cover shows the stereo/Vari-tone version of the 355.

Vibrato *Usually a Bigsby is fitted, although some models have a vibrola.*

Pickups *Hardware on the 355 was gold-plated.*

Binding *Multiple binding on body and headstock indicates a top-quality Gibson and produces distinctive parallel lines.*

Finish *At first the 355 came only in cherry red, but later options included a dark brown "walnut" finish.*

From Trini Lopez to B B King

Gibson has marketed a number of other semi-solid and thinline hollow-body electric models since it introduced guitarists to the idea of such instruments in the 1950s.

In 1964 Gibson brought out two versions of a model named after Latin-pop musician Trini Lopez. The TLD version looked much like a Barney Kessel (see page 135) with its sharp symmetrical cutaways, but both this and the rounded cutaway TLS model were unusual for Gibson in that they featured a headstock with machine heads along one side, in the style of Fender. The Trini Lopez was made until 1972.

Later hollow or semi-solid Gibsons with symmetrical cutaways included the Crest (1969-71), with mini-humbuckers and a sixteenth-fret neck/body join like early 330s; the ES150DC (1969-75), a deep-bodied 335 shape; the ES320 (1972-73), with controls on a semi-circular plate and black humbuckers; and the ES325 (1972-75), like the 320 but with plain metal pickups.

An unusual model in the Les Paul series was the Les Paul Signature (1973-78), which had a semi-solid body with offset cutaways, two low-impedance humbuckers bearing cream covers, and "crown" shaped fingerboard inlays.

Gibson absorbed contemporary guitar trends into the existing semi-solid style at various times. For example, the ES347 followed the late 1970s fad for fine-tuning tailpiece and "coil-tapped" pickups, which give the choice of single-coil or humbucking effect from one unit. In the 1980s, the ES369 adopted the vogue for active electronic circuits, giving boosted tonal options.

The ES Artist (1980-85) and the B B King (launched 1981) were both without f-holes. The Artist featured an active circuit, while Blues Boy's guitar was an expensive signature model.

1959 ES345TN
Built from 1959 to 1980, this semi-solid slotted in between the 335 and 355 and can be identified by its angled split-block fingerboard markers. It offered stereo (the output can feed each pickup to a separate amp) and Vari-tone six-way selector (giving a series of tonal differences). This rare blonde finish was an option only for the first two years of production, and in very limited numbers.

1961 ES330
This model was an odd one out in several respects. Despite its shape and its 1959 launch, it did not have a solid central body-block. It also differed from semi-solids in that its neck was set further into the body, joining at the sixteenth fret (although 330s made from 1968-72 had the usual nineteenth-fret join). Note also the trapeze tailpiece, P90 single-coil pickups, and the lack of headstock inlay.

Fingerboard *The 355's ebony board is inlaid with block markers.*

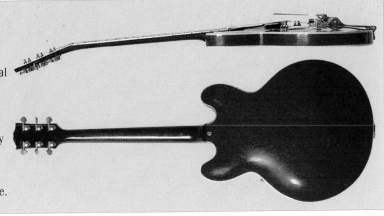

SIDE AND BACK
Generally speaking, Gibson reserved its best spruce tops and maple backs for natural ("blonde") finish guitars, which obviously showed off the choicest woods to best effect. But cherry and sunburst finish Gibsons sometimes turn up that have beautiful woods visible.

1950s ES355TD
Launched around 1959, this semi-solid is a deluxe version of the 335. Until 1970 the mono TD type shown was made alongside a stereo-wired TDSV version fitted with a six-way Vari-tone switch. The stereo 355 continued in production until 1981.

'Split diamond' *This is another indicator of a top-of-the-range Gibson.*

EPIPHONE AND GUILD

Epiphone was first established as a brand for guitars in 1928, named after company president Epaminondas (Epi) Stathopoulo. Epiphone started making electric instruments in the 1930s. Although best known for its early archtop acoustics (see page 34), Epiphone's electric versions of some of these models are often highly rated. After Gibson acquired the Epiphone brandname in 1957 there was a shift toward thinline electrics, and after 1970 the Epiphone name was used for a range of Japanese-made and more recently Korean-made guitars.

Guild began in 1952, and its reputation is based on the quality of its flat-top acoustic guitars (see page 40) and its archtop electrics, some of which are shown here. In 1989 Guild was bought by the Randall electronics company of Wisconsin.

Epiphone Zephyr Emperor Regent

This was made by Epiphone in New York in the early 1950s. Its long name indicates that it is an electric (Zephyr), cutaway (Regent) guitar with an Emperor body shape. The novel switch bank gives a variety of pickup combinations. Note also the unusual pickup surrounds, and Epiphone's attractive octagonal volume and tone knobs.

Epiphone catalog

A spread from an early 1960s brochure shows the Gibson-built electric Emperor on the right.

From Epiphone to Gibson

Gibson took over the Epiphone brandname in 1957 and soon began building Epis in their Kalamazoo factory. Some old Epiphone names survived, including Emperor and Broadway, but most of the new Epiphones were "equivalents" of Gibson models. The Sorrento was like an ES125 TD, the Granada resembled an ES120T, and the Casino was very similar to an ES330. The new Epis often bore small "mini-humbucker" pickups and an Epiphone headstock logo, sometimes with a flowery inlay. Production moved to the Far East in 1970.

Late 1960s Epiphone Riviera twelve-string

The 12-string version illustrated is rare. The six-string model, the E360TD, was almost identical to Gibson's ES335 of the period, including the trapeze tailpiece. The main difference lay in Epiphone's customary use of mini-humbuckers.

1964 Epiphone Sheraton (left)

The top thinline electric guitar from the Gibson-made period, the Sheraton had a maple body, and the mahogany neck's rosewood fingerboard featured pearl and abalone inlays in a classic Epi style Pickups were typical Epiphone mini-humbuckers. The headstock bore Epi's vine design, reserved for top-of-the-line guitars.

Controls *These govern volume and tone per pickup, with pickup selector.*

Tailpiece *An example of Epiphone's distinctive Frequensator unit: "The short fork deepens tone, the longer fork adds brilliance."*

1960s Epiphone Professional (left)

An unusual thinline electric supplied with a special amplifier that could be controlled from the guitar's wide selection of controls. Circuits available included tone boosts, reverb and tremolo. Few controls worked without the Professional's amp, although there was a jack socket on the top of the instrument for normal guitar output.

Headstock *It carries a pearl and abalone motif, and the distinctive "stepped" pegs of Grover Imperial machine heads.*

Inlay *The shape and style of these markers stress Guild's early Epiphone connections.*

1961 Guild Stratford (left)

This guitar, model X350, was made for a few years in the early 1960s. It underlines Guild's early Epiphone links, being similar to the Zephyr Emperor Regent (far left).

1974 Guild X500 (right)

The X500 was launched in the 1950s as one of Guild's first electrics. This model has the "G-shield" logo on headstock and knobs.

1976 Guild Artist Award (right)

This model was introduced in the late 1950s as the Johnny Smith Award. But the guitarist started to endorse Gibson guitars in the early 1960s, and Guild changed the name of the guitar to Artist Award. High-quality materials are used throughout, including spruce top, ebony fingerboard and gold-plated hardware.

Pickguard *This incorporates the pickup, volume knob and (hidden underneath) the socket.*

Tailpiece *This harp-shaped unit was a distinctive trademark on many Guild guitars.*

More from Guild

The Guild company was established in New York in 1952 by Alfred Dronge, who had previously played, taught and sold guitars. His workers were soon producing archtop and flat-top guitars. By 1956 they had out-grown the New York workshop, and moved to New Jersey. During the 1950s several Epiphone craftsmen joined Dronge, and their influence on Guild can be seen in some guitars, especially the fingerboard inlays.

As well as the electric archtops and thinlines shown here, Guild made a number of other models. Thinlines included the small-bodied Gibson Les Paul-like Aristocrat (also known as the Bluesbird) and the Duane Eddy, endorsed by the king of twang. There were also some less expensive jazz guitars such as the maple-topped Capri CE100, plus the Manhattan X175 and Mini-Manhattan X170.

Guild catalog

A page from a 1970s brochure shows two models from Guild's long-running Starfire thinline electric series. These guitars came with either single- or double-cutaway bodies.

THE GRETSCH WHITE FALCON

Gretsch is best known for its electric acoustic guitars made in the 1950s and 1960s. Although many of these classic instruments were designed with strong country music influences, they can command high prices among pop and rock musicians.

Gretsch began in New York in 1883 when a German immigrant, Friedrich Gretsch, set up a music shop. His son Fred Gretsch founded the Fred Gretsch Manufacturing Co., which started making guitars during the 1930s in the company's Brooklyn factory. Fred Gretsch Jr presided over the classic Gretsch period, but Baldwin bought the company in 1967; production ceased in 1981. The operation was back in Gretsch family ownership by 1985, and production of guitars resumed in Japan in 1990.

Dave Stewart
Gretsch guitars have long been fashionable, especially to the rock musician attracted as much by looks and pose value as sound and playability. Striking, stylish Gretsch guitars are often brought in as visually appealing extras for pop videos or photo sessions. Eurythmics' Dave Stewart is a fan of the Gretsch sound and looks, and is seen (left) with a multi-controlled stereo White Falcon.

Switch *This offers a selection of front, back, or both pickups.*

Controls *A volume per pickup and overall tone here, plus a master volume near the cutaway.*

Pickups *These are Gretsch's FilterTron types, which appeared in about 1958.*

Cutaway *The White Falcon originally came only with single cutaway, from 1955 to about 1963.*

1978 7595 White Falcon

The model numbering change came with Baldwin's acquisition of Gretsch in the early 1970s. From about 1974, until dropped in 1981, the Falcon was offered in both single- and double-cutaway versions; model 7593 was single-cutaway mono; 7594 double-cut mono; and this 7595 is double-cut stereo.

White Falcon

Gretsch called the original White Falcon "The Guitar of the Future" when a special prototype was made for exhibition at a musical instruments trade fair in Chicago in the mid-1950s. This show item was designed in part by musician and Gretsch demonstrator Jimmie Webster, responsible for so many of Gretsch's classic instruments and add-on gimmicks during the 1950s and 1960s.

The stunning guitar caused so much interest that Gretsch decided to put this Cadillac of the guitar world into production as the top of their line in 1955. They retained from the unique show guitar the impressive white finish, gold-plated hardware and – borrowed from the very successful Gretsch drum department – a liberal sprinkling of gold-sparkle plastic.

Key dates

The original 1955 Falcon had the normal electric guitar's mono output, and a single, rounded cutaway. Stereo output became an option in 1959. Double cutaways became standard in 1963, and the White Falcon was available with single or double cutaways from 1974. After an absence of eight years the guitar was re-issued in 1990 as part of Gretsch's Japan-based comeback, available in single or double cutaway body styles.

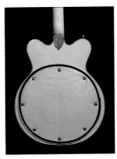

Back

The back of this 1978 stereo White Falcon shows another gimmick from Gretsch inventor Jimmie Webster: the circular, padded plastic, press-studded pad, patented in 1963. It protects the finish from damage and hides the plate covering the guitar's control wiring.

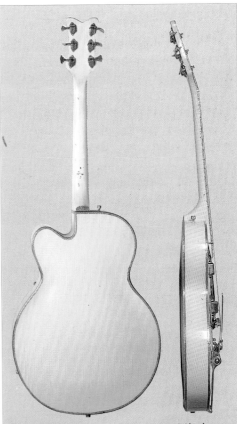

BACK AND SIDE Note the gold glitter trim on this model, near the neck/ body joint (back) and for the binding (side view).

Inlays Some early examples have engraved "humped block" markers.

Logo This long, early type lasted until some time around 1958.

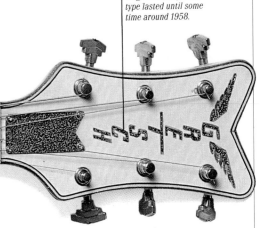

Literature

Early American guitar brochures reflect the electric guitar's pioneering era, and those issued by the Gretsch company are classics. Examples from the 1950s and 1960s were great achievements in hyperbole and salesmanship for what the company's PR people have consistently called the "great Gretsch sound."

1950s 6136 White Falcon (above)

This most ostentatious of Gretsches is owned by David Gilmour, and was probably made in 1957 or 1958. The Gibson bridge is a later addition, and the control layout is of the type usually seen with earlier DeArmond pickups. A stereo version (model 6137) appeared in about 1959.

GRETSCH GALLERY

O f the dozen or so hollow-bodied guitars that Gretsch launched during the 1950s and 1960s, modern musicians have concentrated on seven principal models which might be termed "The Fashionable Gretsches." These are the Double Anniversary, the Country Club, the Country Gentleman, the Hollow Body (which became the Nashville), the Tennessean, the Viking, and the White Falcon.

Quick identification of these models from a distance can be tricky for the newcomer to Gretsch, as the general impression is of a range of similar big-bodied guitars with one or two cutaways and double pickups, a vibrato arm (usually), and an array of controls. So here, as a guide to their distinctive features, we show six fine examples of the main Gretsch models (for details of the White Falcon see pages 144-145).

1959 6122 Country Gentleman (right)
This classic dark brown Gretsch guitar comes from the model's first period of production. Country Gents are rarely seen with a single cutaway, only made for the first few years. These FilterTron pickups are controlled by two volume knobs (lower body), plus master volume, and selector switches for pickups and for tone. It was renumbered as model 7670 from about 1971.

Headstock *Some Gretsch guitars have model name and serial number on a plate mounted here.*

1958 6119 Tennessean
Starting life in 1962 with one pickup, the orange 6119 switched to twin pickups in 1963. The Tennessean was a popular 1960s guitar, a relatively cheaper model in the Gretsch line. It kept its general appearance when it was given model number 7655 (from 1971 to 1980). This fine early example has real f-holes and one volume control on the cutaway; the single switch affects tone.

Inlays *G-Brand models usually feature these cowboy motifs.*

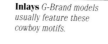

f-holes *The Country Gent had fake painted-on f-holes until about 1970.*

Switch *This gives front, both, and back pickups.*

f-holes *After about 1963, these f-holes became purely decorative, painted on to the guitar's body.*

Control knob *This governs overall volume.*

Pickups *These are the 1950s Dynasonic type, made by DeArmond.*

Finish *This glowing orange finish was officially called "amber red" by Gretsch.*

Controls *A volume per pickup, plus a knob for overall tone.*

1956 6120 Hollow Body (right)
Widely known by its model number, the 6120 was in 1955 the first model in the Chet Atkins series. It moved to a double-cutaway version in 1963, renamed the Nashville in 1967, and bearing model number 7660 from 1971. Some early examples have a brand.

G-brand *Giving firm evidence of country music roots, the earliest Hollow Body models featured western motifs on the headstock and fingerboard inlays, plus a big G for Gretsch "branded" into the body.*

1965 6192 Country Club

This model was distinguished by its gold-plated hardware, and first appeared in 1955. It initially came in sunburst (6192), natural (6193), or "cadillac green" (6196) finishes. Models from the 1970s settled to just sunburst (7575) or natural (7576). A stereo-wired option was also produced at one stage. The Country Club was eventually discontinued in 1981.

Bridge *This is the 1960s Space Control unit.*

Standby switch *In effect an on-off control*

1964 6118 Double Anniversary

This model, unveiled in 1959, had two pickups (the Single Anniversary had one). It could be bought originally as model 6117 in sunburst, or 6118, the beautiful "two-tone smoke green" shown here. The darker green of the pickguard is matched on the back and sides. The 1970s model was 7560.

Headstock *This bears a chromed nameplate.*

1970s 7585 Viking

The Viking was launched in 1965 near the top of the Gretsch range, second only to the White Falcon. Note the specially built curved-arm of the vibrato, and the "Floating Bridge" between back pickup and bridge, supposed to enhance sustain. The Viking lasted to 1975.

Inlays *Typical Gretsch semi-circular markers, known as "thumbnails."*

"T-zone" *This guitar has frets above the fifteenth slanted for "perfect high-note intonation," a Gretsch idea that was quickly dropped.*

Chet Atkins series

Chester Burton Atkins, born in Tennessee in 1924, was a top country music session guitarist by the 1940s. He was a pioneer during the 1950s of the solo electric guitar, and was voted Best Instrumentalist in *Cashbox* magazine's poll for 14 consecutive years.

As a producer Chet worked on Elvis Presley's RCA sessions and is credited in part for the creation of the so-called Nashville Sound of the 1960s. He was elected to the Country Music Hall of Fame in 1973. Chet Atkins has recorded many solo albums and some recently in duet with Les Paul, while a few of Chet's earlier cuts became single hits (such as 'Boo Boo Stick Beat', 1959).

Guitarist Jimmie Webster, demonstrator and inventor for Gretsch, approached Chet Atkins in the early 1950s in an effort to persuade Chet to switch from his D'Angelico instrument to a Gretsch. After some hesitation from Atkins, Webster suggested Chet design a guitar from scratch. The first result was the Chet Atkins Hollow Body 6120 (see left) in 1955, with the guitarist's suggestions including a metal bridge and nut, and a Bigsby vibrato. Later models in the Chet Atkins series included the Country Gentleman and the Tennessean. Chet endorsed Gretsch guitars until the 1980s, when he moved to Gibson who issued a Chet Atkins electric nylon-strung model, and their own Country Gent in 1987.

Dynasonic *This is from a 1950s solid body 6121.*

FilterTron *From a late 1950s White Penguin.*

HiLoTron *On a late 1960s Double Anniversary 6117.*

SuperTron *This is on a mid 1960s Astro Jet.*

WHAT VINTAGE?

Anyone who wishes to date a Gretsch guitar should prepare for frustration. Serial numbers exhibit little sequential logic. Hardware and features often tell more about a Gretsch's period, for example pickups (see left). The DeArmond Dynasonic pickup, with a single, centrally positioned row of polepieces and nearby adjusting screws, was used only in the 1950s, while Gretsch's classic FilterTron humbucker (two rows of polepieces) replaced it later in that decade and continued through to the 1990s in various versions. The HiLoTron, with a one-sided row of screw-top polepieces, came in during the early 1960s, while the SuperTron, without polepieces, appeared later in the 1960s.

RICKENBACKER

The sweeping shapes of Rickenbacker's most famous hollow-body electrics were very different from the lines being drawn by their competitors in the late 1950s. The classic two-pickup 330 and 360 models (for the 12-string, see page 118) are similar: the 360 is a deluxe version with triangular fingerboard inlays and binding added to the neck (and sometimes to the body). Many Rickys have changed little in sound or looks; much of their appeal today lies in their embodiment of the past.

For dating (1961 to 1986), serial letters/numbers were stamped on the jack socket. The first letter gives the year of manufacture, from A (1961) sequentially to Z (1986).

1989 381 V69
Part of the vintage series, started in 1984, this has the original 381's deep, carved-top body. An active version of the V69 had a scratchplate bearing the signature of John Kay, leader of the 1960s group Steppenwolf.

1967 335
Models with numbers ending in "5" have a vibrato: so this is a vibrato-equipped 330.

Tailpiece *This is the R-for-Rickenbacker type, used from the early 1960s.*

Soundhole *This is Rickenbacker's distinctive "slash."*

Frets *These are slanted on this rare 330 variation. Note too the ebony fingerboard, almost always rosewood on normal models.*

Pickguard *A classic split-level unit, with two volumes, two tones, pickup mix, and selector.*

Rick-O-Sound
This simulated stereo effect works by dividing the signal from the pickups and feeding these to two amps. The sockets (left) give the "Rick-O-Sound" effect on a stereo jack, or ordinary ("Standard") output on a mono jack.

1971 331 (right)

This bizarre and short-lived "light-show" guitar, based on the 330 model and made in small numbers, had a body topped with clear plastic, with colored bulbs inside. These illuminated as the guitar sounded particular frequencies. This 331 shown is from Rickenbacker's own collection, and is of the original hand-wired type, with the bulbs arranged in two straight rows. Later examples used a printed circuit board, and featured much brighter bulbs spaced out across the interior. The normal output lead is supplemented by a cable to the flasher unit. The company also made a handful of 12-string and bass versions in addition to a three-pickup variant.

John Lennon (far right)

This UK ad exploits Lennon's regular use in the 1960s of a 325.

1964 Model 1996

This short-scale guitar is the UK "1996" version of the 325, generally referred to as "the John Lennon" after the 325's most famous player. The 325JL reissue of 1990 featured Lennon's autograph and portrait on the pickguard.

Rickenbacker in the UK

In the 1960s a small selection of Rickys was exported to Britain. The UK agent originally requested special features: a proper f-hole; plain black knobs; mono circuitry; and a vibrato. UK-only model numbers were used: 1996, 1997 and 1998, corresponding to US models 325, 335 and 345.

Inlays *Models 330/335 and 340/345 had dot markers; 360/365 and 370/375 used triangles.*

Rickenbacker literature (right)

The page from an early 1980s catalogue (near right) shows the finishes then on offer, including the classic red "Fire-glo" and black "Jet-glo." The 1968 brochure achieves psychedelia in black-and-white.

1968 330SF (above left)

This has a feature that, even for Rickenbacker, is most unusual. The nut, frets, pickups, and bridge are all slanted, to "match precisely the natural angle of the fretting fingers." Today

John Hall, president of Rickenbacker, recalls that there was no response to this experimental option, and so the company went back to less expensive straight frets "since we figured nobody cared."

1959 360F

The F-suffix models ("F" for "full body") lasted from 1959 to the early 1970s. They had single, rounded cutaways and relatively thick bodies, and the usual variations: dot or triangle inlays; two or three pickups; with or without vibrato.

AMERICAN GALLERY

Makers of electric acoustic guitars in the USA have always been dominated by the major producers of such instruments. These large companies have included Gibson, Gretsch, Guild, Rickenbacker, and Epiphone (all of which are featured on previous pages). One major guitar maker, Fender, has consistently failed to succeed with electric hollow-bodied guitars, while other companies have decided to concentrate solely on solid-bodied electrics, leaving hollow-body models to specialists.

Mainly during the 1950s and 1960s, some producers such as Harmony and Kay made all kinds of guitars in large numbers for outside clients. These customers were primarily retail-store chains or mail-order organizations, which had no guitar-making facilities but wanted to cash in on the huge demand by having their own brandnames put on the guitar products. However, both Harmony and Kay made and marketed some guitars with their own logos.

Headstock *The tortoiseshell effect of the plastic facing matches the pickguard.*

Harmony H71 Meteor

This was one of Harmony's most popular thinline hollow-bodied guitars in the 1960s. The natural finish H71 example shown, which has like many lost its pickguard, was partnered by the sunburst H70 version. It was typical of some Harmonys in that the headstock looked rather large in proportion to the rest of the guitar.

1962 Kay Jazz II K775

This model is similar to one used by Eric Clapton in the early 1960s, when he played in a group called The Roosters. The budget-conscious Kay brand started in 1931, and the Chicago-based company also made many cheap guitars for stores and mail-order firms. Their US production ended in the late 1960s.

Block inlays *Harmony's cheaper guitars had dot position markers.*

Pickup selectors *Each switch turns a pickup on or off, giving seven different combinations.*

Pickups *The single-coil units were made for Harmony by De Armond.*

Body *The maple bodies of the H series were finished in red (H77) or mahogany sunburst (H75).*

Harmony catalog

This 1963 publication features an H77 on the cover, along with a Sovereign acoustic and model H22 electric bass.

1964 Harmony H77 (right)

Another Chicago-based company, started in 1892, Harmony was at one time the biggest guitar producer in the USA. American manufacture ceased in 1975. The three-pickup cherry sunburst H77 was the top Harmony hollow electric made from 1960 to 1970.

Controls *Each pickup has its own associated volume and tone knob.*

Tailpiece *Bigsby vibrato was an option.*

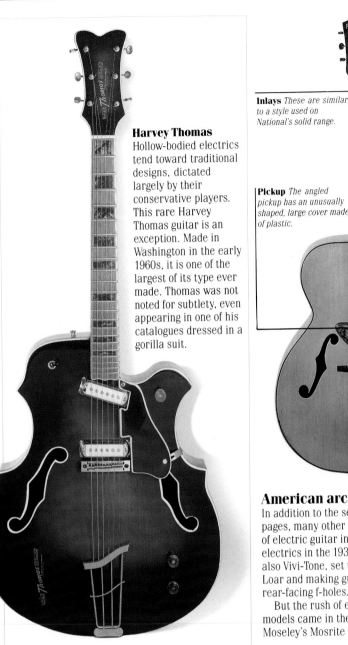

Harvey Thomas

Hollow-bodied electrics tend toward traditional designs, dictated largely by their conservative players. This rare Harvey Thomas guitar is an exception. Made in Washington in the early 1960s, it is one of the largest of its type ever made. Thomas was not noted for subtlety, even appearing in one of his catalogues dressed in a gorilla suit.

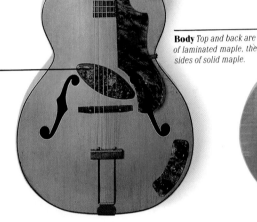

Inlays *These are similar to a style used on National's solid range.*

Pickup *The angled pickup has an unusually shaped, large cover made of plastic.*

Paramount

This was a brandname used in the 1930s and 1940s by a New York company called Lange, and also by Gretsch & Brenner. Paramount guitars were made by various suppliers. This example appears to have been made by Kay. Apart from the headstock logo, it is virtually identical to Kay's model K155, which was produced in the early 1940s.

Body *Top and back are of laminated maple, the sides of solid maple.*

1990 Heritage H535

The Heritage company was formed in 1985 by a number of ex-Gibson employees. A factory was set up in the old Gibson building in Kalamazoo, and a range of electric acoustic and solid models built. Some are even called Parsons Street models after the address in Kalamazoo, and most are based on Gibson lines, such as this ES335-inspired guitar.

Pickguard *This is also made of maple to match the body.*

American archtops and thinlines

In addition to the selected models shown on these pages, many other companies produced this kind of electric guitar in the USA. Producing archtop electrics in the 1930s were National and Vega, and also Vivi-Tone, set up by ex-Gibson designer Lloyd Loar and making guitars with such odd features as rear-facing f-holes.

But the rush of electric archtops and thinline models came in the 1950s and 1960s. Semie Moseley's Mosrite brand appeared on a number of

f-hole models and Coral, a line made by the Daneletro company, could be seen on hollow-body versions of its unusual "long-horn" body shape, as well as on more conventional thinlines.

Harmony made guitars for many other companies, its electric hollow-bodied models bearing such names as Regal and Silvertone. As well as the Fenders pictured below, the Californian maker manufactured the LTD and Montego models. Martin also produced a limited number of f-hole thinlines in the 1970s, as did Ovation.

f-hole *On the Coronado II models the f-holes are bound.*

Pickups *The Coronados came with one (model I) or two (II) pickups.*

1970s Fender Starcaster (below)

In 1976 Fender tried again to market a thinline electric. But the Starcaster was also unsuccessful, mainly due to Gibson's dominance, and was dropped in 1979.

Headstock *A variation on Fender's normal style, with contrasting stripe.*

1968 Fender Coronado Wildwood II (left)

Fender's first attempt at a thinline electric, this was launched in 1966. As well as sunburst or solid colors, it was also offered in grey Antigua or this Wildwood finish.

Finish *This streaked Wildwood effect was produced by dyeing beech during growth.*

EUROPEAN GALLERY

Europian makers of hollow-bodied electrics have for the most part been influenced by guitars from the United States. This is not too surprising, given that most of the invention and innovation among these instruments has originated in the USA.

One factor that sets some European makers apart is their willingness to use the abundant local timbers, often forsaking the American standard of spruce and maple and opting for, say, Scots pine or sycamore.

The art of the European archtop electric has resided firmly in Germany, principally with Hofner's more expensive instruments. This instrument-making company was founded in 1887 by Karl Hofner in the part of the region that was to become East Germany. The firm started to produce guitars in 1925. The Hofner family escaped to West Germany after World War II, establishing a new factory in Bubenreuth in 1951. Their first electric archtops appeared in the 1950s, and the company is still in business today.

Knight Imperial (left)

Made in Britain in the late 1980s, this guitar features Dick Knight's *fleur-de-lys* headstock inlay and carved (not glued) internal struts.

Grimshaw Plectric Deluxe Electracoustic (right)

This late 1950s British guitar by Emil Grimshaw has 24 frets, a spruce/sycamore body, and an extra fingerboard pickup.

Grimshaw catalog

This features a thinline electric guitar and a similar bass guitar from the 1960s.

Other European makers

Many other European makers have catered to the demand for hollow-bodied electrics. In West Germany there were Framus, Hoyer, Klira, and Roger. Hagstrom's Swedish-made Viking was a popular hollow electric, even used by Elvis Presley, while in Italy makers included Eko, Galanti, and Welson.

In the UK there have been few makers of hollow-bodied electrics, although in the 1960s Burns and Wilson did offer a few models. Small makers currently producing such guitars include Chris Eccleshall, Gordon Smith, and M. J. Vanden.

Headstock *This is faced in black plastic, inlaid with the model name.*

Neck *This is made from over 35 strips of beech glued together, a method used on many German guitars of the period.*

Hopf Saturn 63

The Hopf company of West Germany departed from conventional hollow-body electric styling on this mid-1960s guitar. The Star Club in Hamburg featured it in many of their ads, obviously considering it to be a good representative of the German beat scene of the time.

Soundholes *These are unusually shaped, and edged with metal beading.*

Body *Inlaid metal beading is a feature of the body.*

Control panel *This included a three-pin DIN socket instead of the usual 6mm (¹/₄in) jack.*

Vibrato *Of unusual design, the vibrato has twin springs operating the push/pull string anchor.*

1959 Hofner President (left)
Hofner made this UK-only model from the late 1950s to the mid-1970s.

1959 Hofner Committee (right)
This was designed by a committee of six guitarists: Ike Isaacs, Bert Weedon, Roy Plummer, Jack Llewellyn, Freddie Philips, and Frank Deniz.

Pickups *Thin black types were used from around 1957 until about 1960.*

Pickguard *Hofner's plastic unit helped show off the pine top.*

Headstock *The design was described by Hofner as "frondose" (leaf-like).*

Hofner Club 50 (right)
Launched in the late 1950s, Hofner's Club models were scaled-down versions of their large hollow-bodied guitars, but without f-holes. This Club 50 is a special from 1961.

Fingerboard *This is ebony, with ornate mother-of-pearl inlays.*

Controls *The extra knobs and switch are for the built-in battery powered tremolo circuitry.*

1961 Hofner Golden Hofner (left)
The top of Hofner's hollow-bodied electric range, this model was made between 1959 and 1962. It is from an export-only range made by Hofner for Selmer London. Hofner described it as "a masterpiece of guitar perfection."

Back view
The beautiful back of the Golden Hofner has a maple veneer. Note the superb inlay work, with marvelous attention to small details, and the mother-of-pearl heel cap. Only the finest makers take such care over the look of the backs of their guitars.

Pickups *These diamond-logo types were used from about 1961 to 1963.*

Bert Weedon
The British guitarist holds a 1959 Golden Hofner.

Tailpiece *The Golden Hofner's hardware is gold-plated and embossed.*

Controls *This is Hofner's classic "flick-action console."*

ORIENTAL GALLERY

The principal oriental guitar-producing country in the late 1960s and early 1970s was Japan. During that period its makers were primarily concerned with copying the guitars made by the best known American brands. But the Japanese instruments of this period were made for a fraction of the cost of the originals and, inevitably, were generally of much poorer quality.

Later in the 1970s and into the 1980s producers in the Far East — now including makers in Korea and Taiwan as well as Japan — began to manufacture solid-body electrics with more originality and less dependence on US influences. However, when it came to hollow-body electrics, both archtop and thinline types, there was still much reliance on traditional American guidelines.

There were two main reasons for this. First, it is very hard (and relatively expensive) for a maker to be original with such guitars. Second, jazz musicians who favor hollow-bodied guitars are conservative. This combination ensures unadventurously designed guitars.

1989 Washburn J10 This archtop electric model is the top of Washburn's hollow-body line, with strong Gibson influences. The Washburn name originated on acoustics made in Chicago in the nineteenth century. From the 1970s it was used for guitars designed in the US but built in Japan (and more recently also in Korea).

Inlays These are of pearl and abalone, on an ebony fingerboard.

Body This has a spruce top with maple back and sides.

Tailpiece The T-shaped center and angled bars are influenced by Gibson's ES175.

Tailpiece The two string-tension bars are adjusted by these knobs.

Bridge This is adjustable for height.

Controls For each pickup, a volume and tone control.

Pickguard The pickups are fitted to this, floating free of the surface of the guitar.

Body The top is made from spruce.

1989 Antoria Rockstar EG1935

Antoria was a UK importer's brandname, used in the 1970s mostly on guitars made in the Fuji Gen-Gakki factory, which also produced Ibanez guitars. However, this later instrument was made in Korea, and was sold earlier in the 1980s as the Harmony H935. It is clearly influenced by the Gibson 335, although Antoria claim it has "double sustain blocks" inside the body. The model came with or without nickel-plated pickup covers.

Body *An up-market version of the EG1935 featured a more attractive flame maple top.*

1989 Aria TA60

"TA" stands for the "Titan Artist" series, which appeared in 1981. The influence on this model is clearly from Gibson, despite Aria's inscription on the headstock about an "original custom body." The workmanship is good and the pink finish of this example is certainly unusual for this style of guitar.

Fingerboard *The TA60 has small block markers in a rosewood board.*

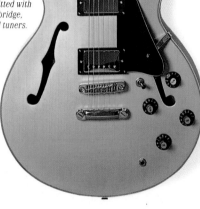

Hardware *The TA60 model was fitted with gold-plated bridge, pickups, and tuners.*

Aria catalogue
Jazz guitarist Herb Ellis has long been associated with Gibson guitars, particularly the ES175. He endorsed the Aria PE175 in 1979.

1990 Yamaha SA1100

This model comes from Yamaha's third generation of the SA ("Semi Acoustic") series, launched in 1977. It is obviously based on Gibson's popular ES335. The fashion at the time it was issued for so-called "blonde" hollow-bodied guitars explains this Yamaha's natural finish.

Fingerboard *This is made from ebony, with block position markers.*

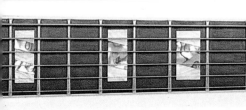
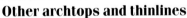

Other archtops and thinlines

This type of instrument usually means a bigger investment for the guitar-maker when compared to that needed for solid-bodied electric guitars. This is principally because the production process can be more time consuming and involved. Oriental makers, whose business so often centers on building guitars to a price, have thus traditionally concentrated on solid guitars.

Despite this, there is still a reasonable number of oriental makers of hollow-body electrics, particularly the thinline, equal-cutaway variety. Among the many additional Japanese brand names that have appeared on such guitars are Tokai, Teisco, Maya, Fresher, Kimbara, Kasuga, Columbus, Cimar, Excetro, and Audition.

George Benson

Guitarist and singer Benson, influenced by Wes Montgomery and Tal Farlow, formed his first jazz group in 1965. He later moved to a popular style, having a huge hit in 1976 with *Breezin.*

1978 Ibanez George Benson GB10 (above left)

This Ibanez model, made in Japan, first appeared in 1977. Influenced in size and shape by the Gibson ES175, it was endorsed and played by George Benson. The guitar has a spruce top supported by a maple back and sides. Note the special inlay at the twenty-first fret. There was also a larger-bodied George Benson, model GB20, which differed in having a single pickup and a pickguard-mounted control. A special anniversary version of the Ibanez George Benson was issued in 1990.

66*Some makers offer
headless basses, add
strings to the original
four, or concoct new
electronics, but simplicity
remains essential to
the bass guitar.***99**

BASS
GUITAR

1990 WARWICK STREAMER LIMITED EDITION, courtesy Bass Centre London.

ANATOMY OF THE BASS GUITAR

Simplicity was the key word for the original design of the electric bass guitar. The American Fender company invented the instrument, marketing their Precision from 1951 (shown here in its modern Japanese-made form). It followed the style set by Fender a year earlier with their Telecaster electric guitar, featuring the straightforward bolt-together construction that turned guitar-making into a production-line business.

Most makers now acknowledge that Fender's original designs were remarkably sound, and indeed the Precision and Jazz basses form the basis for many of the competing models launched since 1951.

The biggest challenge to the Fender style of construction came in the early 1980s when Ned Steinberger from New York came up with his headless, and almost bodyless, bass guitar made from carbon fiber. Since that shock to the bass establishment, the influence of Steinberger's design is seen in some basses that mix a headless neck with a conventional body shape.

Innovations

Bass players have now established a strong identity for their instrument, and the myth of the bass being played by someone not good enough for six-string duties is clearly outdated. Many instruments compete today for the bassist's attention, some using advanced electronics and combinations of exotic woods and space-age plastics. But Fender's innovations live on, both in their own and in countless other bass guitars.

Roundwound strin
Developed by Rotosou and now standard, the give a clearer sound t older "flatwounds."

Scale length *From bridge to nut, this is usually 85cm (34in). Short 75cm (30in) and medium 80cm (32in) scale bases have appeared to ease playing.*

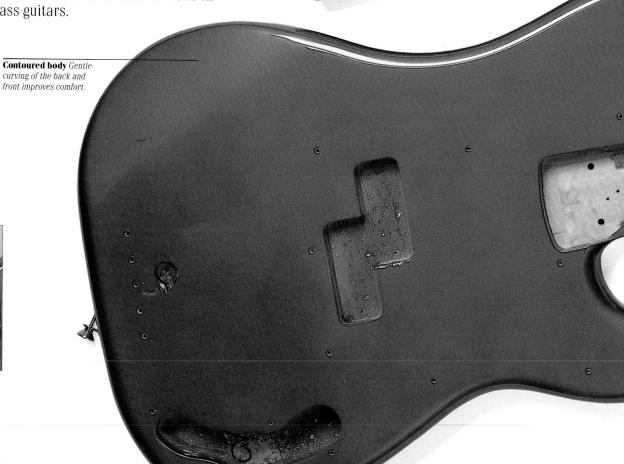

Contoured body *Gentle curving of the back and front improves comfort.*

Through neck
This alternative to the bolt-on style has the neck traveling right through the body.

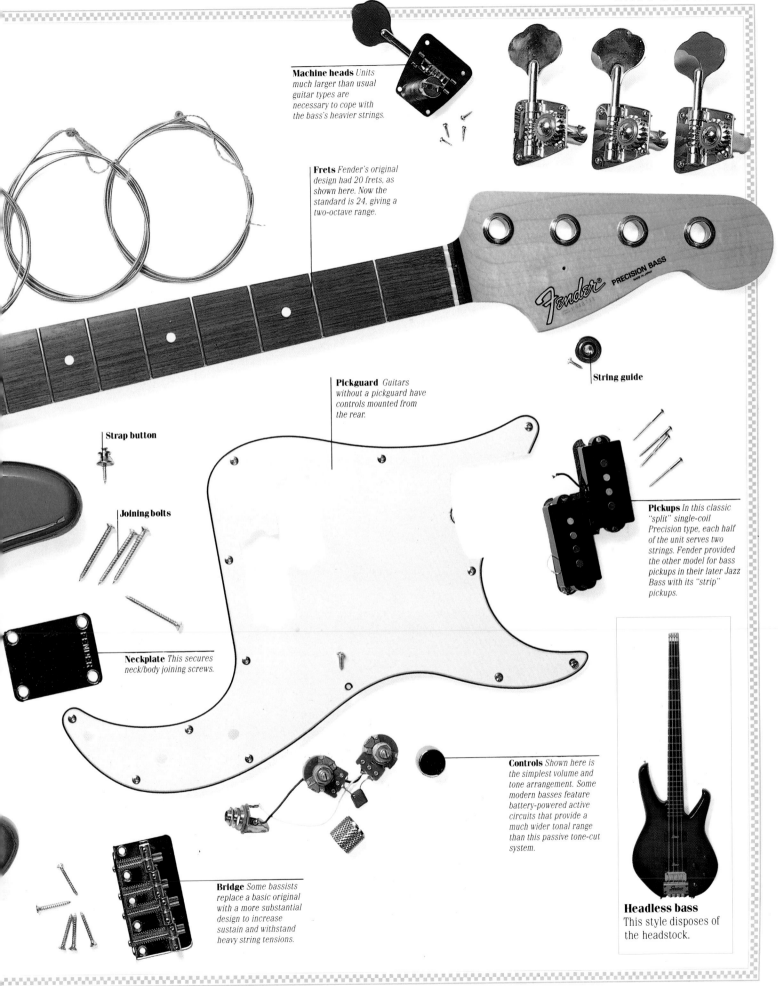

Machine heads *Units much larger than usual guitar types are necessary to cope with the bass's heavier strings.*

Frets *Fender's original design had 20 frets, as shown here. Now the standard is 24, giving a two-octave range.*

String guide

Pickguard *Guitars without a pickguard have controls mounted from the rear.*

Strap button

Joining bolts

Pickups *In this classic "split" single-coil Precision type, each half of the unit serves two strings. Fender provided the other model for bass pickups in their later Jazz Bass with its "strip" pickups.*

Neckplate *This secures neck/body joining screws.*

Controls *Shown here is the simplest volume and tone arrangement. Some modern basses feature battery-powered active circuits that provide a much wider tonal range than this passive tone-cut system.*

Bridge *Some bassists replace a basic original with a more substantial design to increase sustain and withstand heavy string tensions.*

Headless bass
This style disposes of the headstock.

THE FENDER PRECISION

In 1950, Leo Fender and his colleagues had been the first to market a solid body electric guitar (see pages 62-63 and 68-69), but they were not content to stop there. A year later, Leo Fender came up with an exciting new idea, the electric bass guitar.

The Fender Precision was launched in 1951. Players were used to the acoustic double bass — a bulky, cumbersome, and often barely audible instrument, referred to by Leo Fender as "the doghouse." He reckoned that bass players would welcome a louder, more portable instrument that offered precise pitching of notes. So in 1951 Fender offered for sale the world's first commercially available fretted electric bass guitar, aptly named the Precision Bass.

Early Precision players included a number of country-and-western musicians, who formed a large part of Fender's clientele at the time. There was also the occasional jazz player, such as Monk Montgomery of the Lionel Hampton Band. The word spread during the 1950s, and by the early 1960s the bass guitar was established as a new and vital component of modern music-making.

BACK AND SIDE
On the earliest Precision Basses, the big Kluson machine heads work like double-bass tuners: the key is turned toward the player to tighten the string. They were eventually replaced by conventionally geared machine heads.

Body *Note this early Precision's slab body. Contouring did not appear until about 1954.*

Bridge cover *This is usually positioned facing backwards, unlike this example.*

Controls *A knob each for volume and tone, mounted on a chrome panel.*

Pickup *Early Precisions had a single "bar"-shaped four-pole pickup under this cover.*

Pickguard *Early Precisions had a black plate covering much of the body.*

Chrome covers
Until the early 1980s Fender basses were supplied with screw-down covers for the bridge and pickup (as 1952, left). They were intended as rests for the player's hand. But players often discarded them, finding the bridge cover especially awkward and obstructive. For this reason, bare screw-holes are common on such models.

Signed Precision
Leo Fender has autographed the headstock of this Fender Precision Bass. The bass guitar itself dates from 1962, but Fender signed it in 1980 for British bassist Dave Pegg, who visited the G&L factory while on tour with Jethro Tull. Pegg is also well known for his playing with Fairport Convention.

Repackaging the classics

The early history of the Fender company is littered with examples of innovation. The fact that Fender got so much right when there were no rules concerning electric instruments is remarkable. But it has meant that Fender has constantly reissued and re-packaged its original ideas, prompted partly by the copy-cat activities of competitors. Contemporary trends in guitar-making have sometimes influenced additions to the range, including the 1980 Precision Bass Special with active circuitry, but such updates have been rare and short-lived.

Fender's bass regeneration program began in 1968 when they brought out a version of the original Precision Bass, in the style of the 1952 example below, which they named the Telecaster Bass (see page 163).

From the early 1980s Fender has produced many reissues of its essential Precision and Jazz Bass designs, both at their USA plant, and at their oriental factories. These "new oldies" are part of Fender's Vintage series.

1957 Precision
Around this time the Precision changed to the look it kept for more than 30 years: wider headstock; controls and socket built into a new pickguard; four bridge saddles, rather than two; and a new two-piece pickup.

Split pickup
The "P" bass unit was introduced in 1957.

1990 Precision Plus
This radically changed Precision has a new body with deeper cutaways and a longer left horn. Two extra frets have been added to the original twenty. Following most competitors, Fender has added a Jazz pickup near the bridge. There is a pickup selector, "Parallel" button, and fine-tuning bridge.

Body This arctic white finish was one of many options, including gunmetal blue, root beer metallic and black pearl burst.

1952 Precision (below left)
The Precision appeared in 1951 and was pure simplicity. Its four strings were tuned EADG, each an octave below the six-string guitar's lowest four strings. The slab-sided body of the original was finished in a natural "blonde," and the 20 frets were set directly into the solid maple bolt-on neck.

String guide A circular item to help keep correct string tension at the nut.

1955 Precision
From about 1954 the Precision was also offered in two-tone sunburst finish. About the same time, a white pickguard was used. Adopted from the Strat was a contouring of the edge of the body, less harsh than the form of the slab-sided original.

THE FENDER JAZZ BASS

As the Fender Precision Bass took a while to win over musicians who were used to the acoustic double bass, it was not until 1960 that Fender's second guitar-styled bass, the Jazz Model, appeared on the market. This instrument gave a greater range of sounds and offered a more tightly proportioned neck. While it has gone on to wide use in many styles of music, the Jazz Bass has, appropriately, been particularly successful with jazz players, such as Jaco Pastorius (see right) in the 1970s, and Marcus Miller, best known for his work in the 1980s with Miles Davis.

While Fender's great popularity with bassists from the 1960s to date has depended largely on the Precision Bass and Jazz Bass, the company has added several bass models to its range through the years. The Coronado (1966-70) was part of Fender's generally unsuccessful attempt to sell hollow-body electrics, while the Mustang (1966-81) brought the option of short-scale basses. The Telecaster Bass (1968-79) was a revamp of the original Precision and the Musicmaster Bass (1971-82) covered the budget market. The HM Bass (1989) is a kind of three-pickup Jazz Bass.

Jaco Pastorius
This was the player who did most to popularize the fretless electric bass, primarily within the group Weather Report.

1990 Fretless Jazz Bass (left)
While Jaco Pastorius had to remove the frets from his Jazz Bass himself, many makers now offer fretless alternatives to their normal fretted models, like this fretless Fender Japan Jazz.

Pickups *The two single-coil "bar" types each have eight polepieces.*

String mutes *Four screw holes indicate removal of the string mutes.*

Controls *The top of each "stacked" knob controls volume, the outer ring, tone. This layout was discontinued in 1961.*

1961 Jazz Bass
This was Fender's second bass model, introduced in 1960. The offset shape of the Jazz's body is akin to that of Fender's contemporary guitar, the Jazzmaster (see page 76). It also differed from the earlier Precision Bass, with a neck tapering heavily toward the nut, and two separate pickups, giving a deeper sound.

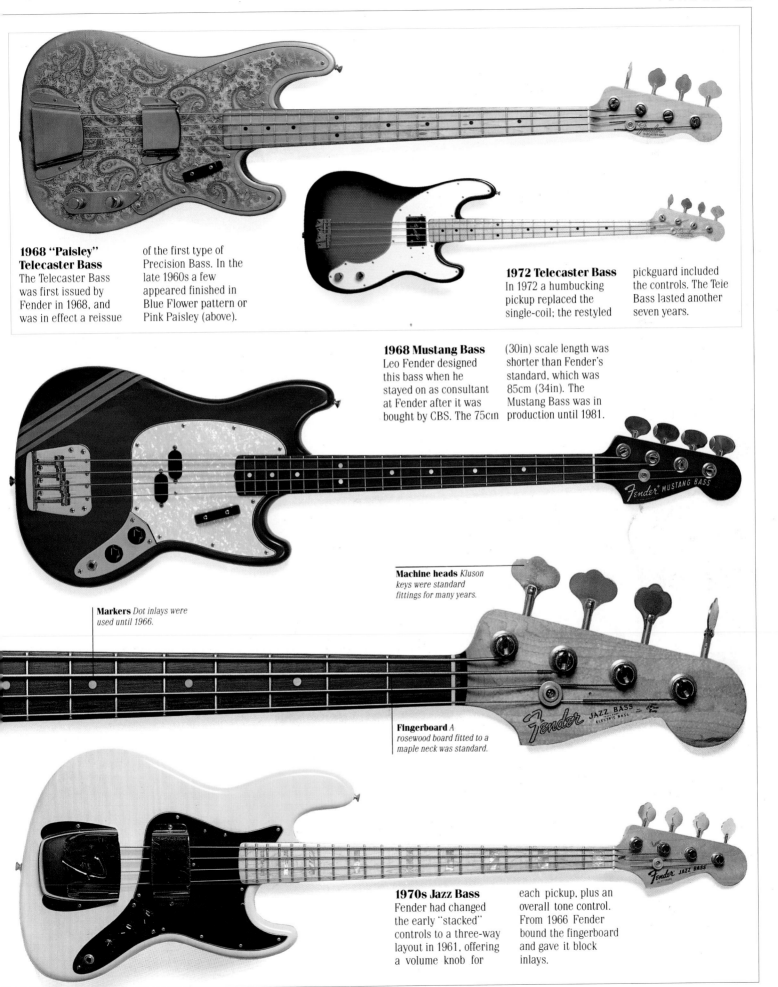

1968 "Paisley" Telecaster Bass
The Telecaster Bass was first issued by Fender in 1968, and was in effect a reissue of the first type of Precision Bass. In the late 1960s a few appeared finished in Blue Flower pattern or Pink Paisley (above).

1972 Telecaster Bass
In 1972 a humbucking pickup replaced the single-coil; the restyled pickguard included the controls. The Tele Bass lasted another seven years.

1968 Mustang Bass
Leo Fender designed this bass when he stayed on as consultant at Fender after it was bought by CBS. The 75cm (30in) scale length was shorter than Fender's standard, which was 85cm (34in). The Mustang Bass was in production until 1981.

Machine heads *Kluson keys were standard fittings for many years.*

Markers *Dot inlays were used until 1966.*

Fingerboard *A rosewood board fitted to a maple neck was standard.*

1970s Jazz Bass
Fender had changed the early "stacked" controls to a three-way layout in 1961, offering a volume knob for each pickup, plus an overall tone control. From 1966 Fender bound the fingerboard and gave it block inlays.

RICKENBACKER

When Rickenbacker launched its first bass guitar in 1957, the instrument had still only been in existence for six years. But the Californian company's offering to bass players was as idiosyncratic as any of its distinctive six-string electrics. The 4000 model had a long-horned body unlike any other bass guitar before; this and the harmoniously curved headstock set the classic Ricky bass style that the company has followed with only occasional variations ever since.

The simple single-pickup, two-control 4000 model lasted until 1984. But by far the most popular version of the Rickenbacker bass is the twin-pickup 4001 model (which first appeared in 1961) and its many descendants such as the current model 4003. Two British players in separate decades – Paul McCartney in the 1960s and Chris Squire in the 1970s – helped to establish Rickenbacker's popularity with bass players. Rickenbacker made special export versions to cater to the British market.

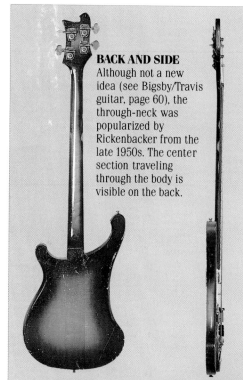

BACK AND SIDE
Although not a new idea (see Bigsby/Travis guitar, page 60), the through-neck was popularized by Rickenbacker from the late 1950s. The center section traveling through the body is visible on the back.

Rush
The Canadian group's bassist Geddy Lee is seen here in concert using Rickenbacker's bass-and-guitar twin-neck, the 4080. This was Rickenbacker's first production twin-neck guitar, combining six-string and four-string necks. It was launched in 1975.

Through-neck *The mahogany neck section travels right through the body.*

Pickup *This is the pre-1970s "horseshoe" type with split cover.*

Controls *A volume and tone control per pickup, plus pickup selector.*

Mute *When activated this "muffles" the sound.*

Body *Maple "wings" are glued to the mahogany through-neck.*

1964 4001S (above)
This model earned Rickenbacker great fame among bass players when it was used by Paul McCartney in the 1960s and later, and by Chris Squire of Yes in the 1970s. Originally designed as an export-only version of Rickenbacker's 4001 model differs from the 4001 in its dot fingerboard markers and the lack of binding.

Tailpiece *The 4005s were the only basses to use the R-for-Rickenbacker unit.*

1978 4005
Rickenbacker's first hollow-body bass (1965-84) followed the design of its non-

solid six-string electrics (see page 148). The late 1960s UK export-only version was called the 3261.

Inlays *The 4003S model is similar, but has dot markers rather than these "triangle" types.*

Catalogs
The 1968 US catalog (below) shows the line-up of 4000, 4001 and 4005 basses, with a chart detailing their features. The 1964 UK catalog (top), published by the importer Rose-Morris & Co, includes the model 1999 bass (second from right), the export version of the 4001S.

1990 4003 (above)
This model was launched in 1979, replacing the 4001 in 1986. Like the 4001 it features deluxe binding and "triangle" fingerboard markers.

Headstock *Note how the shape echoes that of the distinctive body.*

Fingerboard *Dot position markers are mounted on a 20-fret rosewood board.*

Body *4001 models are bound here.*

Pickup *The "single cover" style was introduced in the 1970s.*

Fingerboard *The 4001 has "triangle" markers.*

1973 4001
The company added this two-pickup model in 1961, four years after Rickenbacker's

first bass, the 4000. An even more deluxe version, the limited edition 4002, appeared in 1981.

GIBSON

Gibson has never been as successful with its bass guitars as with other guitar types. In the 1950s and 1960s, Fender was the undisputed leading maker for basses. Players have regularly marked Gibsons down as "must try harder" basses. Until the mid-1970s this was usually due to the typical combination of humbucking pickups and short scale-length that Gibson used. Some bassists found these features respectively too thick-sounding and too fiddly.

Other musicians made strengths from these apparent weaknesses, notably in the 1960s when Cream's Jack Bruce used the Gibson EB3's murky sound to great effect. And the short scale-length of many early Gibson bass designs has meant that guitarists who double on bass and guitar usually find them easier to use. Gibson issued some rather more modern designs in the mid-1970s and 1980s. Later in the 1980s they bought the innovative bass company Steinberger and the small Tobias operation. Gibson's own bass range continues in a modest way.

1970s Les Paul Triumph Bass
This model replaced the Les Paul Professional Bass (1970-71), which had control knobs mounted separately from a smaller panel. The Triumph was launched in 1971, its large control panel containing volume and tone knobs, plus phase, tone, and high/low impedance switching. The model lasted until 1979.

Pickups *This model IV has two; model II had one. The original chrome hand-rests are missing.*

Construction *In the same way as the early Firebird guitars, the first series of T'bird basses was made with an extended neck which went right through the body. This had "wings" added each side to complete the overall body shape.*

Controls *Volume per pickup, plus tone. The knobs are not the originals.*

Gibson catalogs
The 1972 item (far right), rather late for psychedelia, contains details of the solid EB bass series. The spread from the 1983 catalog (right) features the Victory Bass, launched two years earlier.

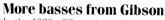

More basses from Gibson
In the 1960s Gibson issued a six-string bass, the EB6 (with solid or hollow body), but many basses were just four-string versions of guitar models, such as the Signature semi of 1973, RD basses of 1977, or Victory Bass of 1981. Originality had been reinstated in the 1970s when Gibson brought out a range of new-design basses, the Grabber, Ripper, and G3, and in the late 1980s with the mini-body 20/20 designed by Ned Steinberger.

1971 EB3

Gibson's third bass appeared in 1961, an SG-style solid that was effectively a top-of-the-line version of the EBO, with a volume and tone control for each of the two pickups. The extra bridge pickup gave it a brighter sound. The EB3 also featured a large four-position rotary control to select preset tonal varieties. It stayed in Gibson's catalogue until dropped in the late 1970s.

Headstock *This slotted type was used in the early 1970s, but Gibson soon reverted to the normal solid style.*

Scale-length

The solid EB basses are notable for their short scale-length of 76cm (30$\frac{1}{2}$in). A few bassists find this easier to play, but tone is less defined. Long-scale "L" versions of EB basses, at 88cm (34$\frac{1}{2}$in) length, appeared in the 1970s.

1963 EBOF

The EBO was Gibson's second solid bass, issued in 1959 with a twin-cutaway slab body, like a contemporary Les Paul Junior. It changed to this SG shape in the early 1960s, keeping the single pickup and simple volume and tone controls. The EBOF version pictured, made for a short time around 1963, has a built-in "fuzztone" distortion unit. The EBO finished production in the early 1970s.

Fuzztone *The "in/out" switch turns the distortion circuit on and off, while the knobs control its intensity.*

Headstock *This has back-facing "banjo" machine heads.*

1956 EB1

Gibson's Electric Bass, or EB1¡ was the company's first bass guitar. The traditional shape led to its "violin bass" nickname (see also Hofner, page 170). It even came with a base spike to allow it to be played upright. It was made from 1953 to 1958, and reissued in 1969.

Body *The body is made of solid mahogany, with painted "f-hole."*

Controls *The large humbucking pickup fed a single volume and tone.*

Neck *Unlike most Gibson basses of the time, the T'bird had a long scale.*

Body *A cherry finish was officially offered from 1965. EB2s also come in sunburst, natural, walnut and burgundy.*

Headstock *All the reverse-body T'birds, including the reissues in 1976 (Bicentennial) and 1988, have this "turned up" headstock. Non-reverse T'birds have a more Fender-like unit.*

1964 Thunderbird IV

The T'bird pictured is now owned by John Entwistle, and was his main stage and studio bass in The Who from 1972 to 1976. Gibson's most distinctive bass was launched in 1963, a bass version of the Firebird. Until 1965 it featured the so-called "reverse" body styling, and moved to a "non-reverse" body from 1965 until 1969.

1967 EB2

This bass appeared in 1958 alongside the ES335 guitar, the first instruments to feature semi-solid construction. A block of wood inside the hollow body cut feedback. The single-pickup EB2 was withdrawn in 1961, but the model reappeared in 1965 in one- or two-pickup versions.

AMERICAN GALLERY

It is hardly surprising that the bass guitar should flourish so readily in the country where it was invented. Although Leo Fender got so much right with his original Precision Bass in the early 1950s, the later improvements to the bass guitar that have occurred in the succeeding decades have tended to come from the United States.

Some came from Fender himself. For example, his Music Man StingRay Bass, which remains a firm favorite with players, did much to persuade bassists that active electronics were effective and useful. The idea is to have a small battery-powered pre-amplifier on board the bass, which boosts the output and allows a much wider degree of tonal variation.

Alembic had earlier offered such circuits, but in its limited production runs of very expensive instruments. It was the Alembic company, in the mid-1970s, that finally established the idea of a guitar-maker specializing in bass guitars. This coincided with a realization by players that new sounds and new musical directions could free the bass guitar from its role as backing instrument, and at last give the instrument a new and more distinctive voice.

1990 Jackson Bass
Best known for its introduction of the "superstrat" six-string guitar. Jackson also offers a line of basses, made with maple center-block and poplar sides. This Custom Shop model has a graphic finish, ebony fingerboard with "shark-fin" inlays, and bound neck and head.

Finish *This spaceship design is typical of Jackson's graphic work.*

1990 M V Pedulla MVP4
The current Pedulla company, based in Massachusetts, was formed in the late 1970s by Michael Vincent Pedulla and his brother Ted. Having started with acoustics and a few electrics, they hit on a good bass design and now specialize in basses. The long sculpted horns and Bartolini pickups are typical, and this Custom has a beautiful "flamed" maple body.

1990 Zon Legacy Elite (left)
This Californian company is named after founder Joseph M. Zon, and specializes in making graphite-necked bass guitars. The Legacy Elite comes with Bartolini humbuckers, a distinctive body shape and, in common with many modern basses, Schaller hardware from Germany.

Inlay *The oval designs are typical of Alembic's fingerboard markers.*

1989 Alembic Mark King Signature
Alembic was the first specialist bass maker. Their 1970s basses introduced active electronics, the use of exotic woods, brass hardware and carbon-fiber necks. Alembic was started in the 1960s in California by Ron Wickersham, sharing a workshop with the Grateful Dead. This Mark King model, a typical Alembic design, was launched in 1989.

Body *This is made from cocobolo, an exotic wood which comes mainly from Nicaragua and Costa Rica.*

Through-neck *Alembic was among the first to use this type of design.*

Controls *These consist of volume, two tones, and a pickup balance, plus two tonal variation switches.*

Headstock *Music Man's logo has two guitarists forming a large M.*

1970s Music Man StingRay Bass

After selling Fender to CBS in 1965, Leo Fender designed instruments for the Music Man company, set up by ex-Fender men in 1972. An early product was the StingRay Bass, which did much to popularize active electronics and furthered Leo Fender's already glowing reputation among bassists. Music Man was acquired by the Ernie Ball company in 1984. The still popular StingRay Bass continues.

Body *A choice of finishes offered natural, sunburst, walnut, black or white.*

Pickguard *This elegant shape is a trademark of the StingRay.*

Pickup *The StingRay has a large humbucker. Music Man's Sabre bass features two pickups.*

Ampeg Basses

The Ampeg company are best known for their amplifiers, and in particular their valve bass-amps. Not so well known are their bass guitars. These began in the early 1960s with an upright electric bass. In the middle of the decade the New Jersey-based company produced some strange looking bass guitars, including in 1965 one of the earliest fretless basses, the AUB1. From 1969 to 1971 Ampeg teamed up with guitar designer and repairer Dan Armstrong to make so-called "see-through" clear plastic guitars and basses.

Fingerboard *It has 24 frets, an unusually large complement for this period.*

Body *A very small number of these guitars were made in black plastic.*

Pickguard *Made from Formica, a material rarely used on guitars.*

Pickup *The rubbery housing is partly broken away on this example.*

1970 Ampeg Dan Armstrong (left)

Dan Armstrong, the designer of this bass and its accompanying six-string electric, used Lucite, or clear plastic, for the bodies of his peculiar instruments in an attempt to improve sustain. However, there is no doubting the visual impact of these short-lived guitars (1970-71). Armstrong resurfaced in 1990 with a design for the oriental Westone company.

1969 Ampeg Bass

Ampeg's unusual bass guitars with large scrolled headstocks first appeared in 1965. Early models had bridge-mounted transducers, but later models (1968-69) had conventional pickups. The Ampeg bass shown may have had some modifications.

Fretless neck *These Ampegs were among the first fretless basses.*

f-holes *These are cut right through the "burnished" body.*

Spector

This flyer from New York bass-maker Spector showed their NS range.

More American bass-makers

While we have shown here guitars from some of the better-known bass-builders in the USA, there are many other specialist makers throughout the country. As we have seen, it was Alembic who made instrument makers aware that bassists were different from guitarists, and could be served by companies specializing in bass guitars.

Some of these small specialists have been absorbed into bigger companies, such as Spector (see left), started in the 1970s by Stuart Spector and at one stage marketed by Kramer, and the California-based maker Tobias, begun in 1978 by Mike Tobias and bought by Gibson in 1990.

The big US guitar companies usually offer a line of bass "versions" of six-string guitars. Honorable exceptions include G&L, where the bass guitar's inventor Leo Fender continues to come up with fresh-looking basses, and Peavey, which in the late 1980s was active in attracting bassists to endorse a varied range of new models.

EUROPEAN GALLERY

Some European companies and workshops have followed the lead of the US Alembic set-up in establishing the idea that makers can specialize in building bass guitars. These makers nearly always treat the bass guitar as an individual instrument, not merely a four-string version of the six-string electric guitar.

For instance, bass-maker Wal, working in southern England, designed their Custom bass (opposite) with little reference to the six-string guitar. Its co-designers Pete Stevens and the late Ian Waller decided to develop a bass as a bass and, as they once described it, "not to do as most manufacturers do: make a six-stringed instrument, and then put a long neck on it and call it a bass."

This attitude reflects that of the inventor of the bass guitar, Leo Fender, who chose to design the bass guitar as a new instrument in its own right. Of course, the electric bass leans on general six-string guitar design, but in detail the two are quite separate. The finest bass-makers worldwide know this well.

1968 Vox Stinger IV
This Italian-made Vox succeeded their original British-built Wyman Bass. There was also an active version, called the Constellation IV. Note the very narrow neck and huge headstock.

1989 Jaydee Mark King
Built by UK maker John Diggins, this model was named for Level 42 bassist Mark King, who was an early user of a Jaydee. Note the wooden pickup covers and three-pin socket for studio use.

SIDE AND BACK
Note the pleasant grain to the wood used for the back, the strap button at the body/neck joint, and the machine heads on two strips. The Beatles' set-list can be seen on the side view.

Paul McCartney

The Beatles' bassist bought his first Hofner "Violin Bass" in Hamburg, probably at the end of 1960. It had a long Hofner logo going down the headstock and the two pickups were close together. It was used on many of the Beatles' live performances. The bass pictured below was given to Paul by Hofner at the Beatles' Royal Variety Show performance in London in November 1963. This Hofner was also used in the studio, where it later competed with Paul's Rickenbacker 4001 bass. However, McCartney can be seen using it during the Beatles' 1969 "roof-top concert" in the film *Let It Be*. It was put into service again by Paul for his 1990 World Tour.

Fingerboard *Hofner changed to a bound fingerboard from 1965.*

1962 Hofner 500/1 (above right)
A bass belonging to Paul McCartney still with a 1966 Beatles set-list taped to the side. This German bass model appeared in 1956 and is still made, although its popularity peaked in the 1960s.

1989 Warwick Thumb Bass (below)
In 1982 Hans Peter Wilfer started the Warwick company in Germany. The Thumb Bass (launched 1985) typifies Warwick's distinctive bodies of attractive natural-finish woods. Neck and body are bubinga; fingerboard and neck stripes are wenge. Other models include Streamer (1984), Buzzard (1986), and Dolphin (1989).

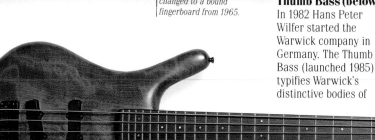

1990 Wal Custom
London repairer Ian Waller teamed up with Pete Stevens in the mid-1970s to design the Wal Custom, with its unusual leather pickguard. The company became Electric Wood in 1978. The current Custom appeared in 1980. This is a recent fretless example.

1963 Burns Bison Bass
The huge Bison (1962-64) was the finest bass from UK company Burns. It had a sycamore body, low impedance circuitry and, unusually for a bass, three pickups. Black was the standard finish.

Beatles set-list
Shown in more detail, from the model pictured below, this dates from 1966.

Framus catalog
This 1966 item shows the Framus Star Basses.

OTHER EUROPEAN BASS GUITARS
Rolling Stones bassist Bill Wyman was a busy endorser of basses in the 1960s. He lent his name to the German Framus company's Star Bass (see catalog page, left), and also endorsed the Vox Wyman Bass from the UK.

Britain's bass makers have been successful in recent years. In the 1970s Hayman made popular semi-pro basses, their 4040 model evolving into the Shergold Marathon bass. In the 1980s, good small makers like Overwater, Nightingale and Goodfellow appeared, while in 1990 Status, known for their headless basses (see page 175), issued their first bass with a headstock, the Matrix model.

Pickups *These metal-covered units were used between 1961 and 1964.*

Body *Despite the lack of soundholes, the body of the so-called "Violin Bass" (model 500/1) is hollow.*

Controls *These incorporate two volumes, plus three slide-switches offering different tones.*

ORIENTAL GALLERY

I t was around the turn of the 1960s and the early 1970s that various Japanese manufacturers established themselves as producers of copies of American guitars, basses included. The earliest examples were poor, and the expression "Japanese copy" quickly became derogatory.

Most of these early Japanese copyists chose the obviously successful American models. Fender's Precision and Jazz basses were by far the most common target.

Gradually, the Japanese began to get better and better at copying, and slowly their reputation improved. By the middle of the 1970s some Japanese makers had begun to produce their own designs, rather than strict copies, although the influence was still coming from American basses. A good example is the way in which Japanese makers such as Aria popularized the through-neck design feature in the late 1970s, which had been introduced by specialist US bass makers like Alembic.

The 1980s saw many Japanese and US companies moving their production bases into other oriental countries, in common with six-string manufacturing, guided principally by cheaper labor costs. Budget and mid-price basses from the East now dominate the market, and these sources offer some strong competition further up-market as well.

Headstock *This is faced with a colored finish matching the body.*

1990 Aria MAB40
This active bass is from Aria's Korean-made Magna series. It features probably the most popular bass pickup configuration of the last few years. The split unit at the front is based on Fender's Precision type, while the "bar" pickup at the back comes from the Fender Jazz Bass design.

Woods *The alder body is bolted to a maple neck with rosewood board.*

Fingerboard *This is rosewood, with 24 frets, and dot markers.*

1989 Charvel 1B Bass
Since the mid-1980s, Charvel has been the brandname used by the US Jackson company for guitars manufactured in Japan. This simple, straightforward bass has a single split pickup. The headstock is of the pointed "droopy" design used on most Jackson guitars.

1990 Ibanez
This Japanese instrument bears the Soundgear brand, used by Ibanez for up-market basses. The heavily sculpted body and bright metallic finish is typical of Ibanez's higher-priced six-string guitar lines of the late 1980s. The ebony fingerboard is another sign of quality.

Pickup *This is a humbucking type of Aria's own design.*

1980s Aria SB1000 (left)
The SB1000 has been a long-standing and successful bass for Aria. The lighter wood of the through-neck visible on the body is testament to its late 1970s design. Aria is the brandname used by the Arai company of Japan. Until 1987 many of their guitars were made at the Matsumoku factory in Japan; now they are produced in Korea as well as Japan.

Body *This is made from an exotic wood called sen, and the through-neck is of a maple/walnut laminate.*

Controls *Two volumes and a tone control govern the active circuit.*

Yamaha catalog
This page from a 1983 catalog features Yamaha's BB2000 bass. The pictures at the top show the through-neck.

1987 Yamaha BB5000

This bass is from Yamaha's Taiwan-made BB series of the mid and late 1980s. The 5000 did much to popularize the use of five-string basses, and like the Music Man (see page 177) it places the fifth machine head on the opposite side of the headstock to the normal four. The up-market look of the gold-plated hardware is balanced by the simple passive controls.

1990 Yamaha TRB5P (right)

Compare this to the five-string on the left, and the changes made to the design of such basses becomes apparent. The neck is less narrow than usual, meaning wider string spacing. Note also the chamfered horns, fashionable at this time. It also comes in four- and six-string bass versions, and like all modern Yamahas is made in Taiwan.

Truss rod cover *This bears the model number. The 1A was active; the 1 a normal "passive" type.*

Neck *This has a rosewood fingerboard with unfussy dot inlays and 22 frets.*

1986 Westone Thunder 1A Bass

The Japanese Matsumoku company had been making guitars since the 1960s, putting the brandnames of customers like Aria, Epiphone and Vantage on the headstocks. Their Thunder Bass was a very successful, medium-priced, simple instrument, seen here in its active version. Matsumoku ceased Japanese production in 1987, and the Westone name was revived in Korea.

Other oriental basses

Guitars made in the East sometimes end up with different names on the headstocks of otherwise identical instruments. This is because some manufacturers there often produce guitars and basses for a number of different customers throughout the world. Each of these customers will almost certainly want their own logo to appear on the resulting instrument.

With that fact in mind, you are likely to see a large number of bass guitars made in the Orient. These are principally from Japan and Korea, and to a lesser extent from Taiwan, where the biggest single maker is Yamaha. Japanese basses tend to be the most expensive. While most companies which originally produced guitars there have moved further afield in search of cheaper costs, brands such as ESP, Fernandes and Tokai were still being made in Japan in 1990.

By far the most prolific country manufacturing guitars and basses in this part of the world is Korea. The brands used on the basses pouring from its factories have included Washburn (since the late 1980s), Squier (since 1987), Epiphone (since 1986), Hohner, Charvette, Cort, Starforce, Marlin, Hondo, Columbus, Tanglewood, and Fenix.

Washburn catalog
This 1980 brochure page shows two versions of the Washburn Stage B20-II.

Body *Maple was used under solid colors, and an ash/maple/walnut laminate for a natural finish.*

Controls *A volume, and a tone control each for active and passive modes.*

Bridge *The simple unit is adjustable for height and length.*

HEADLESS BASSES

The Steinberger Bass, which appeared in the early 1980s, completely revised makers' ideas about what a bass guitar should look like, and how it should be made. Tiny and without a headstock, it was made from what has become known generally as "graphite." To be more precise, the material that Steinberger popularized is a molded epoxy resin strengthened by carbon and glass fibers. On instruments such as Status basses the carbon-fiber weave within the resin is clearly visible.

The material is claimed to have twice the density and ten times the stiffness of wood, and to be stronger and lighter than steel. This leads to a clean, brilliant tone for guitars, virtually eliminating "dead-spots" (notes that do not ring true) and any muddiness in the tone. The headstock was removed primarily for balance and tuning convenience, and the tuning gears were moved to the body.

The novelty of the tiny body faded, but the idea of non-wood materials and the headless neck certainly has lasted, making Ned Steinberger the second most important name in the history of the bass guitar, after Leo Fender.

Tuning clamp *In place, it offers normal tuning. Flicked off, it moves the low E down to low D.*

1989 Kubicki Factor
This Californian-made bass appeared in 1985. There is a "headstock," but it exists so that an unusual flick-switch can offer an optional extra two frets below the open E of the lowest string. Tuners are at the bridge, and the three controls are a six-position tonal selector, stacked volume/pickup-pan, and stacked bass/treble. The Kubicki company was bought by Fender in the 1980s.

Tuners *There are four high-ratio direct gears.*

Anchor plate *This pivots at the rear, holding the bass in any position.*

Materials *The one-piece neck/body is made from molded reinforced epoxy resin.*

Controls *A volume per pickup, plus single tone.*

SIDE AND BACK
Note the pivot screw for the anchor plate, and the jack socket located on the back.

Steinberger's story
Ned Steinberger was an industrial engineer who worked for Spector, a New York bass-making firm, in the late 1970s. After leaving, he experimented for three years, finally completing his Steinberger Bass design in 1980. Ned had concluded that the all-important constituent of an electric bass is the neck, and that a headstock is likely to cause unwanted changes to the resulting bass's sound. He also reckoned that a guitar's solidity is the key to its sustain and clarity, and so chose to use fiber-reinforced epoxy resin for his Bass.

In the late 1980s Steinberger was bought by Gibson, who kept it running as an independent company.

1985 Westone Rail
This peculiar Japanese headless bass has a novel sliding pickup. The central body block housing the pickup can be moved back and forth on the chrome "rails" after the securing screw on the side is loosened. Despite its modern appearance, the Rail bass is made of wood, with neck bolted to body. It is without active pickups.

Pickup *The unit can be slid up and down the rails, to provide different tones.*

1990 Hohner Jack Bass
This Korean-made all-maple headless bass was launched in the late 1980s and is clearly modeled on the British Status design (see below). The hardware is licensed from Steinberger and the pickups are EMG Selects, designed by the successful US company and made in Korea.

1980s Steinberger XM2
Gradually during the mid-1980s the novelty of the mini-bodied headless bass began to fade. Even the inventor of the instrument, Steinberger, produced models like this XM2 with a relatively conventional body shape. The material is more conventional, too – the XM2's body is made from maple.

Steinberger TransTrem (above)
This special unit has a slotted ratchet protruding from the pivoted bridge. Moved with the arm, it positions the bridge at preset angles, instantly changing the length and therefore the pitch of all the strings.

Clamp *Strings are locked into place just above the nut.*

Fingerboard *This has 24 metal frets and is made from phenolic fiber.*

Wooden "wings" *The cocobolo front of this Series II has a splendid "curl" to the grain.*

1983 Steinberger Bass
The radical redesign of the bass guitar was launched in 1982. It has no headstock; the tuners are on the body. Pickups have built-in pre-amps. Made almost entirely from graphite, the Steinberger weighs 3.6kg (8lb), about 450g (1lb) less than a Fender Precision. It inspired many "headless" basses and guitars.

Through-neck *The central neck section is made from carbon-fiber reinforced resin.*

1990 Status Series II
Status basses were the first British guitars to be made from graphite. Maker Rob Green started with the Series II bass in 1983, combining graphite and wood. Success has led to such models as the all-graphite 2000 and resin-composite-bodied 4000.

MULTI-STRINGED BASSES

The five-string bass is now an established instrument in its own right. In the early 1990s, demand for the five-string led one American specialist bass maker to produce around 60 per cent of his basses as five-string models.

Despite Fender's early use of extra strings with their Bass V and Bass VI instruments (from 1965 and 1962 respectively), the multi-string bass revolution began in the early 1980s when touring bassists found themselves having to reproduce low-pitched bass-synth sounds from recordings.

Unlike the Fender V's extra high C-string, the 1980s five came with an additional low B to supply those extra deep notes (although a few companies now offer high C as a fifth-string option again). Early attempts crowded five strings into the space originally intended for four, but later models sensibly spaced the strings out across a wider neck, easing the player's right-hand technique.

The six-string bass, too, has changed radically from Fender's first offering. That and similar 1960s guitars shown here were simply six-string guitars tuned down an octave. Later types, again developed in the 1980s, added an extra high string (usually tuned to C) as well as the low B of the five-string. Makers also eventually adopted a wide string-spacing for six-string basses, resulting in some instruments with enormously wide necks.

Machine heads *Different-sized pegs ease access to the eight tuners.*

Neck *The scale length is a medium 80cm (32in).*

Fingerboard *This is made from ebony, and has abalone inlays.*

Body *The ash top and back are set on a mahogany core.*

1979 Ibanez MC 980
On this eight-string bass the usual four strings are paired. The second string is pitched an octave above the normally tuned string. Played with a plectrum, this produces a full sound. Eight-string basses are rarely seen, though makers have included Hagstrom and Rickenbacker. The MC980 was one of two late 1970s eight-string models from Ibanez.

Controls *Volume and tone; active on/off; active treble and bass; pickup selector.*

Bridge *A specially machined brass unit with eight saddles.*

Body *The "wings" are made from exotic wood – for example, shedua, walnut or koa – on a mahogany core.*

Through-neck *This is a five-piece laminate of maple and rosewood.*

Controls *Volume; active tone; pickup balance.*

1989 Ken Smith BT Custom Five
Ken Smith Basses started in 1981 in New York, and did much to popularize the idea of five- and six-string basses. Smith makes two ranges, the BT and the cheaper Burner, both in four-, five-, and six-string versions.

1962 Fender Bass VI
Only the earliest of Fender's six-string basses had this type of pickup and three selector switches. The 1963 version, with Jaguar-style pickups and four switches, lasted until 1975.

1980 Shergold Modulator Six-string Bass
Like the Fender, this was another guitar tuned down an octave, this one British. A slot in the Modulator's body accepted changeable modules to create different sounds.

1989 Tune Six-string Bass
This Japanese model represents the modern six-string bass. It is tuned like a bass guitar with an extra-low and an extra-high string, and the strings are widely spaced as on a four-string bass.

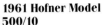

1961 Hofner Model 500/10
This is typical of the first generation of six-string basses, in that it is tuned like a normal guitar, although an octave lower, and has narrow string-spacing. This German electric acoustic, made by Hofner, was a six-string version of the normal Model 500/5 electric acoustic bass, which had been introduced a few years earlier.

Finish *Both this six-string bass and the four-string version came in brown sunburst or natural.*

Pickups *Hofner basses of this period have two close units.*

Pickguard *Some units from this period are made from clear plastic.*

Controls *This is Hofner's classic 1960s "Flick-action" set-up. One knob cap is missing.*

More than four
The idea of five- and six-string basses was championed by small New York makers such as Carl Thompson, Ken Smith, and Vinnie Fodera. Bassist Anthony Jackson, who has played on records by Paul Simon and others, was among the first to realize the potential of the multi-string bass. In 1974 Carl Thompson built Jackson his first six-string bass. Vinnie Fodera, working at Ken Smith Basses in the early 1980s, built other six-strings for Jackson. Vinnie formed his own Fodera company in 1983, which now markets Jackson's "Contrabass." By 1985 most bass makers offered five-string options, some also six-string models.

Screw holes *Those here and at the bridge indicate removed covers.*

1970 Fender Bass V (above)
Unlike the early six-string basses, this five-string, launched by Fender in 1965, has normal bass string-spacing. The extra string was a high C, whereas most modern five-string basses opt for a low B.

Fingerboard *This is ebony, with pearl inlay.*

Nut *This brass unit is scalloped between the string slots.*

Fingerboard *This is rosewood; harder ebony is usually used.*

1989 Ernie Ball Music Man StingRay 5 (left)
There is a stylish simplicity to this fretless five-string.

UNUSUAL BASS GUITARS

There was a time when a bass guitar was a bass guitar: a simple, straightforward instrument that did its job, and little more. But during the past 20 years bass players have pushed their instruments further and established a far more important role for the bass in modern music. This has led far-sighted bassists to seek better, more versatile instruments, which in turn has meant that bass-makers have had to try that much harder.

A handful of makers took the opportunity to see just how far they could push the bass and its new-found freedom – and here we show a number of examples, by no means all of them successful. Some makers are attempting to take the bass guitar back a step to an acoustic life that it never really had; others are trying to forge links between the bass and the computerized recording systems of the 1990s; while a fanciful few want to take the bass right out into uncharted territory.

1990 Washburn AB40

Launched in 1989, this Japanese bass has a shallow acoustic body with a piezoelectric pickup mounted in the bridge. Washburn were among the first to market what is, in effect, a bass equivalent of the thinline electro-acoustic guitar (see page 46). A cheaper Korean-made version, the AB20, was also offered.

Fingerboard *This is made from rosewood that has been "ebonized," in other words stained to a darker color.*

Top *This is made from spruce; back and sides are maple.*

Soundholes *Washburn describe these as acoustically placed sound slots, saying they accentuate frequencies to give "a warm, woody tone."*

Bridge *Each saddle has a piezoelectric pickup.*

1978 Zemaitis Bass (right)

Tony Zemaitis has been a full-time guitar-maker since 1965, based in England. This acoustic bass was specially built for Pink Floyd's David Gilmour in 1978. Zemaitis is well known for his acoustic guitars and for his distinctive metal-front solids, as used by Ron Wood of the Rolling Stones.

Truss-rod cover *This is engraved with owner David Gilmour's name.*

Fingerboard *The ebony board is fretless, with inlaid fret markers.*

Controls *Volume, plus active treble and bass.*

Body *Maple back and sides support a spruce top.*

Label *Zemaitis' signed and dated label is visible through the "heart" soundhole.*

Bridge *This and the separate tailpiece below are made from ebony.*

1970s Eko BA4NPE

The soundhole of this acoustic bass guitar from Italian maker Eko bears some signs of influence from the Maccaferri guitars of the 1930s (see page 42). This model was launched in the late 1970s, offered in fretted or, as here, fretless versions (N = no frets). This model also has piezoelectric pickups (PE) in the bridge to allow amplification as well as acoustic use.

Top *This is made from spruce, while the back and sides are mahogany.*

Bar *Holds neck rigid for cleaner synth signals.*

Pickups *Jazz-type pair, plus "hex" synth pickup.*

Controls *These include a knob to adjust the balance between the synth sound and the ordinary bass sound.*

1985 Roland G77 Bass Synthesizer (above)
Roland's second, short-lived bass synth was launched in 1985, matching in looks the 707 guitar version (see page 184). A separate synth control unit completed the set-up.

1982 Roland catalog
This shows Roland's first bass synth (1980-84). The bass "controller" (G33 or 88) fed the GR33B control unit (bottom right).

1989 Wal MIDI Bass (below)
British bass maker Wal built an Australian MIDI Bass system into this instrument. Fret contacts and a special bridge feed information to a control unit that enables the bass to "play" the sounds of an external synthesizer.

Pickups *A normal bass sound can be achieved from these.*

Through-neck *This becomes uncommonly wide at the body end.*

Wal fingerboard
The frets are divided into four. Each section is in effect a separate switch, registering string contact as played.

1984 Vigier Nautilus Arpege Bass (below)
Launched at the end of 1983, this French bass offered a novel system where 19 different control settings could be stored and recalled at the flick of a few switches. Its failure implied that bassists did not need such complexity.

Controls *A huge array gives wide tonal options and storage/recall faciliities.*

Vigier controls
The raised red "window" among the controls shows the player the preset number (1-19) that is being written to or recalled.

1990 Ashbory Bass
This British bass has a tiny body and toughened silicone strings. The bridge's piezoelectric pickup offers a range of sounds, from a passable imitation of a double bass to electric bass tones.

Neck *The Ashbory has a 55cm (22in) scale length, and fretless fingerboard.*

Strings *Made from high-grade toughened silicone, these are dusted with talc for smooth playing.*

Controls *Volume, bass, treble; plus active/ passive switch.*

"Linking a guitar to a synthesizer involves the conversion of every nuance of a player's style into electronic impulses that a synth will recognize quickly and accurately.**"**

BEYOND GUITAR

1989 CASIO PG300 GUITAR SYNTH, courtesy Sensible Music.

BUILT-IN SPECIAL EFFECTS

I t was in the 1960s that special effects and gimmicky sounds for the electric guitar first became available. These came via separate foot-operated pedals offering tone-boosts, distortion, "wah-wah," and so on.

Some makers chose to build effects into the guitar itself, and the more comprehensively equipped versions of these instruments can be considered the forerunners of the guitar synthesizer.

Unfortunately, the amount of wood removed from the bodies of these guitars to make way for the extra electronics adversely affected their natural sustain and tone. Also, while the additional circuitry certainly made the fashionably funny noises, it was invariably at the expense of decent, normal guitar sounds.

The instruments shown here must have seemed good ideas at the time, but they were all short-lived, and provided strong arguments that electronic effects were best kept separate from the guitar.

BACK AND SIDE
The Godwin's removed rear cover plate shows the mass of electronics inside. The guitar was made just before the extreme miniaturization of electronic chips. This is the reason for the large, deep body.

Pickups *Two single-coil units give normal guitar sounds, which are independent of the organ section.*

Controls *13 knobs and 19 switches are almost certainly record numbers for a guitar.*

Headstock *Kay's diamond-shaped inlay resembles that used by Gibson.*

Controls *Three knobs and five switches adjust the effects sent either to amp or to headphones.*

Headstock *Only the basic model bore the Danelectro brandname on the headstock.*

Kay LP Synth
Made in Korea in the early 1980s, this cheap guitar was loosely based on the Gibson Les Paul Recording model. However, unlike the Gibson, it had four built-in, battery-powered effects: tremolo; distortion; repeat; and "whirlwind."

Guyatone "Rhythm Guitar"
This Fender-influenced Japanese guitar was made in the early 1970s. It came complete with an on-board drum machine offering five preset rhythms via a rotary selector and "Start" switch. The black knobs controlled drum volume and tempo.

Body *Despite the absence of f-holes, the Violin Guitar's body is hollow.*

Hofner 459/VTZ "Violin Guitar"
The German company's better-known 500/1 "Violin Bass" inspired a guitar equivalent in the mid-1960s. The active version shown here incorporates controls for treble and distortion boosts, plus overall selector switch.

Electric Sitars
During the psychedelic era of the late 1960s Indian music had a heavy influence on rock musicians. Guitarists liked the sound of the sitar but most found it impossible to play. One enterprising American company, Danelectro, came up with instruments that played like guitars, but gave a sitar sound. This effect came from a special bridge, designed by leading US session guitarist Vinnie Bell.

Shown here are both Danelectro models, the Coral Sitar with sympathetic drone strings (left), and the cheaper, basic Danelectro Sitar.

Frets *Each is divided into six segments, to sense individual string contact.*

Vox Guitar Organ
The UK company Vox pioneered the guitar organ, producing the first commercial instrument in 1966. In effect it combined a Vox Continental organ with a normal Vox Phantom solid guitar. Like the later Godwin, it was plug-powered.

Godwin Guitar Organ (above left)
For years makers had been trying to produce a guitar that sounded like an organ. This Italian attempt from 1976 used the Vox method, in which the frets are wired to a set of organ tone generators. A string touching a fret completes a circuit and produces the relevant organ note. The Godwin had a huge array of knobs and switches giving organ pipe sounds and electronic effects. This extremely heavy guitar does manage to impersonate a church organ.

ROLAND GUITAR SYNTHESIZERS

As keyboard synthesizers evolved in the 1970s, certain manufacturers of these instruments saw the possibility of applying the technology to the guitar. This was in effect a development of the guitar organ idea, producing keyboard sounds from a guitar. But early guitar organs (see page 182) were unreliable. They were also very heavy, because makers put all the bulky circuitry into the guitar. Synthesizer electronics, however, were becoming increasingly small, and generally reliable.

Roland, a leading Japanese synthesizer-maker, was established in 1974. The company soon began experiments with guitar synths, and developed the concept of a two-piece outfit consisting of a guitar (they called it a "controller") and separate synthesizer box. A series of such models appeared between 1977 and 1985: all the guitars were made for Roland by Fuji Gen-Gakki, best known for their Ibanez and Greco instruments. Roland must have believed very strongly in the idea. For eight years the company developed the concept and tried to create a market, while no other makers seemed confident enough to provide any real competition.

Chart *This shows an "edit map," used to identify parts of the synthesizer when creating new sounds.*

SIDE AND BACK
The back of the G707 shows its bolt-on neck, and the plates for access to controls and selector switch. The side shows the rubber knee-rest pad.

Roland G707 Guitar (above)
This was the third and last generation of Roland's guitar synths with a purpose-built guitar. It was launched in 1984 for £2200/ $3150. The price and unconventional shape contributed to its lack of popularity with guitarists, and it lasted about a year.

Hex pickup *This special unit sends signals to the guitar's synth section. It contains a separate pickup for each string.*

Controls *The Mode switch selects guitar or synth sounds only, or a blend of the two controlled by the Balance knob. The three small knobs control the synth section: two for tone; one for an electronic vibrato-like effect.*

Body *Options of red and black were offered in addition to the original silver finish.*

Roland GR700 Synthesizer
The 707 guitar links to this outsize pedalboard, which contains the synthesizer circuitry.

The numbered footswitches along the bottom are used to enter, change or select pre-programed sounds.

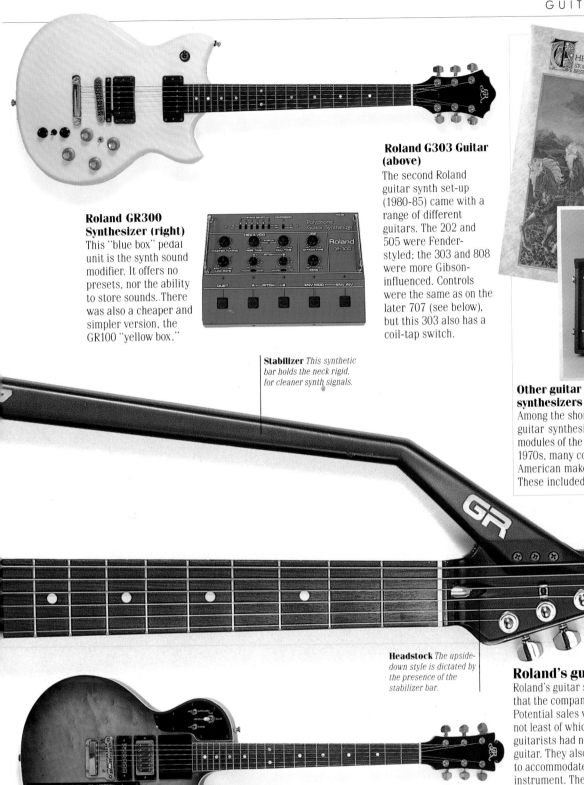

Roland GR300 Synthesizer (right)

This "blue box" pedal unit is the synth sound modifier. It offers no presets, nor the ability to store sounds..There was also a cheaper and simpler version, the GR100 "yellow box."

Stabilizer *This synthetic bar holds the neck rigid, for cleaner synth signals.*

Roland G303 Guitar (above)

The second Roland guitar synth set-up (1980-85) came with a range of different guitars. The 202 and 505 were Fender-styled; the 303 and 808 were more Gibson-influenced. Controls were the same as on the later 707 (see below), but this 303 also has a coil-tap switch.

Other guitar synthesizers

Among the shortlived guitar synthesizer modules of the late 1970s, many come from American makers. These included the Avatar from the Massachusetts ARP keyboard company (color brochure cover above), and the 360 Systems polyphonic synthesizer from California.

Headstock *The upside-down style is dictated by the presence of the stabilizer bar.*

Roland's guitars

Roland's guitar synths never achieved the success that the company clearly believed they deserved. Potential sales were hindered by various factors, not least of which was that, with Roland's system, guitarists had no choice but to use the supplied guitar. They also had to modify their playing style to accommodate the idiosyncrasies of the instrument. The outfits were expensive, too. Some players thought that having to buy an extra guitar just to obtain the new synth sounds was an expensive luxury.

Roland's insistence on synthesizer terminology seemed to imply that guitarists could become synth experts overnight. In reality, most guitarists like things simple and direct, and were often baffled by these seemingly complex instruments.

The Roland guitars were of high quality, but this wasn't enough to tempt many players away from their beloved Fenders and Gibsons. The peculiar styling didn't help popularity, giving the impression that Roland wanted to create a market rather than sell to the existing one.

Roland GS500 Guitar/GR500 Synthesizer

The pioneering Roland design (1977-80) presented an array of synthesizer controls, with "poly-ensemble" feature, giving impressive orchestral chord sounds and infinite sustain. The huge separate control unit (right) was based on Roland's keyboard synthesizer range.

SYNTH- AND MIDI-GUITARS

In the mid-1980s several British and Japanese companies decided that there was enough interest in the guitar synthesizer to warrant their involvement. Roland, virtual creators of the genre, decided to abandon the dedicated guitar system, opting instead for a rack-unit driven by a hex pickup suitable for any electric guitar. Ironically, most of the competition chose Roland's original idea, and offered purpose-built guitars. Some refined this still further by offering completely self-contained guitar synths, with all sound generation circuitry built into the guitar.

The introduction of MIDI – the Musical Instrument Digital Interface – in 1983 broadened the potential sounds available to the synth-guitarist. MIDI is a communication system agreed by all the major makers that enables synthesizers to be linked and to control one another. MIDI-equipped guitar "controllers" can, therefore, use the sounds from suitable synthesizers when connected to them via MIDI. In theory, any brand of MIDI guitar can be used with any brand of MIDI synthesizer.

BACK AND SIDE
A multiplicity of plates on the back of the body gives access to control circuits. The "Card" plate lifts to allow insertion of a ROM card for additional sounds.

Synthesizer panel
The window displays preset numbers, selected by the black buttons. Blue buttons transpose sounds up or down an octave, and there is a built-in tuning system.

Vibrato *This is a Japanese unit licensed from Floyd Rose.*

Casio DG20 Digital Guitar

Casio's DG20 and the DG10 were 1987 budget attempts at guitar synthesis. The DG20 had plastic "strings" triggering on-board synth sounds, an internal speaker, built-in rhythm unit, drum pads, and MIDI output.

Casio MG500 MIDI Guitar (above)

This, and the Fender-style 510, came out in 1987. It was an electric guitar with facilities for controlling external synths via MIDI. This model was made for Casio by Fuji Gen-Gakki.

Synthaxe

A British attempt (started in 1984) to change the way guitarists play, this model has equally spaced frets and separate "trigger" and fretting strings. The appearance and cost, some £9000 ($15,500) complete, has deterred many players from buying this unusual MIDI controller.

Control panel *The DG1's built-in synthesizer is controlled from this panel.*

Stepp DG1

This British invention was the first self-contained guitar synth (1986-88). Its own sounds were synthesized, but it also had limited control over external MIDI synths. The later DGX did not have the built-in synth, but wider MIDI control.

The player's position

Despite the great advances made in sound synthesis, guitarists have been slow to embrace the new technology. This has been due in part to hi-tech manufacturers failing to grasp what guitar players really want. Applying keyboard synthesis techniques and computer technology directly to the guitar has so far failed to work completely successfully, and only a minority of guitarists appear willing to accept the inherent compromises of this method.

Most guitarists want simple instruments; makers seem intent on complicating them. It is possible that the guitar and the synthesizer will never be married successfully unless the attitudes of both manufacturers and guitarists change significantly.

Fingerboard *This is made of high quality ebony.*

Casio PG380 Guitar Synth (above)

Tokyo-based Casio entered the keyboard market in 1980. They launched this self-contained guitar synth in 1988, the first to combine a quality electric guitar with an on-board synthesizer. It could also control external synthesizers from its MIDI socket.

Yahama G10 MIDI Controller

The Japanese Yamaha company dabbled in guitar synthesis in 1988. The short-lived G10 had an ultrasonic fingerboard tracking system, and had to be linked to a MIDI converter unit and external synth.

GLOSSARY

Alternative terms in brackets following key word. Cross-references in *italic*.

Abalone Shellfish, source of *mother-of-pearl*; most valued part is small "green heart".

Acoustic General term for any hollow-bodied acoustic guitar.

Action Height of strings from fingerboard; thus high action, low action, good action, etc.

Active Short for active electronics, or active circuit. Small *pre-amp* boosts *signal* and/or widens tonal range.

Alnico Magnet material used for pickups: iron plus 'aluminum, nickel, and cobalt. Nickname for Gibson's oblong *polepiece* unit.

Anodized Finish given to metal by electrolysis. Often refers to Fender's 1950s gold-tinted aluminum *pickguard*.

Archtop Guitar with arched top formed by carving or pressing.

Bakelite Synthetic resin invented by Belgian-American chemist Leo Baekeland in 1909. Used in some guitars from the 1930s to the 1950s.

Banjo tuners Descriptive term for rear-facing and/or reverse-gear *tuning pegs* on guitars.

Bar (blade) pickup A pickup with single magnetic "bar" rather than individual *polepieces*.

B-bender String-pulling device giving pedal steel-like effect on electric guitar.

Belly See *soundboard*.

Belly bridge Type of *flat-top* bridge: from front view, the central section is deeper than the sides.

Bigsby Almost generic term for a simple, single-spring, non-recessed *vibrato system*.

Binding Protective and decorative strip(s) added to edges of guitar body, neck.

Bird's eye Type of maple with small circular *figure*.

Blade pickup See *bar pickup*.

Blocks Square or rectangular *position markers*.

Blonde Natural *finish*.

Bobbin The frame around which pickup *coils* are wound.

Bolt-on neck Neck/body joint popularized by Fender (using bolts or screws).

Bookmatched Wood split into two thin sheets and joined to give symmetrically matching grain patterns.

Bound (of body, neck etc) See *binding*.

Bout Outward curves above (upper bout) and below (lower bout) guitar's *waist*.

Bracing Pattern of wooden struts inside hollow body giving strength and affecting tone.

Bridge pin Secures string to certain bridges, usually on *flat-top*.

Bug Pickup added to acoustic.

Bullet Describes appearance of *truss-rod* adjustment socket at headstock.

Camber Degree of curve, or "radius," to a fingerboard.

Capacitor (cap) Electrical filter used in tone controls.

Capo (capo tasto, capo dastro), Movable device which fits over neck, shortening *string length*.

Center block Solid wooden block running through inside of *semi-acoustic* body.

Chamfer A bevel or slope to body edges.

Changer Unit at bridge end of neck on pedal steel guitar housing string *fingers*.

Coil(s) Insulated wire wound around *bobbin(s)* inside pickup.

Coil-tap Usually describes switch to cut out one *coil* of humbucker, changing sound.

Contoured body Gentle carving away of solid guitar body, aiding player comfort.

Control cavity Hollowed-out area in solid body for controls, pickups etc.

Controls Knobs and switches on outside of guitar, front-mounted on *pickguard* or rear-mounted through back of body.

Course Usually means double string played as one; can refer to single or triple.

Custom color A selected color finish for a guitar, as opposed to natural or *sunburst*.

Cutaway Curve into body near neck joint aiding access to high frets. Sharp (florentine) or round (venetian) describe shape; double (equal) or single number of cutaways.

Ding Small knock or dent.

Dobro Generic term for (and brand of) *resonator* guitar, from US inventors the DOpyera BROthers.

Dog-ear Nickname for some *P90* pickups derived from shape of mounting lugs on cover.

Dot-neck Fingerboard with dot *position markers*; nickname for Gibson ES335 of 1958-62.

Double-octave Twenty-four-fret fingerboard.

Dreadnought Large acoustic designed by Frank H. Martin and Harry Hunt in the 1910s. The term is used generically for the shape.

Droopy headstock Long, down-pointing headstock popularized on 1980s *superstrats*.

Earth (ground) wire Connected to bridge or tailpiece, this earths the strings to reduce background noise.

Ebonol Synthetic material resembling ebony, used for fingerboards.

Ebonized Wood stained darker to look like ebony.

Electro-acoustic Acoustic with built-in *piezoelectric* pickup and controls.

Electric acoustic Electric guitar with hollow body.

End block Provides stable join for *ribs* of acoustic body.

Fan-strutting *Bracing* pattern of fan shape common on "classical" guitars, popularized by Torres in the nineteenth century.

f-hole Soundholes approximating "f" shape, usually on archtops and electric acoustics.

Figure Pattern on surface of wood; thus, figured maple, etc.

Finger String holder which moves to alter pitch on pedal steel guitar.

Finish Final coats of paint and/or lacquer.

Flame Dramatic *figure*, usually on maple. (See also *tiger-stripe*.)

Flat-top Acoustic with flat (i.e. not arched) top; usually with round *soundhole*.

Floating bridge Not fixed, but held in place by string tension, usually on archtop.

Floating pickup Pickup not fixed to top, but on separate *pickguard* (sometimes added to archtop acoustic).

Fretless Bass guitar fingerboard without frets.

Friction peg *Tuning peg* kept in place by friction of peg in hole.

Glued neck (set neck) Type of neck/body joint popularized by Gibson.

Golpeador (golpe) Protective "tap" plate added to flamenco guitars.

Hardtail Slang for Fender Stratocaster with non-*vibrato* bridge.

Hardware Anything added to the basic guitar: bridge, tuners, controls, etc.

Harmonic bar Inside soundboard of acoustic, usually one above and one below soundhole.

Headless Design with no headstock, popularized by Ned Steinberger in the early 1980s.

Heel Curved deepening of the neck for strength near body joint, especially on "classical" guitars.

Herringbone Decorative patterned *binding* used on Martin and other guitars.

Hex pickup Provides suitable *signal* for guitar synthesizers.

Horn Pointed body shape formed by *cutaway*: thus left horn, right horn.

Hot-rodding Slang for *mod*.

Humbucker Twin-*coil* pickup which reduces background noise ("bucks the hum"); thicker sound than *single-coil*.

Impedance Measure of electrical resistance. A few electric guitars had low impedance circuits to match recording equipment; the vast majority are high.

Inlay Decorative material cut and fitted into body, fingerboard, headstock etc.

Jack plate Mounting plate for output jack stock, usually screwed on to body.

Jumbo Large-bodied *flat-top*.

Knee-lever Large switch on pedal steel guitar operated by player's knee.

Laminated Joined together in layers; usually wood (bodies, necks) or plastic (*pickguards*).

Lining Strips, usually slotted, joining top and back to *ribs* of hollow body.

Locking trem Type of *vibrato system* that locks strings to prevent pitch slip during use.

Logo A brandname or trademark, usually on headstock.

Long scale See *scale-length*.

Machine head Geared *tuning peg*.

Medium scale See *scale-length*.

Mint Entirely as new; perfect condition.

Mod Short for modification; any change made to a guitar.

Mother-of-pearl (pearl) Lustrous internal shell of some molluscs, eg *abalone*, used for *inlay*. Synthetic *pearloid* versions exist.

Moustache bridge Descriptive of shape of decorative bridge base.

Neckplate Screw-holding plate for joint between body and neck (Fender-style).

Neck-tilt Adjustment on Fender *neckplate* to alter neck angle.

Nut Bone, metal or synthetic guide determining string *action* and spacing at headstock end of neck.

PAF Gibson pickup with "Patent Applied For" sticker on base.

Passive Normal, unboosted tone circuit (opposit of *active*).

Pearl See *mother-of-pearl*.

Pearloid Fake pearl, made of plastic and pearl dust.

Piezo-electric A pickup with special crystals (discovered 1880) that generate electricity under mechanical strain; i.e. string and body movement.

Pickguard Raised protective panel on body.

Pin bridge Unit where strings are secured by *bridge pins*.

Plantilla Spanish term for outline shape of guitar body.

P90 Early Gibson *single-coil* pickup, originally coded PU90.

Polepieces Pickup's magnetic poles, one per string, sometimes screw-adjustable for height.

Position markers Fingerboard *inlays* of various designs to assist accurate fingering.

Potentiometer (pot) Alters voltage by a spindle turning on an electrically resistive track. Used for volume and tone controls, etc.

Pre-amp Pre-amplifier; when present, boosts *signal* in guitar circuit.

Pre-CBS Fender guitars made before CBS takeover in 1965 (and thus, "post-CBS").

Pressed top Arched top made by machine pressing rather than hand carving.

Purfling This term usually means *binding*.

Pyramid bridge Unit on flat-tops with pyramid-shape carvings either side of saddle, popularized by Martin.

Quilted Undulating *figure*, usually on maple.

Radius See *camber*.

Refinished (refin) New *finish* added, replacing original.

Resonator Generic term for guitar with metal resonator in body to increase volume.

Ribs Sides of acoustic or electric acoustic body.

Rose hole Decorative wood or parchment in *soundhole* of early guitars.

Rosette Decorative *inlay* around *soundhole*.

Router Machine to cut *control* cavities into body. Thus routing, routed etc.

Saddle(s) Unit(s) on bridge where strings make contact.

Scale-length Double the distance from *nut* to twelfth fret. Bass guitars often called short scale (76cm/30in), medium scale (81cm/32in), or long scale (86cm/34in).

Scallop Gentle sloping of sides of *bracing*, for lightness and tonal modification.

Scalloped fingerboard Wood scooped out between frets; eases some playing styles.

Scratchplate Protective panel fitted flush on to body. (Not common usage in USA.)

Selector Any control that selects from options, usually of pickups.

Semi-acoustic (semi-solid, semi) Electric guitar with solid wooden block running down center of *thinline* body. First examples were Gibson's ES335 and EB2.

Semi-solid See *semi-acoustic*.

Serial number Added by maker for own purposes; sometimes useful for dating.

Shielding Special paint or sheeting in *control cavity* to reduce electrical interference.

Short scale See *scale-length*.

Signal Transmitted electrical information, for example between control circuits, or guitar and amplifier, etc.

Single-coil Original pickup type with one *coil*.

Slab (finger) board Fender type (1959-62) in which join between neck top and fingerboard base is flat (later curved).

Slash soundhole Scimitar-shaped *soundhole*, used primarily by Rickenbacker.

Slotted headstock Headstock with cut-outs allowing access to tuning peg posts.

Snakehead Headstock narrower at top than bottom (usually refers to early Gibson type).

Soap-bar Nickname for *P90* pickup without mounting lugs.

Solid General term for any solid-body guitar.

Soundboard (table, belly) Top of an acoustic.

Soundbox Body of an acoustic.

Soundhole Hole in body top that increases sound projection. Various types; most are round or 'f'-shaped.

Spaghetti Early Fender *logo* with thin, stringy letters resembling spaghetti.

Stop (stud) tailpiece Type of *tailpiece* fixed to solid or semi-acoustic guitar top, not to body end (as on archtops and some electric acoustics).

Strap buttons Where strap is attached, on sides (or side and back) of guitar.

String guide (string tree) Small "hook" at headstock to maintain downward string tension at *nut*.

String length Sounding length of string, measured from *nut* to bridge *saddle*.

Strutting See *bracing*.

Sunburst Decorative finish: pale-colored center graduates to darker edges.

Superstrat Updated Fender Stratocaster popularized by Jackson in the 1980s: more frets, deeper cutaways, changed pickups, *locking trem*.

Table See *soundboard*.

Tags Hang-tags and/or other literature originally accompanying a guitar.

Tailpiece Unit separate from bridge that anchors strings, usually attached to body end. (See also *trapeze tailpiece*, *stop tailpiece*).

Thinline Narrow-bodied electric acoustic; term coined by Gibson for Byrdland model, 1955.

Through-neck Neck that travels complete length of guitar, with "wings" added to complete body shape.

Tied bridge As on early and "classical" guitars, with strings knotted to bridge.

Tiger-stripe Dramatic *figure*, usually on maple. (See also *flame*.)

Transducer Converts one form of energy to another; used generically (and erroneously) for *piezo-electric* pickups.

Transverse strutting *Bracing* across top or back of acoustic or electric acoustic, applied from side to side.

Trapeze tailpiece Simple *tailpiece* of trapezoidal shape.

Tremolo (tremolo arm, trem) Erroneous but much-used term for *vibrato system*.

Truss rod Fits inside neck; adjustable to correct bending as result of string tension.

Truss-rod cover Decorative plate covering truss rod's access hole, usually on headstock.

Tune-O-Matic Fully adjustable Gibson bridge.

Tuning pegs Overall term for tuners (see *friction pegs*, *machine head*).

TV White or limed Gibson *finish* designed to stand out on black-and-white television in the 1950s.

12-fret/14-fret Refers not to the number of frets, but to the position at which neck joins body (mainly acoustics).

U-neck/V-neck Cross-section of neck: U is rounded at back; V has pronounced point.

Vibrato system (tremolo arm, trem, wang bar, whammy) Bridge and/or *tailpiece* which alters pitch when attached arm is moved. Bigsby, Fender, Floyd Rose are best known.

Waist The incurved shape near the middle of the guitar body.

Wang bar See *vibrato system*.

Whammy See *vibrato system*.

Wrapover bridge Unit in which strings are secured after wrapping around circular bar.

X-braced Pattern of *bracing* in "X" shape, popularized by Martin.

Zero fret Extra fret in front of *nut*: improves tone of open strings; makes later *action* adjustment harder.

OWNERS

We are very grateful to the following individuals, companies, and institutions who allowed us to photograph their guitars. They are listed according to the alphabetic order of the code used to identify their guitars in the Photographic Index below.

AH Alan Hayward; AI Adrian Ingram; AL Adrian Lovegrove; AM Andrew Manson; AN Andy's (Andy Preston); AR Alan Rogan; ARI Aria UK (John Joyce); AS Ashmolean Museum (Vera Magyar); BA Barnes & Mullins Ltd (Bruce Perrin); BAS Bass Centre, London (Barry Moorhouse & staff); BC Brian Cohen; BG Barrie Glendenning; BM Bill Marsh; BP Bill Puplett; BR Bryant's Music (Gaic Belli); BU Buzz Music (Buzz Peters); BW Bruce Welch; CA Casio UK (Sue Stanton, John Wright); CB Clive Brown; CD Chris Dair; CE Chris Eccleshall; CH Chandler Guitars; CHA Chappell of Bond Street (Phil Thompson); CK Clive Kristen; CM Charles Measures; CO The Cocteau Twins; COU Country Music Hall of Fame (Chris Skinker); DB Dave Brewis; DC Don Clayton; DCR David Crozier; DG David Gilmour; DGR Dave Gregory; DP Dave Pegg; ED Edinburgh University Collection (Arnold Myers); FA Frank Allen; FC FCN Music Ltd (James Coppock, Andie Brook-Mellor); FE Fender A&R London (Tom Nolan); GG Gerald Garcia; GH George Harrison; GI Gibson London Showroom (Jamie Crompton, Anneka Creüter, Robert Usher); GJ Gerald Johnson; GK Gerry Kelly; GM Graeme Matheson; GU Guitar Gallery UK (Charles Measures, Doug Chandler); GW Gary Winterflood; HO Hogan Music (Gerry Hogan); HOH Hohner Ltd (Martin Brassell); HOR Horniman Museum (Frances Palmer, Margaret Birley); HT Henry Thomas; IA Ian Anderson; JA Jeff Allen; JD Jerry Donahue; JE John Entwistle; JM Juan Martin; JMI John Mills; JO John Hornby Skewes & Co Ltd (Dennis Drumm); JS John Smith; JT John Tuck; JTE Juan Teijeiro; JU Juan Teijeiro Music; KH Keith Henderson; MA Macari's (Nigel May); MD Malcolm Draper; ME Metropolitan Museum of Art (Laurence Lidin, Marcie Karp); MF Mo Foster; MG Michael Gee; MM Michael Messer; MU Music Ground (Rick Harrison, Stuart Palmer & staff); MW Malcolm Weller; OC Ollie Crooke; PB Pete Banacin; PC anonymous private collector; PD Paul Day; PK Pete Kent; PM Phil Manzanera; PMC Paul McCartney; PMI Paul Midgeley; PP Per Peterson; RC Richard Chapman; RCL Rod Clements; RE Reflections Marketing (Mal Chapman); RG Rory Gallagher; RIC Rickenbacker International Corp (John C Hall USA, Trevor Smith, Linda Garson UK); RO Rockbottom (Neville Crozier); ROS Rose-Morris & Co Ltd (Mark Smith); ROSE Rosetti Ltd (Christine Kieffer, Doug Ellis); RR Ray Rover; RS Robert Spencer; RU Raymond Ursell; SC Simon Carlton; SE Sensible Music; SH Steve Howe; SL Steve Lewis; SN Simon Nicol; SO Sotheby's London (Adam Watson); SRO Stuart Ross; TB Tony Bacon; TF Tim Fleming; TG Tony Gad; TP Tim Phillips; VS Vince Smith; WA Washburn UK (Gavin Mortimer); YA Yamaha-Kemble Music UK (Martyn Booth, Mike Clement); YS Yoshi Serizawa.

PHOTOGRAPHIC INDEX

Our three main photographers were Matthew Chattle, Garth Blore and Paul Goff. Additional pictures were taken by Jeffrey Veitch, Richard Conner, Shoichiro Kataoka and Chris Taylor. All but 12 of the guitars in this book were photographed in the UK.

Page number is followed by a key, m: = main guitar, bx: = in box, t-b: = top to bottom, l-r: = left to right, and b: = below main guitar. Owner's initials are in capitals (for example AH – see key above). Illustrations of players, makers, etc, are

listed after the guitars, ill:, followed by the supplier. Catalogues reproduced are from the collections of Paul Day, Bill Puplett and Tony Bacon, and are not individually noted. Title page: 1979 Gibson Kalamazoo Award, courtesy Bill Marsh.
12 l-r: ED; ED; RS. ill: G Morlaye *Quatriesme Livre* 1552, facsimile by Editions Chanterelles (1980). 13 bx: AS; AS. l-r: HOR; AS; AS. 14 l-r: RS; AS. 15 l-r: RS; AS; RS. 18 m: AM. 20 m: BC. l-r: HOR; SH. 21 t-b: BC; MW. 22 m: BC/SO. bx: ME. ill: Ibbs & Tillet. 23 l-r: JM; MW; JTE; BC. b: MW. 24 l-r: JU; YS; JMI. 25 l-r: GG; RU; SH. ill: RU. 26 m: IA. ills: C F Martin & Co. 27 all IA. 28 m: IA. 29 t-b: SH; SH; GU. bx: IA. 30 m: COU. 31 all AH. 32 t-b: BM; BM; PC. 33 l-r: BM; AI; DB. b: AL; AL. 34 l-r: SH; BM; AL. 35 l-r: BM; BM. bx t-b: AL; AL; MU. 36 m: PC. ill: Gibson Guitar Corp. 37 l-r: RC; BM; PC. PC. b: BM; BM. 38 m: COU; 39 l-r: AL; GH; CM; DG. b: PC. 40 l-r: RCL; MU; SH. 41 l-r: MU; MU; MU; MU. bx t-b: SH; DG. +GM 42 l-r: VS; MU; BG. 43 t-b: MU; CK; AM; DP. +RC 44 t-b: ROS; DG; TF. 45 t-b: YA; WA; ROS. 46 l-r: HOH; BR. t-b: CO; GI. 47 l-r: GI; BA; WA; PD. 48 m: PC. bx r: MU. +CB. 49 l-r: PD; PD; MM; GM. bx r: MU. 50 m: HO. 51 t-b: DG; DG; PC; PC; SH. 54 both RIC; ill: RIC. 55 ill: RIC. 56 m: AI. 57 t-b: GJ. ill; CBS Records. 58 t-b: AL; BG; COU. 60 m: COU. 62 m: DG. ill: *The Guitar Book, Revised,* Tom Wheeler, Harper & Row. 66 m: FE. ills: Gibson Guitar Corp. 67 bx: GW. 68 m: DG. 69 all DG. 70 l-r: AR; DB; FE; PMI. 71 l-r: RO; MU; PMI. PMI. +JD. 72 m: GW. bx: GW. ill: Dave Peabody. 73 l-r: KH; DGR; GW; DCR; SL; FE. 74 l-r: FE; PMI; PMI; DG. 75 l-r: PD; RG; FE; BW. bx t-b: RC; GW. 76 m: DG. 77 l-r: CO; MU; PD. bx t-b: PD; PD. 78 m: PD. 79 t-b: PD; BU; PMI. ill: Ernie Ball Inc. 80 m: JS. 81 t-b: MU; ROSE; PC; GJ. bx: GW. 82 t-b: GJ; GW; GW. 83 l-r: GW; ROSE. b: GW. 84 m: SRO. bx t-b: MU; DB; ROSE. 85 l-r: CB; CB; SC; RC. bx: SH. 86 m: GJ. 87 bx t-b: PM; DGR. l-r: GU; GU. b: RO. 88 l-r: GJ; GI; CB. 89 t-b: PD; PD; CD. 90 l-r: PD; PD; DGR. 91 l-r: PD; PD; RIC. t-b: DG; MU. 92 l-r: CH; MD; PD. 93-4 all PD. 95 l-r: DC; MU. t-b: DG; PD. 96 m: JO. bx: RO. 97 t-b: PD; JO; WA. 98-108 all PD. 109 all PD except Tokai: SC. 110 all PD except Jackson: JO. 111 all PD except SG2000S: YA. 112 l-r: HOH; YA; YA. 113 all PD except Encore: JO. ill: WEA Records. 114 all PD. 115 l-r: PD; MA; PD; FE. b: PD. 116 all PD. 117 all PD except Corn Flakes: SN. 118 t-b: RO; GH. 119 l-r: CO; rest PD. 120 t-b: MF; MD. ill: Kaman Music Corp. 121 t-b: PD; FE. 122 t-b: PM; rest PD. 123 all PD. 126-7 m: CE. ills: RIC. 128 m: SRO. 129 l-r: BG; GU. b: RC. 130 l-r: GU; GU; BM. 131 t-b: PC; JS. 132 l-r: BM; SRO. 133 l-r: PC; SH. 134 m: GU. 135 l-r: DB; GU. 136 m: PK. 137 l-r: PC; GU. b: GU. 138 m: GW. 139 l-r: SRO; GW; FA. b: RO. 140 t-b: AL; AR. 141 t-b: GU; GW. 142 l-r: AL; GU; DB. 143 l-r: SH; AL; FA; AL. 144 m: DG. ill: BMG Records. 145 PD. 146 l-r: PC; PK; PC. 147 l-r: DGR; GK; AN. 148 t-b: PMI; MU; PP. 149 l-r: RIC; DGR. b: RIC. 150 l-r: RO; PD; RCL. 151 l-r: PD; AL; CHA. t-b: TP; GM. 152 l-r: AL; AL; PD. 153 l-r: RO; RO; BP; PD. ill: Ian Purser. 154 t-b: WA; TB. 155 l-r: MU; ARI; YA. 158 m: FE. bx: BAS. 159 bx: BAS. 160 m: DG. 161 l-r: DP; CO; FE. b: BAS. 162 t-b: FE; DG. ill: CBS Records. 163 t-b: BAS; TB; PD; MU. 164 m: DB. ill: Polygram. 165 t-b: RIC; RIC. FA. 166 m: JE. bx: BAS. 167 l-r: BU; RO; FA. b: RO. 168 l-r: BAS; BAS; BAS; JO. 169 l-r: SE; BAS; RCL. 170 l-r: RO; BAS. b: BAS. 171 m: PMC. l-r: PD; BAS. 172 l-r: BAS; FC; BAS; ARI. 173 l-r: BAS; YA; BAS. 174 t-b: FE; PB. 175 l-r: PD; HOH; BAS. b: BAS. 176 l-r: BAS; CO; HT. 177 l-r: CO; PD; BAS; CO. t-b: BAS. 178 l-r: WA; DG; SE. 179 t-b: TG; OC; BAS. BAS. 182 m: PD. 183 l-r: all PD. bx l-r: DG; PD. 184-5 all PD. 186 m: PD. 187 t-b: PD; PD; YA. l-r: RE; RE.

We would also like to thank the following: Ian Allen (The Bass Place); Kent Armstrong; Martin Barre; David Bergstrom (Kaman Music Corp); Nick Boyles (Big M Productions); Peter Browning (Spanish Guitar Centre); Chris Burden; Martin Chuzzlewick; Cheryl Clark (G&L Guitars); B. J. Cole; Max Comrie; Andy Cooper, Paul Gilby (computer advice); Gary Cooper; Mike Cooper (Scott Cooper); Richard Downs (Larrivee Guitars); Donald Gallagher; Pete Gleadall; Rob Green, Steve Lovett (Status Graphite); Clive Gregson; Vincent Hastwell; James Hunter (Dick Institute); Fiona Hurry (McCartney World Tour 90); Sheila Jones, Kate Taylor (MPL); Scott Jennings (Guitar Gallery USA); Henry Juszkiewicz, John Hawkins, Robi Johns (Gibson Guitar Corp); Stephen Kaufman (IMC); Max Kay; Dixie Kidd (Dixie's Music); Joseph Lauricella (Fodera Guitars); Adrian Legg; Cliff Little; Emil Lobo; Mike Longworth, Dick Boak (C. F. Martin & Co Inc); Ivor Mairants; Hugh Manson; Neville Marten (Guitarist); John Martin (Eleventh Hour Management); Chris May (Overwater Guitar Co); Ted Muir; Tony Muschamp; David Newton; Marc Noel-Johnson (Music Village); Denis O'Brien (EuroAtlantic); Les Paul; John Pearse; Michael Pedulla (M.V. Pedulla Guitars); Nick Peraticos; Marco Pironi; Bob Pridden; Peter Pulham (Music World); Tony Quinn (Eligible Music); Patty Rich (Taylor Guitars); Santa Cruz Guitars; Miki Slingsby; Dan Smith, John Maher, Jack Shelton (Fender Musical Instruments); Kate Smith (Handmade Films); Nigel Spennywyn (Peter Cook Music); Sue Stanton (Stanton-Alexander PR); Ned Steinberger (Steinberger Sound); Pete Stevens (Electric Wood); Maurice Summerfield; Dave Sumner; Phil Taylor; Alan Townsend (Roland UK); Nigel "don't even look at them" Tufnell; Martin Turner; Robert Usher; Jerry Uwins; Woody Wahlen (Warwick Bass Guitars); Adrian Walker, Paul Colbert, and all staff (Making Music); Guy Wallace (Ernie Ball Inc); Elizabeth Waters (NAMM); Elizabeth Wells (Royal College of Music); James Werner; Tom Wheeler (Guitar Player); Marty Wilde: John Williams; Kenny Wylie (Salamander Music); Phil York (Dreadnought Guitar Co); James Yorke (Victoria & Albert Museum); Tony Zemaitis; Joseph M. Zon (Zon Guitars).

BIBLIOGRAPHY

The following books were used during research:
Ken Achard *The Fender Guitar* (Musical New Services, 1977); *The History and Development of the American Guitar* (Musical New Services, 1979). Tony Bacon (Ed) *Rock Hardware* (Blandford, 1981). Tony Bacon, Laurence Canty *What Bass* (Track Record, 1990). Tony Bacon, Paul Day *The Guru's Guitar Guide* (Track Record, 1990). Alexander Bellow *The Illustrated History of the Guitar* (Colombo, 1970). Julius Bellson *The Gibson Story* (Gibson, 1973). Clifford Bevan (Ed) *Musical Instrument Collections in the British Isles* (Piccolo Press, 1990). Ian Bishop *The Gibson Guitar from 1950* (Musical New Services, 1977); *The Gibson Guitar from 1950 Vol. 2* (Musical New Services, 1979). David D. Boyden *The Hill Collection of Musical Instruments in the Ashmolean Museum* (Ashmolean/W. E. Hill, 1969). Donald Brosnac (Ed) *Guitars made by the Fender Company* (Bold Strummer, 1983/6). John Bulli *Gibson SG* (Bold Strummer, 1989). Ian Darr, Digby Fairweather, Brian Priestley *Jazz: The Essential Companion* (Paladin Grafton, 1987). Paul Colbert (Ed) *What Guitar* (Track Record, 1990). Dave Crocker, John Brinkmann, Larry Briggs *Guitars, Guitars, Guitars – a pictorial reference manual* (All American Music, 1988). Paul Day *The Burns Book* (PP, 1979). Fred Dellar, Alan Cackett, Roy Thompson *illustrated Encyclopedia of Country Music* (Salamander, 1986). Ralph

Denyer *The Guitar Handbook* (Dorling Kindersley, 1982). Andrew Duchossoir *The Fender Stratocaster* (Mediapresse, 1988); *Gibson Electrics Vol. 1* (Mediapresse, 1981); *Guitar Identification: Fender, Gibson, Gretsch, Martin* (Mediapresse, 1983). Tom Evans, Mary Anne Evans *Guitars: from the Renaissance to Rock* (Oxford University Press, 1977). Susan Caust Farrell *Directory of Contemporary American Musical Instrument Makers* (University of Missouri Press, 1981). David George *The Flamenco Guitar* (Society of Spanish Studies, 1969). Frederic V. Grunfeld *The Art and Times of the Guitar* (Da Capo, 1974). *Guitar Player Rock Guitarists* (Guitar Player Books, 1975); *The Guitar Player Book* (Grove Press, 1983). *Guitar World 1990-91 Guitar Buyer's Guide* (Harris, 1990). Phil Hardy, Dave Laing *The Faber Companion to 20th-Century Popular Music* (Faber & Faber, 1990). Franz Jahnel *Manual of Guitar Technology – the History and Technology of Plucked String Instruments,* English translation J. C. Harvey (Verlag das Musikinstrument, 1981). George S. Kanahele *Hawaiian Music and Musicians: an illustrated history* (University Press of Hawaii, 1979). Rich Kienzle *Great Guitarists* (Facts On File, 1985). Allan Kozinn, Pete Welding, Dan Forte, Gene Santoro *The Guitar – the History, the Music, the Players* (Columbus, 1984). Mike Longworth *Martin Guitars – a history* (Four Maples Press, 1988). Norman Mongan *The History of the Guitar in Jazz* (Oak, 1983). Wendy Munro *Chambers Pocket Guide to Language of Music* (Chambers, 1987); *Chambers Pocket Guide to Music Forms and Styles* (Chambers, 1987). Arnold Myers *Historic Musical Instruments in the Edinburgh University Collection: Volume 1, Illustrations* (Edinburgh University 1990).I Tony Palmer *Julian Bream: a Life on the Road* (Macdonald 1982). José L. Romanillos *Antonio de Torres, Guitar Maker – his life and work* (Nadder, 1987). Norbert Schnepel, Helmuth Lemme *Electric Guitars made in Germany,* English translation J. P. Klink (Musik-Verlag Schnepel-Lemme, 1988). Andrés Segovia *An Autobiography of the Years 1893-1920* (Marion Boyars, 1977). A. P. Sharpe *The Story of the Spanish Guitar* (Clifford Essex, 1968). Richard Smith *The Complete History of Rickenbacker Guitars* (Centerstream, 1987). Stanley Sadie (Ed) *The New Grove Dictionary of Musical Instruments* three volumes (Macmillan, 1984). Maurice Summerfield *The Classical Guitar* (Ashley Mark, 1982), *The Jazz Guitar* (Ashley Mark, 1978). Akira Tsumura *Guitars – The Tsumura Collection* (Kodansha, 1987). Harvey Turnbull *The Guitar: from the Renaissance to the Present Day* (Batsford, 1974). James Tyler *The Early Guitar* (Oxford University Press, 1980). Tom Wheeler *American Guitars* (Harper & Row, 1982); *The Guitar Book* (Macdonald & Jane's, 1974).

The following magazines were used during research:
Beat Instrumental* (UK); *Classical Guitar* (UK); *Guitar International* (UK); *Guitar Player* (USA); *Guitar World* (USA); *Guitarist* (UK); *Making Music** (UK); *One Two Testing** (UK); *Sound International** (UK). (*no longer published)